The Beat Goes On

The Beat

Goes On

Popular Music and the City of Norwich 1955-60

Colin Miller

POPPYLAND PUBLISHING

This edition 2022 published by Poppyland Publishing, Lowestoft, NR32 3BB.

www.poppyland.co.uk

ISBN 978 1 909796 98 0

Designed and typeset in 10.5 on 13.5 pt Gilgamesh Pro.

Printed by Severn Printing.

Picture credits:
Archant Newspapers Ltd (Archant) 53, 111, 122, 143, 155.
author's collection vi, 27, 50, 57,64, 77, 78, 93, 103.
Brown, E 41*.
Cavanagh, D 33.
Cooper, A 81, 84, 119.
Jones, P 63.
Library of Congress 8*, 9*, 12*, 24*.
Picture Norfolk 23±, 28±, 29±, 61, 62, 102, 120, 132, 135.
Seved, W 136*.
Tooke, C 5.
Warriner, R 34.
unknown 140*.

*under Creative Commons Licence or public domain.
±with the permission of M Bartle.

Contents

The author during his student days at Leicester University, 1959–1963.

Introduction and Acknowledgements

This book is about a special moment in time, the late 1950s. A moment that was special for me as well as for most young people throughout the whole of Great Britain. And now that I am in my eighties, I look back on that time with immense pleasure. In this book I have tried to retell the story of the years 1955 to 1960 from a teenage point of view, partly based on my memories but mostly on the experiences of young people in the city of Norwich as recorded in contemporary local newspapers, the *Eastern Daily Press*, the *Eastern Evening News* and the *Great Yarmouth Mercury*. I have tried to be as accurate as I can, but I have no doubt there will remain errors of fact and interpretation. Nevertheless, I hope that the content of this book will map in some detail the development of the youth culture that was emerging at that time and the influences that precipitated those changes. A culture characterised by changing fashions in dress, behaviour, music and dance. Changes that led into that era we now call the Swinging Sixties.

As author I wish to acknowledge that this book would not have been produced without the help and advice that I received from many sources. Firstly, I must thank my wife, Dr Celia Miller, for her interest, encouragement and professional expertise, especially for her helpful efforts in checking the accuracy of my manuscript and for correcting my numerous grammatical mistakes. I must thank Gareth Davies from Poppyland Publishing for his faith in the book and for his advice during the publishing process. My sincere thanks is due to Albert Cooper, musician and singer extraordinaire, for our many conversations and for his recollections of the late 1950s when he sang the blues with Antoinette Hannent (Black Anna) at the *Jolly Butchers* on Ber Street in Norwich. A thank you also to Kingsley Harris, coordinator of the *Music from the East Zone* archive, and Ben Craske, archivist at Archant Newspapers for their comments and advice. A special thank you must go to Clare Everitt, Picture Norfolk Administrator, and the staff at the Norfolk Heritage Centre for their help in negotiating me through the maze of resources at the Millennium Library in Norwich.

My thanks go also to the individuals and organisations that have permitted me to source photographs and illustrations from their collections, especially Picture Norfolk and the Photographic Archive of Archant Newspapers. Where necessary, I have made every effort to identify, trace and acknowledge all the current copyright owners for their permission to reproduce these photographs and illustrations, but this has proved an almost impossible task in some cases. I would be pleased to hear from any current copyright holders regarding errors or omissions made in this book and I will make every effort to ensure that these are rectified in any reprint. I have also included some unattributed illustrations that are either from my personal collection of ephemera relating to Norwich or are contemporary photographs taken by myself.

The Author Remembers 1955-56

In 1955, I was fifteen years old, a teenager when the term 'teenager' was beginning to assume a wider meaning than just a person of a certain age. At the time I was living at home with my parents in Rollesby, a village on the Norfolk Broads in a district called the Fleggs, eight miles from Great Yarmouth and fifteen miles from Norwich. My father was a bricklayer and my mother, a housewife and part-time Saturday cleaner at a seaside holiday camp. In 1955 most fifteen-year-olds were on the verge of leaving school to enter the grown-up world of adult responsibilities and full-time labour. For many young men, an apprenticeship or a brief period in training would be followed by conscription at eighteen years of age into a year and a half of national service in the armed forces. For most young women, the prospect of temporary employment until marriage beckoned, followed by the unenviable tasks thereafter of bringing up a family and running a home. My situation was different. In 1951 I had passed the Common Entrance Examination, the infamous eleven plus, which enabled me to join the three hundred or so privileged pupils at the grammar school in Great Yarmouth. At fifteen years of age, I was about to take my 'O' level examinations hoping to enter the school's sixth form and, in time, to continue my studies at university. This kind of opportunity was rarely available to children with my rural working-class background. Had I not passed the eleven plus, I would undoubtedly have followed my father's example and sought employment as an apprentice bricklayer.

I was a typical yet relatively innocent teenager. I did the things that most teenagers did. I had smoked my first cigarette, drank my first half-pint of beer, hung out on street corners with my friends and discovered the attraction of girls. At fifteen years of age, I was allowed a modicum of independence by my parents. I visited the cinemas of Great Yarmouth and Norwich at least once a week, sometimes on my own but more often accompanied by a family member or a friend. I was also permitted to join my teenage colleagues most weekends at a Saturday dance in one of our nearby local village halls, providing I was home by 11.00pm. According to my mother, anyone out after 11.00pm was up to no good. Nevertheless, it was an exciting time, not just because I was fifteen. Change was in the air. Post-war austerity was finally ending and rationing of all essential commodities had ceased. Most bomb sites had been cleared, and the entertainment industry was getting into full swing. Full employment meant that the struggle to survive experienced by many families immediately after World War II had diminished and a surplus of money existed in most pockets, including the pockets of working-class teenagers. Rapidly changing fashions in music, entertainment and dress provided unlimited opportunities for that surplus to be spent, especially those opportunities targeted deliberately at the teenager. Opportunities that inevitably resulted in young people developing their own fashionable trends in music, dance and clothes; markedly different from those of their parents.

My evolving culture—my habits, preferences and beliefs—was primarily that of a working-class teenager, influenced to some degree by my attendance at a grammar school. I followed the trends shared by my friends in the village and my classmates at the grammar school. I enjoyed music of all forms although I had scant appreciation for classical music, despite the efforts of the grammar school's music master. I much preferred music that I could dance to, as well as the popular songs of the day. I enjoyed playing music, although piano lessons when I was eleven were a failure. When I was fourteen, my grandmother gave me her old ukulele-banjo and a collection of sheet music. Although I was unable to read music, the fingering for the appropriate chords was indicated by a diagram above the score. I was soon proficient with many of George Formby's comic songs, and thereafter I was expected to take my turn to perform at family parties and occasionally in public. However, the biggest influence on my choice of music was the radio. When I was unwell and confined to bed, a casualty of the nationwide flu epidemic of January 1955, in one of his rare but memorable acts of generosity, my father bought a second-hand radio for my bedroom. From that moment on, I was able to listen to the programmes and stations of my choice, especially Radio Luxembourg's English language programmes that were broadcast every evening from 7.00pm. The radio in our living room remained permanently under the strict control of my parents and their selection of programmes was not always appreciated by a rebellious teenager. The radio in my bedroom allowed me the freedom to listen to the programmes I enjoyed.

I liked music of all forms, from brass bands to sentimental songs. By the summer of 1956 I had also discovered rock 'n' roll, although, at the time, I did not know it. Rock 'n' roll was not yet established as an identifiable genre by me or my friends. I clearly remember one Saturday night standing on the terraces of the Great Yarmouth Speedway Stadium on Caister Road watching stock car racing with tears in my eyes when the public address system began playing *Why Do Fools Fall In Love*, by Frankie Lymon and the Teenagers. I had just been rejected by my first long-term girlfriend. I also had a liking for Gene Vincent's *Be Bop a Lula* although I was not sure what the lyrics meant. But I did not recognise either as an example of rock 'n' roll. They were just simply songs that I liked and songs that had struck

The Regal in Febuary 1941, showing the film Feather Your Nest starring George Formby.

a chord with my feelings at the time. My eventual passion for rock 'n' roll in all its forms began in earnest in November 1956 when the film *Rock Around the Clock* came to the Regal Cinema in Great Yarmouth. I had heard about the film, which was the talk of the grammar school classroom, so, inevitably, I joined the long Saturday night queue of excited teenagers outside the Regal waiting impatiently to buy their tickets to see the film. The film itself was a surprise, with music and dancing that excited its audience into shouting and clapping, and dancing in the aisles. I was immediately converted and wanted to hear more, and to learn the dance that I soon knew as the jive. My newly discovered passion for the genre was consolidated when my village friend, Richard, purchased a long play record by another American singer, Elvis Presley, which he played repeatedly on his proudest possession, a record player. In no time at all, we knew the words to all the songs, which we sung while wiggling our legs and hips in the manner made famous by the singer. His parents were not impressed.

New Year
1955

With a definite feeling of optimism and the hope for a better future to come, the citizens of Norwich, young and old, celebrated the arrival of 1955 at family parties in their homes and at dances in the ballrooms, hotels and function rooms of the city. An enthusiastic greeting which was repeated by revellers at noisy social gatherings in the community halls of the surrounding villages.

Many hundreds danced at carnival events at both the Samson & Hercules and Lido Ballrooms. At the latter, where there was a Carnival of Balloons, four thousand balloons were let down among the dancers at midnight. The doors of the ballroom were closed by 8.15pm and hundreds of people had to be turned away. ... Hundreds had to be turned away too from the new premises of the Norwich Industries Club in Oak Street where 1500 people celebrated under paper hats, streamers and balloons. The programme included a fancy-dress parade and entertainments for the members' children.[1]

At the Samson & Hercules, Ronnie Caryl and his Orchestra played music for a Grand Carnival Dance to a sell-out audience in the main ballroom. while a New Year's Eve Dinner Dance was held in the Flixton Rooms for those who could afford it. The New Year's Eve Dance at the Gala was also sold out. At the International Club's party in the Music House, the arrival of the New Year was announced by the appearance of a papier mâché model of a flying saucer suspended above the dance floor. Maestro and his Dance Band played music for Old Time Dancing at the Ailwyn Hall, Los Gatos did Latin American at the Cottage in Thorpe St Andrew, while the Stompers played jazz at the RAFA Club on Lobster Lane.

Festive events in the city featured a choice of three pantomimes, *Dick Wittington and his Cat* at the Hippodrome, Billy Dainty as Simple Simon in *Puss in Boots* at the Theatre Royal and *Snow White and the Seven Dwarfs* on roller-skates at the Norwich Rollerdrome. Roller-skating had become an extremely popular activity with the youth of Norwich, mainly because there was a shortage of leisure facilities providing suitable activities for young people, and especially activities for girls. The cast of *Snow White* consisted mostly of local skaters aged between 5 and 26. As well as the Norwich Rollerdrome, major indoor and outdoor rinks were available at the Palais de Dance in Lowestoft and at the Wellington Pier Gardens in Great Yarmouth.

> The immense popularity of roller skating among the young in East Anglia is not really surprising for there are no ice rinks, no indoor swimming baths, no general squash courts (as yet) to satisfy the needs of those who like to take their relaxations energetically. [2]

In the cinema, the selection of films on offer included *The Robe* at the Norvic in wide-angled cinemascope starring Richard Burton and Jean Simmons; Edmund Purdom and Ann Blyth in *The Student Prince* at the Regent; manic comedian Norman Wisdom in *One Good Turn* at the Odeon, and at the Carlton, Bing Crosby and Danny Kaye in *White Christmas*. For most of Norwich's residents, irrespective of age, 'going out' throughout the year was simply a choice between dancing at the city's many dance halls and hotel function rooms, visiting the cinema or theatre, eating out at a growing number of restaurants, or joining a singsong in a local public house. Norwich's eleven cinemas provided a choice of close to fifty different films every week.[3] Great Yarmouth boasted five cinemas with two more nearby in the adjacent town of Gorleston. Because the home film industry was slow to

Production photograph from the film White Christmas, 1954. Paramount Pictures Corporation.

recover from the damaging effects of wartime bombing, most major films were American products and an advert for American culture. As well as its cinemas, Norwich's two theatres provided an additional selection of serious plays, variety shows and the occasional concert from a celebrity singer or band. Going out was not restricted by a lack of choice to one night a week, although for most working adults it was a weekend only activity.

In the home, the BBC provided a choice of three radio stations to entertain the whole family throughout

Nat King Cole, 1947

the day and for most of the evening, the Home, Light and Third Programmes. For the more adventurous listener looking for something more exciting and different, it was usually to be found in broadcasts from Radio Luxembourg, the American Forces Network (AFN) and the Dutch radio station at Hilversum. Watching television was not possible in most of Norfolk's homes until 1 February 1955 when the first temporary transmitter at Tacolneston, near Norwich, became operational, and then only to households within a 20-mile radius of its tower. Television for the rest of Norfolk was not possible until the end of 1956 and, consequently, until then television played a minor role in the development of Norfolk's teenage culture. As well as a radio, many homes possessed a record player of some sort. The old wind-up gramophones playing 78 rpm shellac records were gradually being replaced by electric powered radiograms and record players playing vinyl records at 45 or 33 rpm. Record buying was on the increase especially among the young. At the start of 1955, the newly established popular music charts were dominated by songs from ballad singers, such as Dean Martin, Teresa Brewer, Billy Eckstine, Nat King Cole, Johnny Ray and Frankie Laine from America, and Ruby Murray, Dickie Valentine and David Whitfield from the UK, performers who were appreciated by people of all ages. The most popular song of January 1955 was Rosemary Clooney's version of *Mambo Italiano*, a song that reflected the growing interest in the ballrooms for Latin American dances. The lone exception and a sign of changing times was the first ever rock 'n' roll recording to make the popular music charts in both the UK and America; *Shake, Rattle and Roll* performed by Bill Haley and his Comets in a style of music preferred by the younger record collector. Despite being rarely heard by listeners to the BBC's Home and Light programmes, the song's success clearly demonstrated the growing influence of American culture; continental radio stations, primarily Radio Luxembourg; the many young American servicemen stationed in the UK; a growing number of youth focused magazines, and an effective but informal 'word-of-mouth' communication system passing up-to-date information between young people about trends and fashions in music and dress.

Notes

1. *Eastern Evening News*, Saturday 1 January 1955.
2. *Eastern Evening News*, Thursday 3 February 1955.
3. Peter Cossey (2015) *Continuous Performances*, p24.

A Blackboard Jungle

On Monday 7 November 1955, the film *Blackboard Jungle* began a week-long run at the Regent Cinema in Norwich. Based on Evan Hunter's novel of the same name, it dramatised the life of a war veteran, Ricard Dadier (played by Glenn Ford), an English teacher in a tough American inner-city school. His teenage pupils were portrayed in both film and novel as out-of-control delinquent youths with little interest in education, prone to violent episodes, addicted to alcohol and sexually promiscuous. Dadier, christened Daddy-O by his students, tried hard to involve them in various aspects of learning and literature in the face of almost overwhelming verbal and physical abuse. Under the heading 'Sheer sadism in the classroom,' film critic, Stargazer, in the *Eastern Evening News*, commented that:

> America has some astonishing educational problems judging by Blackboard Jungle, the X certificate drama coming to the Regent. Maybe this picture has some meaning in America but in comparison our catapult carrying schoolboys are Little Lord Fauntleroys. If anything, it makes the teachers look stupid with little resemblance to their English colleagues.[1]

The film was released in the USA on 20 March 1955 and in the UK the following September. Deemed suitable only for an adult audience, it was awarded an X certificate by the British Board of Film Censors restricting admission to the over-eighteens. Despite much local opposition, the film was performed in front of capacity audiences at its showings in Norwich.

While Stargazer may have considered the film to be of little relevance to British society, its release is considered by many social historians to be a defining moment in the development of British popular culture, especially the culture of the young. The storyline of the film reflected a growing concern among conservative middle-Americans that its post-war teenage generation was out of control, a view highlighted previously in films such as *The Wild One* and *Rebel Without a Cause*. Marlon Brando's threatening behaviour as the leader of a motorcycle gang in *The Wild One* was considered so anti-social that the film did not feature in most UK cinemas until the mid-1960s. Once released, *Blackboard Jungle* reinforced a real fear in the minds of many Britons that the spread of American culture would promote similar anti-social behaviours among Britain's own teenagers, particularly working-class teenagers. However, for most of British youth, *Blackboard Jungle* was significant solely because it provided them with their first experience of rock 'n' roll music, if only briefly, and a sense of excitement rarely felt in the dull days of post-

Marlon Brando, in A Streetcar Named Desire
Library of Congress, Prints & Photographs
Division, Carl Van Vechten Collection,
[LC-12735]

war austerity. After much deliberation, the film's producer, Richard Brooks, had selected Bill Haley's recording of the song *Rock Around the Clock* as the backing music for the opening and closing credits after it had been recommended to him as a suitable choice by Peter Ford, the rock 'n' roll loving teenage son of Glenn Ford. To give the storyline a contemporary feel, Brooks had replaced the book's references to singers Perry Como, Tony Bennett and the Hilltoppers, the foremost exponents of popular music at the time, with music from Bill Haley and his Comets that more accurately reflected the developing interest by young white Americans in rhythm and blues, the music of the African-American community in the USA.

The song *Rock Around the Clock* was written by C Freedman and JE Myers in 1952 and was recorded by Bill Haley and his Comets for Decca Records on 12 April 1954. Initially released as the B side to *Thirteen Women and Only One Man*, a song about the fourteen survivors of a major nuclear war, it became a minor hit in the USA. It would have gone unnoticed in Britain had it not been for its role in *Blackboard Jungle*, the first film to feature rock 'n' roll music in its soundtrack.[2] Thanks to its exposure in the film, Haley's recording of *Rock Around the Clock* gained overnight success in both the USA and the UK. On 12 November 1955, it reached number one in the UK singles popular music charts and remained in that position for eight weeks until 7 January 1956. Bill Haley's three appearances in the UK Top Ten during 1955 with *Shake, Rattle and Roll*, *Mambo Rock* and *Rock Around the Clock* established him categorically as the man who introduced rock 'n' roll into Britain.

Despite the apparent success of Haley's recording of *Rock Around the Clock*, its immediate influence was limited to those young people over the age of eighteen who had been able to see the film *Blackboard Jungle*. It was hardly ever heard on the BBC's radio programmes. An agreement made in 1935 between the various musicians' unions in both Britain and the United States resulted in a ban on British bands touring America and American bands touring Britain. Individual American artists could tour Britain only if they were backed by a British band. While this ban was in place, Bill Haley and his Comets were unable to play live performances in the UK. Furthermore, the BBC's policy for promoting live music rather than relying on music recorded on disc meant that the song rarely featured in their broadcasts of music. A 'needle time' agreement, between the BBC and the musicians' union, had imposed a limit on the amount of time allocated for broadcasting music on records; a time during which all musical tastes had to be accounted for, not just popular music. As a result, frequent airplay of *Rock Around the Clock* was only possible for some continental radio stations not party to this agreement and who had no limitations imposed on broadcasting recorded music in their programmes; stations such as Radio Luxembourg, Radio Hilversum and the American Forces Network (AFN). Fortunately, these were easily received by listeners in East Anglia because of the region's proximity to the continent. As a result, they became extremely popular with younger listeners and highly influential in determining their choice of music.

In Norfolk, the local newspapers failed to mention Bill Haley's success, preferring instead to restrict their record reviews to new releases from classical musicians, swing orchestras, jazz bands and ballad-singing crooners.[3] In 1955, older people were buying more records than were the young and the record reviewers had them in mind when writing their columns. It was also patently clear that they considered classical music and even jazz to be enduring and worthy, while popular music, especially rock 'n' roll, was transient and of inferior quality, barely worth a mention. Jazz had an intellectual side and was suitable for the middle-classes, but rock 'n' roll was the music of working-class youth and had little cultural value. Unfortunately, the subject matter of *Blackboard Jungle* also ensured that there would always be an unbreakable link in the minds of many older people between rock 'n' roll music and unacceptable teenage behaviour.

Blackboard Jungle was just one among many factors that were inducing the youth of 1950s Britain into developing a culture of their own, based heavily on music and fashion, different in so many ways from the traditional culture of their parents; a trend encouraged by the producers of popular entertainments, records, sheet music and clothing. Post-war austerity was ending, rationing was a thing of the past and almost full employment for the whole adult population ensured that a small cash surplus remained at the end of the working week for most people from all levels in society to spend on entertainment and leisure. The 1944 Education Act also meant that increasingly young people were being educated for longer and in cohorts based on age, not necessarily on social class. At school, in college, at university and at work, as well as during most of their recreational activities, young people of a similar age stayed together, played together, copied each other and adopted the same fashions and beliefs as their peer groups, often significantly different from those of their parents. This became more marked when television finally became available and many older people chose to stay at home rather than venture out to a public house, the cinema or a dance hall for their entertainment. Going out at the weekends became an activity mainly for the young. Furthermore, the teenage quest for excitement that was becoming most evident in their choice of music and leisure pursuits was not just simply a reaction to the dull days of post-war austerity but also to the justifiable fear that their lives could be ended in an instant by the outbreak of a nuclear war with Russia. The mantra of the day was 'enjoy life now as the future is uncertain.'

The major driving force behind this cultural change was money. While the better-off middle classes consistently had money available to spend on entertainments and leisure, and commercial enterprises had focused on catering for their needs, full employment, and often well-paid employment, meant that Britain's working classes, and especially young working-class men and women, now also had a financial surplus, however small, to spend on entertainment. Those young people who left school to begin their working life at fifteen and remained living at home with their parents had more money in their pockets than ever before to spend in coffee bars and public houses, at the cinema and dance hall, visiting hairdressers and buying records, magazines, shoes, make-up and clothes, creating a demand for products more suitable for the younger working-class consumer.

> It is indisputable that youths and girls out to work are much better off than their counterparts in the 1930s. Especially in the 'blind alley' jobs young people can earn something approaching an adult wage. ... Criticism of high wages for boys and girls is based more firmly on the grounds that they receive far more money than their responsibilities, which in turn leads to a complete disregard of the value of money. Young people who live at home and pay very little for the privilege have much more spending money for themselves than they can hope to have after they marry.[4]

For those who remained as students in higher education, well-paid temporary employment during the long vacations was readily available to supplement their grants and allowances, providing them also with a degree of financial independence. Early marriage was discouraged.

> A girl who marries in her teens misses dances and dates. No use counting on a 'good time' in marriage. She can't live for pleasure and bring up a family, and there are people who hold the view that by waiting until the twenties she makes a more contented wife.[5]

Advice often ignored as the average age at marriage in the 1950s was twenty-three for men and twenty for women.

The most obvious change to the culture of young people was in their choice of popular music, although at the start of 1955 there was little evidence for that change.

Popular music for most people in 1955 was an eclectic mix of many distinctive styles: favourites from the two World Wars and the period in between, sentimental ballads about everlasting love, big band numbers and songs from musical theatre, together with a few comedy and novelty numbers that were enjoyed by listeners of all ages. Inevitably, as dancing was a major leisure-time activity for both young and old, compositions and songs performed by dance bands featured heavily in the newly established popular music charts.[6] The immediate post-World War II era was a golden age for British dance bands. Most of Britain's successful singers began their careers as vocalists in a dance band, Dickie Valentine and Alma Cogan with the Ted Heath Band, Lita Rosa with

The forties and fifties were a golden age for dance bands.

the Harry Roy Orchestra, Michael Holliday with Eric Winstone's Band and David Whitfield with the Stanley Black Orchestra. The songs that they sang not only vied for commercial success but also provided a convenient rhythm for dancing a Waltz, a Foxtrot, or the Quickstep. Not only were new songs regularly heard in the ballrooms and dance halls, big and small, but most days on the radio. Programmes featuring live bands, including *Billy Cotton's Band Show*, *Music While You Work*, Jack Payne's *British Band Box*, *Melody Hour* and Victor Sylvester's *Music for Dancing*, were providing a non-stop diet of up-to-date popular music and song on the BBC radio's Light and Home services. Nevertheless, before 1956 their content included little American produced rock 'n' roll or music targeted specifically at a teenage market.

While live performances on the radio by American musicians were restricted and the airtime for their recordings limited, films from Hollywood did give American singers an opening into the UK popular music market, especially the high-quality Hollywood musicals of the early 1950s. Doris Day earned her popularity through films. Her most successful recording, *Secret Love*, featured in the musical *Calamity Jane*. Frank Sinatra consolidated his status as an all-round singer and entertainer with an award-winning acting appearance in the film *From Here to Eternity* and the release of an album of popular music entitled *Songs for Swinging Lovers*. An emerging record industry enabled their music to be heard outside of the cinema. Ballads were the most popular of all with numerous successful hit recordings flooding in from America performed by the likes of Guy Mitchell, Frankie Laine

and Johnny 'Cry-baby' Ray. Where it was available, television expanded the choice of music on offer, especially after 1955 when independent commercial stations were established in some British regions to compete with the BBC. But television was not a feasible proposition for most families in Norwich until well after 1955. A reliable television signal for most of Norfolk was not available until the end of 1956. Norfolk viewers had no commercial alternative to the BBC until the long-awaited arrival of Anglia TV in October 1959. Nevertheless, the presence of a large force of young American servicemen stationed in the many airfields within easy reach of Norwich ensured that music from the USA was readily available locally.

By 1955, the many factors and influences necessary to effect change in the culture of young people in Britain were in place, especially influences affecting their choice of music. For some middle-class young people that change was already underway with the popularisation of jazz in its many forms, traditional and modern. What was needed was a catalyst to kick off that change for the rest of the teenage population, and the film *Blackboard Jungle* and Bill Haley's recording of *Rock Around the Clock* ideally served that function. They identified a musical genre that appealed to working-class teenagers—rock 'n' roll—and, consequently, provided an ideal business opportunity for the entertainments sector. By the end of 1955, change was in the air, even in Norwich.

Notes

1. *Eastern Evening News*, Tuesday 8 November 1955.
2. The term rock 'n' roll was initially used to identify black rhythm and blues music played by white artists that was intended for a white listening audience. The term was first used in this manner by the American DJ Alan Freed.
3. Crooner: a male singer of popular songs that he delivered in a soft sentimental manner made possible with the use of microphones; usually backed by an orchestra, jazz combo or piano.
4. *Eastern Evening News*, Monday 2 January 1956.
5. *Eastern Evening News*, Friday 13 April 1956.
6. The *New Musical Express* published its first list of the week's best-selling records in November 1952.

We Heard it on the Radio

For most people who were living in Norwich during the early 1950s, entertainment in the home meant listening to the radio, usually to the BBC's three stations, the Light, Home and Third programmes. The Light programme for popular music, situation comedies and variety shows, the Home for regional and national news, light dramas and general entertainment and the Third for classical music, poetry, serious dramas and in-depth discussions. The most popular was the Light programme, appealing as it did to the average working-class family, while the Home service had a definite middle-class bias and the Third unashamedly targeted the intellectual minority. For most ordinary people, in the workplace or at home, the radio provided a musical background while they worked during the day, and in the evening, it entertained them with a mix of music programmes, plays, situation comedies, quizzes and variety shows.

Of the programmes broadcast by the BBC's Light programme on Monday 17 January 1955, a typical day on the radio, more than half of the programmes lasting 30 minutes or more consisted of live or recorded music in a range of styles, aimed at an adult audience. Programmes on that day included *Housewives Choice*, a record request programme introduced by Norman Hackforth; a concert from the band of the Coldstream Guards; Spanish influenced music from Troise and his Mandoliers; and no less than three programmes involving theatre organs, an instrument initially developed to provide a musical accompaniment in the cinema to silent movies. Subsequently it had evolved into a solo instrument providing a musical entertainment in between films. The remaining music programmes featured music from the dance bands of Victor Sylvester, Jack Salisbury, Cyril Stapleton and Jack White, and the BBC Midland Light Orchestra. Although The Tommy Whittle Quintet played bebop jazz in a late-night show, no music programme on that day was intended specifically for the teenage listener. The situation was vastly different for those listeners who could receive broadcasts from Radio Luxembourg. Its early evening English programmes were clearly aimed at the interests of ordinary working-class families and the record buying teenager. These popular music programmes were introduced by a new breed of presenters, commonly called Disc Jockeys (DJs), that included Jack Jackson, David Jacobs and Pete Murray, and played the style of music bought by the young.

While children were adequately catered for in its radio programmes, the BBC virtually neglected the teenage listener. The teenage phenomenon was still in its early days. Despite not being targeted specifically at the teenage listener, a minority of the programmes broadcast by the BBC did become essential listening for young people. Among these were *Journey into Space* and *The Goon Show*. *Journey into Space* was an early evening science fiction adventure programme serialised by Charles Chilton and was broadcast by the BBC on the Light Programme from 1953 until 1958 in six series. The storylines told of the adventures of Jet, Doc, Mitch and Lemmy, the four-man crew of a futuristic spaceship, as they explored the Solar System for the first time. In 1955 it was into its third series entitled *The World in Peril* where they attempted to thwart an invasion of Earth by Martians. While it added little to the development of a teenage culture, it did reflect the growing fascination of young people in science and the beginnings of space technology.

The Goon Show, on the other hand, captured exactly the prevailing mood of young people and their growing disillusionment with authority and bureaucracy. *The Goon Show*, featuring Peter Sellers, Harry Secombe and Spike Milligan, was first broadcast in 1951 under the title of *The Crazy People*. By 1955 it was already into its fifth series, had changed its name to *The Goon Show* and had evolved into a standard format consisting of a single 30-minute storyline in three acts, separated by two musical interludes and linked together by a narrator, Wallace Greenslade. The stories related the crazy misadventures of a patriotic idiot, Neddy Seagoon, who was often led astray by two devious adversaries, Count Jim Moriarty and Hector Gryptype-Thynne. As his adventures unfolded, Seagoon encountered many other equally strange characters including Eccles, an educationally challenged teenager; Bluebottle, a boy scout from East Finchley who was always dramatically killed during every episode only to reappear fit and well in the next; Major Bloodnok, ex-Indian Army, coward, womaniser and drunkard with flatulence; and two semi-senile pensioners, Henry Crun and Mini Bannister, who were involved in an unlikely romantic attachment and had a penchant for dirty dancing. The surreal and anarchistic humour of the show was radically different from anything else on the radio and appealed to its younger listening public.

Shows with titles such as *Six Charlies in Search of an Author*, *I Was Monty's Treble*, *The Siege of Fort Night*, *The Great Tuscan Salami Scandal* and *The Nadger Plague* ridiculed authority and made fun of everyone and everything in 1950s British society. Nothing and nobody were safe. The class system, foreigners, politicians, the colonial civil service and scientists were all fair game. The voices of the characters and their catchphrases became part of teenage vocabulary. The silence of many secondary school classrooms was often broken by a disembodied Goon-like wail, a 'sapristi nabolis' uttered as inspiration struck or an Eccles-like 'fine, fine, fine,' much to the annoyance of the teachers. Outside the classroom, catchphrases like "You dirty rotten swine, you've deaded me," "You can't get the wood you know" and "He's fallen in the water" became part of normal conversation, while Goon inspired words, such as 'lurgy' and 'the nadgers,' were added to every English dictionary. At the peak of their popularity in 1956, the Goons even succeeded in entering the popular music charts with two nonsense songs entitled I'm *Walking Backwards for Christmas* and *The Ying-tong Song*. While *The Goon Show* was intended to be a comedy programme it was unlike anything else around at the time and suggested clearly to most young people that British society was not perfect; that the persons and institutions of authority, which were often treated as being sacrosanct and unquestionable, could be challenged, ridiculed and seen as figures of fun. It was a show with an anarchistic bent that not only echoed a growing tendency towards rebellion against authority among mid-1950s British youth, but also their yearning to be entertained by something different.

For young people especially, Radio Luxembourg provided something different. Radio Luxembourg was an American style radio station, financed by advertising, which relied on its popular appeal for success. Its programmes were a mix of serialised adventure stories, talent and other competitions, evangelistic religious programmes, but with a heavy bias towards popular music programmes. Its emphasis on promoting popular music on record, especially the latest recordings from America, heavily influenced the choice of music by the young.

Saturday Night is for Dancing

By 1955, bands playing live music could be heard most nights of the week in a multitude of venues in Norwich, both big and small, despite the limiting absence of a major concert hall. Dance bands and orchestras played live music for dancing weekdays as well as at weekends to capacity audiences in the many dance halls and ballrooms of the city. The variety shows at the Theatre Royal and the Hippodrome regularly contained at least one live musical act, often featuring a nationally known singer or orchestra. Many of the larger public houses and hotels with a suitable function room included a live band as an attraction for the over-eighteens, often providing them also with music for dancing. In a few, the increasingly popular sound of jazz could be heard.

For most of Norwich's young men and women, 'going out' at the weekend meant going to the cinema or dancing at the Samson & Hercules, the Gala, the Lido or the newly opened Norwich Industries Club. In 1955, the largest dance hall in the city was the Samson & Hercules[1], located in an historic building opposite the Cathedral's main Erpingham Gate in a district called Tombland. It was called the Samson & Hercules because of the statues of the two legendary heroes that supported the canopy covering the porch of the building's main entrance(see

The Ronnie Caryl Orchestra at the Samson 1954-55.

p.41). Built in 1657 as the residence of Christopher Jay, Mayor of Norwich, the current building was converted into a dance hall and swimming pool in 1936. The Samson was partially destroyed by a fire in 1944 and thereafter remained under-used until it was purchased by local entrepreneur Geoffrey Watling and refurbished in 1954 as an entertainment complex consisting of a ballroom and various function rooms[2]. Music for dancing was provided in the first instance by the resident dance orchestra, Ronnie Caryl and his Band. When Caryl departed from the Samson in April 1955 for a summer season at the Middleton Towers Holiday Camp in Morecambe, he was replaced by a succession of local dance bands, including the locally popular Jack 'Tubby' Rogers Band featuring the Eastern Area Final winner of the *Melody Maker* Singer of the Year Competition, Bernard Dugdale, as vocalist. Full-time employment seven days a week during the summer season at one of Britain's many seaside holiday resorts was an attractive and financially beneficial proposition for any dance band—a booking no band could refuse.

The Gala Ballroom on St Stephens Road also opened its doors for the first time in 1954 with the Les Hague Orchestra as its resident orchestra; an up-tempo dance band that included several musicians destined to be highly influential in the future development of popular music in the city.

They've taken over at the Gala. Les, himself, is a guitarist, former member of the late Felix Mendelsohn's band and of the Army Entertainments Services in the Middle East. His trumpet player is Brian Green who has several broadcasts to his credit, while the piano and vibraphone departments are in the care of Peter Fenn. Bob Barbour plays the bass and guitar and sings in three languages. The drummer is Rex Cooper, well-known in this area as a skin and sticks expert.[3]

The Gala was also home to the Eileen Page School of Dancing.

The Lido on Aylsham Road, adjacent to the Carlton Cinema, was opened as an indoor swimming pool on 31 May 1934. During the winter months the pool was covered, and the premises were used for dancing. After the war, the pool was permanently covered, and the Lido was used all year round as a dance hall. In 1955, the all-purpose resident band was Billy Duncan and his Dance Orchestra, with leader Duncan billed as the man with a voice like Nat King Cole. Every Tuesday evening it was Rhythm Club night, with up-tempo music aimed at the younger dancer. With over two thousand members, this extremely popular club allegedly regularly entertained over one thousand dancers at its Tuesday evening meetings.[4]

The Norwich Industries Club was the first workingman's club in Norwich and was built on land at Oak Street leased from the Great Hospital.[5] The club was opened on 20 December 1954 by the Lord Mayor, Horace Allen, and the first variety show performed at the club featured singer Ann Shelton[6] with music from the newly installed resident dance orchestra, the Trevor Copeman Band, a 10-piece ensemble formed by Norwich-based trombonist Trevor Jones and drummer Colin Copeman.

Smaller halls also added to the live music on offer most nights of the week, including the Arlington, a dance hall on Newmarket Road, advertised as providing strict tempo music for good dancers, and the Ailwyn Hall on Lower Clarence Road where Maestro played music for Old Tyme Dancing every Saturday night. In Great Yarmouth too, in the winter as well as in the summer, regular dances were held in the Britannia Pier Ocean Ballroom with its resident band, Charles Bosomworth and his Oceanaires, at the newly re-floored Floral Hall in Gorleston with the Eddie Gates Orchestra and at the Wellington Pier Winter Gardens to the music of Bert Galey's Dance Band, as well as in many of the larger seafront hotels. In 1955, most public dances catered for all ages and all styles of dancing. Only at the Norwich Industries Club was there a 'Teenagers Only Night' every Thursday.

For most people in the 1950s, dancing was an essential social skill. In a more strictly controlled society with rigid social conventions, dances not only provided a chance for people of all ages to meet and talk, but also were one of the few opportunities where young men and women could mix without arousing any adverse comments. Many a young person met his or her future partner on the dance floor. Dancing classes for all ages were readily available in Old Time, Latin American and modern ballroom at numerous dance schools in the city including weekly tuition at Peggy Carr's, Norman's, PF Daniel's, and Eileen Page's Schools of Dancing. Young people favoured the modern ballroom dances, the Waltz, Foxtrot and Quickstep, with an occasional old time Veleta, Gay Gordons, Palais Glide or Saint Bernard's Waltz for variety. Responding to the younger dancer's desire for more exciting forms of dance, the craze of the moment was for Latin American dances, especially the Mambo. An American influence was apparent in the increasing popularity of jive among a few of the younger dancers. The larger dance halls frequently hosted dancing competitions. Every year, the National Veleta Championship was held at the Samson with separate events for juvenile and adult competitors. Hundreds of spectators came to watch. Often dancers as young as 10 years of age took part.

The ambition for most young men with a surplus of money in their pockets was to own the smartest suit possible to wear at the weekend dance or out on a date, often the most expensive they could afford in an often all too personal style, yet a step up from the notional 'Sunday best.' In his book *Country Boy*, the author recalls the purchase of his first suit in 1955.

A Saturday night dance at the Samson & Hercules.

As it was a birthday present, I was allowed to choose both the style and material. Since I had very little colour sense and was particularly naïve regarding fashion, the result was a tailor-made suit unique to me and one that I was particularly proud of. My choice of material was a bright light powder blue woollen cloth checked with red, the jacket was double-breasted with large, pointed collars and the trousers had 24-inch bottoms with turn ups and were designed to be held up by a pair of braces. The whole I believe cost £15 from Burton's Tailoring Limited, a considerable expense at the time. Worn with a pair of black shoes, a white shirt and blue woollen tie I considered myself to be the height of elegance at local dances and socials.[7]

The latest London fashion in men's suits was for a return to an Edwardian look. In the late 1940's, many Saville Road tailors, and Hardy Amies in particular, had attempted to revive a New Edwardian style in expensive suits for middle- and upper-class men featuring long draped jackets with velvet cuffs and collars, ornate waistcoats and narrow legged trousers. By the early 1950s, many working-class young men with money to spare were attempting to copy this look in their own suits. An extreme form of this dress combined the New Edwardian look with elements drawn from the fashions of America, notably the draped look of the flamboyant Zoot suits favoured by many off-duty African-American servicemen serving in American airbases in Britain, especially the large airbases in Norfolk, Suffolk,

Cambridge and Lincolnshire. Minor variations based on this style of clothing were adopted in the first instance by groups of London teenagers, who became commonly known as Teddy Boys, a working-class movement that gradually spread to other parts of Great Britain, even to the backwaters of way-out rural East Anglia. As well as Edwardian style suits, other fashion accessories adopted by

US soldier inspecting a couple of "zoot suits", 1942.

Teddy Boys included Mississippi gambler style bootlace ties, bright colourful and, often, luminescent white, pink, or lime-green socks, and elaborate hairstyles.

The most popular hairstyle among fashion conscious young men was the Tony Curtis, a hairstyle aping that of the American cinema actor who gave his name to the cut. Hair was worn long with extravagant sideburns down below the ear. The sides were combed towards the back to meet in a line behind the head, reminiscent of the rear end of a duck, hence its assumed name, the DA or 'Duck's Arse.' Everything was held in place by the application of copious amounts of Brylcreem, a white coloured greasy hair gel. The top was often curled over at the front into a quiff. Individuality was achieved by personal variations of the quiff. In some it was curled over into a tube that fell forward onto the forehead, sometimes a double tube, others had it cut into a spikey triangular crewcut while some simply folded their hair back into a wave as high as they could get it. Many from the older generations of the time considered that young men's attention to hairstyle was not a masculine trait and predicted that it would be a short-lived fashion. When visiting a local barber's shop, Whiffler from the *Eastern Evening News* discovered that:

> One or two youths have their hair permed in this saloon each week. However, I am glad to hear that this practice is dying out. To have the proper Tony Curtis style with curls over the forehead, a perm is essential apparently. Looking after it properly is just too much bother and although the Tony Curtis is still seen about, other styles have almost vanished. Long hair is going out slowly. The DA is dead, I was told.[8]

There were Teddy Girls as well, commonly called Judies. Their fashion was for smart jackets, pencil slim skirts or tight fitting shiny black trousers turned up to mid-calf, all worn with a scarf tied tightly around the neck. Young women who wore trousers were often regarded as odd by older generations.

The wearing of slacks by girl students at Norwich Art School has been frowned upon by the school authorities." "People look on the art student as being a wild and woolly being who doesn't conform to ordinary standards. What the artist wears is always under suspicion. The Art School is situated right in the centre of the city and people notice oddities of dress very quickly.[9]

Nineteen-year-old Jackie Collins, sister of film star Joan Collins, was asked by Hunstanton Town Council not to wear her skin-tight slacks when walking around Hunstanton following complaints from members of the public. At the time, screen actress Jackie was on location in Hunstanton filming scenes for the Ealing Studio's comedy *Barnacle Bill*.[10]

Despite their bad reputation, the fashions of the Teddy Boys and Girls were in demand by the young and had steadily spread beyond London into all parts of the country. A suit in the Edwardian style caused a great stir when it appeared in the window of a St Stephens Road clothing store in Norwich.

The suit, which appeared to be made of good worsted material, was of midnight blue and light blue revers, flap pockets and gauntlet cuffs. One of the revers on the jacket was flat and had the normal V cut while the other was rolled and had no cut in it.[11]

In his column 'Through the Porthole' in the *Eastern Evening News*, Peggotty described his first encounter with a Teddy Boy walking towards the sea along Great Yarmouth's Regent Road.

His style of dress was to say the least startling for the streets of Yarmouth. His black trousers were so drainpipe narrow that I seriously wondered how he got them on. On his feet were a pair of black shoes with block toe-caps reminiscent of my Army boots, and he wore a (grubby) white shirt and a piece of black tape that served as a tie. But the eye-catching thing about his dress was the jacket. It was so long that we were not fully decided if it was a long jacket or short overcoat and it was only because it was a warm day, we agreed it was a long jacket. Its colour—pink, with collar and cuffs edged in black. Of course, the Edwardian style might have meant that it was his grandfather's and had been stowed away some years, and it is also possible that it was specially made for an ardent supporter of the former Kirkley F C who played in pink and black, I seem to recall.[12]

Even if they could not afford a complete outfit, most young men adopted the fashion of the moment and copied some aspect of the Teddy Boy uniform; either the hairstyle, the colourful socks, belts with decorative buckles or the tight-fitting trousers. For most, to be a Teddy Boy was simply choosing to follow a specific fashion in clothes, but for a minority their culture included gang violence and a disrespect for authority. Their notoriety came to the fore in 1953 when two gangs of Teddy Boys fought on Clapham Common resulting in many injuries and one death. Thereafter, any young person guilty of a misdemeanour was inevitably described as a Teddy Boy by the press; and anybody wearing Edwardian style clothing was regarded with suspicion.

The significance of the film, *Blackboard Jungle*, and the Teddy Boy movement was that they marked the point in time when it became clear to everybody, young and old, that Britain's teenagers were developing a culture of their own, separate from that of their parents; an evolving culture characterised by distinct fashions in dancing, music and clothes, and a culture not easily understood or welcomed by the older or more conventional thinking members of society. However, it was a culture whose development was encouraged by commercial interests keen to benefit from the increasing affluence of young people, especially working-class young men and women.

Notes

1. Normally referred to as the Samson.
2. Geoffrey Watling (1913-2004). Born Queens Road, Norwich on 2 April 1913; businessman and former Lord Mayor of Norwich. Became Chairman of Norwich City Football Club in 1957. Lived at Felthorpe Hall from 1963 until his death in 2004.
3. *Eastern Evening News*, Saturday 19 March 1955.
4. Kingsley Harris, coordinator of the East Anglian Music Archive, points out that the Tuesday Rhythm Club at the Lido was often referred to in the press as a jazz club and could, therefore, claim to be the first jazz club in Norwich, specializing in up-tempo and Swing music for dancing. Following the 1935 ban on live performances by American jazz bands in Britain, a National Rhythm Club Movement was formed by enthusiasts in the UK to establish small groups of like-minded people to listen to, play and discuss jazz on record. It published two magazines, Swing Music and Hot News and Rhythm Record Reviews. John Chilton, in his book Who's Who of British Jazz, records that singer Beryl Bryden helped establish a Norwich Rhythm Club in 1939 and was its secretary in 1941. It is unclear whether this was that at the Lido or a separate club located elsewhere.
5. The Great Hospital was founded in 1249 as part of the Cathedral complex to provided accommodation for retired and sick priests. It now provides sheltered housing for retired Norwich residents.
6. Singer, Anne Shelton, topped the popular music charts with Lay Down Your Arms in September 1956.
7. Colin Miller (2005), *Country Boy* p76.
8. *Eastern Evening News*, Thursday 24 May 1956.
9. *Eastern Evening News*, Thursday 15 November 1956.
10. *Eastern Evening News*, Monday 8 April 1957.
11. *Eastern Evening News*, Friday 19 October 1956.
12. *Eastern Evening News*, Thursday 27 September 1956.

Jazz at the Butchers

Interest in music from America grew in post-war Britain despite the restrictive broadcasting policies of the BBC that limited the amount of recorded music in its radio programmes, especially recorded music from the USA. American music gained its popularity primarily in the cinema, a medium dominated by films from Hollywood, and on the radio, especially through the nightly broadcasts by Radio Luxembourg. But the substantial number of American servicemen stationed in the UK during and immediately after the Second World War were also influential in promoting American popular music, especially among the teen and twenty age range in London and the urban areas of the south and east of England. The music enjoyed by America's young servicemen appeared to be far more exciting than the sedate easy-listening dance music, romantic ballads and novelty songs that dominated the British popular music scene of the 1940s and early 1950s. As a result, jazz in its many manifestations—Mainstream Modern, Traditional and Big Band Swing—became popular, particularly with students and those young men doing their compulsory national service in the armed forces.

By 1955, both Traditional and Modern Jazz could be heard inside the bars and backrooms of several well-known public houses in Norwich, attracting a modest but enthusiastic following. The best known of these was the *Jolly Butchers* on Ber Street run by an amiable sixteen stone teetotal Italian-born landlady, Anna Hannant. Better known to her customers as 'Black Anna' because of her habit of always wearing black clothes, Anna was landlady from 1935 until 1976, initially with her husband Jack until his death in 1947. Anna's interest in jazz began when American servicemen were billeted at the *Jolly Butchers* during World War II. With their encouragement, she began to entertain her guests by singing American folk and blues songs to a piano accompaniment in a gruff deep-throated voice reminiscent of Sophie Tucker. Knowledge of her talent soon spread outside Norwich and the *Jolly Butchers* became a magnet for anyone interested in jazz. Steve James in the *Eastern Evening News* commented that:

The Blue Plaque at the site of the Jolly Butchers public house.

27

The Butchers Arms public house on Ber Street.

Anne's reputation as a jazz singer is known in places where they "jam" far beyond Norwich; Cambridge and Oxford students are among the motley crowd who come to the Jolly Butchers to mix their beer with jazz.[1]

Located in a former red-light district of Norwich, the customers at the *Jolly Butchers* were a colourful mix of American servicemen, prostitutes, gay men, lesbians, students, local drinkers and jazz afficionados. In a small, smoky, crowded and often noisy bar, with its walls covered in postcards and a mannequin's head hanging down from the ceiling, Anna and her guest vocalists sang jazz songs without the aid of a microphone to a piano accompaniment. Anna's piano players included her regular accompanist, John Ayres, and two twenty-year-old Lowestoft art students, Colin 'Barney' Bates and Derek Warne.[2] Beryl Bryden was a frequent visitor singing solo and, occasionally, in duets with her long-time friend, Anna. By 1955, Beryl Audrey Bryden was already well-established as an international jazz singer with a singing voice likened to that of Bessie Smith. Her talent was such that she was christened 'Britain's Queen of the Blues' by none other than Ella Fitzgerald. Born at 17 Rowington Road, Norwich on 11 May 1920, Beryl was converted to jazz during her teenage years. In 1945 she moved to London in search of a career as a jazz singer, and frequently guested with many of the up-and-coming London-based bands, including the iconic George Webb's Dixielanders. Her professional career began in earnest in 1953 when she was invited to join Maxim Saury's Jazz Band in Paris. A frequent visitor to Norwich, she guested with most of the city-based jazz bands as well as with Anna at the Jolly Butchers.[3]

The popularity of jazz in Britain had evolved from modest beginnings. In 1942, a would-be jazz pianist George Webb, a machine-gun fitter at the Vickers Armstrong factory at Crayford in Kent, established the Bexleyheath and District Rhythm Club, allegedly the first jazz club in the country. A club where like-minded British musicians could meet to listen to, study and play the authentic jazz music of early twentieth century New Orleans from which the popular wartime big band swing had evolved.[4]

*Black Anna (Antoinette Hannant)
Norwich's Queen of Jazz.*

Weekly sessions were held in the backroom of the *Red Barn* public house in the Kent village of Barnehurst. The club's band, the Dixielanders, began to attract not only those enthusiasts who were interested in learning about and listening to live jazz music, but also ordinary entertainment-seeking members of the public. In time, the *Red Barn* became a popular destination for a rapidly growing audience of followers who had been newly converted to the exciting sound of jazz. The well-known trumpeter Humphrey Lyttelton, a former Grenadier Guardsman, joined the band in 1947. In 1948, George Webb retired temporarily from performing to manage new groups and promote jazz throughout London and the south-east of England. With Humphrey Lyttelton as its new leader, the Dixielanders moved to the more convenient location of the Leicester Square Jazz Club in London where jazz was heralded by many of its followers as the music of the labouring classes and was adopted by a bohemian mix of students, young middle-class liberals and left-wing activists as their music of choice. The *Red Barn* provided a model for subsequent jazz clubs to follow and a network of similar pub-based venues with their resident bands were soon functioning in London, the South-East of England and eventually into Norfolk. The concentration of jazz clubs in the function rooms of public houses meant that, in the first instance, jazz was played to a listening audience drawn from the over-eighteen age range. As such, by 1955 its appeal crossed all age ranges and was not exclusively music for the young.

The most successful of Norwich's jazz bands was the Collegians; a conventional six-piece band playing traditional jazz in the style of Louis Armstrong, featuring trumpet, clarinet, trombone, bass, banjo and drums. The Norwich based band was established in 1948 and began playing gigs at the *Boston Gliderdrome* in Lincolnshire before becoming the resident band of the East Coast Jazz Club at the *Cat and Fiddle* public house on Magdalen Street.[5] A piano was later added to the ensemble and singer Colin Burleigh joined the band in 1952 after completing his National Service with the RAF. The East Coast Jazz Club was the first club specialising in the traditional form of jazz to be established in Norwich and was the brainchild of two jazz enthusiasts, Bryan Land and Laurie Green.[6] The club's initial meeting at the *Cat and Fiddle* was held on Tuesday 25 November 1952. Proceedings began with the club's new honorary president, the well-known music critic Sinclair Traill, giving a talk about the origins of jazz illustrated by recordings played on a gramophone.[7] This was followed by a live concert from the Collegians featuring guest singer Beryl Bryden, who had made a special journey from London to attend. The mainly seated 70-strong audience included a large contingent of American servicemen. Thereafter, club nights were every Tuesday with music from the Collegians and other invited guest artists. The club membership quickly rose to well over one hundred, a respectable membership at that time.

Interest in jazz by young people grew, especially as it became increasingly linked with dancing. By the mid-1950s, jazz band balls had become a popular attraction for the younger members of the jazz community, initially in London and then throughout the rest of the country. Conventionally, these were jazz sessions involving more than one band that were held in larger premises where audiences were able not only to sit and listen to the music but also to dance, usually a toned-down version of the Lindy Hop,[8] not always with the approval of the more traditional jazz enthusiasts. As these events were often located away from the public house, they also enabled the under-eighteens to access and enjoy the sound of live jazz. Norwich's first jazz band ball was organised by the East Coast Jazz Club and held in the Chantry Hall on Chantry Road on Monday 16 February 1953 with the Collegians as the headline band.

In the same year, a second jazz club was established at the *Gibraltar Gardens*, a riverside public house on Heigham Street, and was creatively named the Gibraltar Gardens Jazz Club.[9] Club nights were held every Monday from 8.00pm until 10.00pm with music from the club's resident band, the Stompers, later to be known as the Mustard City Stompers. Seeking a more advantageous location in the centre of Norwich, the club moved its base from the *Gibraltar Gardens* to premises in the cellar of the *Orford Arms* public house on Red Lion Street where it was renamed as the Norwich Jazz Club. The opening session at the Orford was held on Monday 5 May 1954 with music from the Mustard City Stompers supported by the Collegians and guest vocalists Beryl Bryden, Colin Burleigh and Anna Hannant from the *Jolly Butchers*. Despite the loss of the Norwich Jazz Club and the Mustard City Stompers, jazz nights continued at the *Gibraltar Gardens* featuring traditional jazz from the new resident Gibraltar Jazz Band and a modern jazz combo called the Norwich Modernists. The Norwich Jazz Club's stay in the Orford cellar was short-lived. Following complaints about excessive noise from the bands, it was once again relocated, this time to a function room at the RAFA Club headquarters in Spencer House on Lobster Lane.[10]

By 1955, jazz nights had also become a regular feature in the function room of the *Cottage* public house on the outskirts of the city at Thunder Lane in Thorpe. Jazz frequently replaced conventional dance bands on Friday and Saturday nights, often featuring the Collegians as the main attraction. Monday nights were devoted to the less popular sound of modern jazz performed by the Norwich Modernists and their guest artists. The Modernists were newly installed as the resident Monday night band after relocating to the *Cottage* from the *Gibraltar Gardens*.

> Jazz fans, you may know, are divided into 'Trads' (Traditionalists) and 'Moderns.' The Modernists bring a star down here Monday night—Joe Harriott, alto sax with the new Ronnie Scott orchestra. He'll be playing at the Cottage, in Thorpe, accompanied by a group led by Peter Fenn on piano, with Bud Cooper (drums) and Bob Barbour (bass).[11]

Unlike the leading full-time London-based bands of Humphrey Lyttelton, Cy Laurie, Ken Colyer and Chris Barber, Norwich's jazz bands were mostly semi-professional groups playing music that they loved on a part-time basis rather than as their primary occupation. Most band members had a daytime job and played jazz in the evening. Some musicians, like Peter Fenn, were later able to convert their interest in jazz into a full-time musical career. Even in Norwich, jazz, both traditional and modern, still only had a minority appeal. However, due to the efforts locally of clubs, like the Norwich Jazz Club, and nationally through exposure on radio and on record, the popularity of jazz was on the increase, especially with urban middle-class youth. In the rural areas, the management of most village and community halls were unable to afford to engage the larger and more costly urban-based jazz bands to perform at their dances, neither were there enough competent local musicians with the right instruments who were able to play this specialist form of music. Consequently, live jazz was primarily an urban form of entertainment and, until the late 1950s, rarely featured in most of Norfolk's rural dance halls.

Notes

1. *Eastern Evening News*, Saturday 26 June 1954. Anna Hannant was occasionally referred to as Anne in the press.

2. Lowestoft born pianist Derek John Warne joined the Ted Heath Orchestra in 1959. He later became musical director for the Dickie Henderson Show, the Mike Reid Show and Top of the Pops. Derek was cofounder of the Norwich Jazz Club in 1980; not to be confused with the original Norwich Jazz Club that was formed in 1954 in the cellar of the Orford Arms Public House on Red Lion Street. Jazz pianist Colin 'Barney' Bates was born at Llangollen in 1932 and moved to Lowestoft in 1952 where he formed his own band, the Colin Bates Jazzmen. In 1957, he moved to London where he joined the Cy Laurie Band before moving on to join with Terry Lightfoot's Band. Colin went on to have a lengthy career in music, playing the piano in numerous jazz bands including those of Kenny Ball and Aker Bilk.

3. Beryl Bryden had a long and successful career in music, singing with many top jazz bands right up to her death from cancer in the St Mary's Hospital, Paddington, London on 14 July 1998.

4. Rhythm Clubs were formed primarily for the study of jazz on record. Jazz Clubs, on the other hand, also included among its activities live performances by jazz bands with an audience, sometimes providing music for dancing.

5. The Boston Gliderdrome was built in the 1930s as an open-air skating rink. Roofed over during World War Two, it became a major dance venue, popular with locally based British and American servicemen. The original building was destroyed by fire on 24 May 1959 and replaced by a purpose-built entertainments centre.

6. The East Coast Jazz Club was most probably the first club in Norwich specializing in traditional jazz.

7. Music critic and author, Eric Sinclair Traill (1905-81) was chief editor of Jazz Journal and founding director of the National Federation of Jazz Organisations in Britain.

8. Lindy Hop: a wild partner dance of the jazz era that originated in 1920's Harlem, and was characterised by frenzied kicks, twirls, lifts and athletic body movements; a fusion of black American dance moves with the Charleston. The Lindy Hop was so named to commemorate Charles Lindbergh's 'hop' across the Atlantic in 1927.

9. In correspondence with the author, Kingsley Harris records that the Gibraltar Gardens Jazz Club was formed by a break-away group from the Norwich Jazz Club led by Brian Land. What led to the break-away is unknown?

10. Kingsley Harris also records that there is evidence to suggest that the Norwich Jazz Club was forced to move not due to the noise but because, at that time, the Orford Cellar was not licenced for music and dancing.

11. *Eastern Evening News*, Saturday 3 December 1955. Fenn, Cooper and Barber were also members of the Les Hague Orchestra. Competent musicians often played in more than one ensemble.

Oversexed, Overpaid and Over Here

The presence in East Anglia of large numbers of US servicemen during and after World War II undoubtedly had had an impact on the culture of Norfolk's youth. Towards the end of the war, over 50,000 young Americans were billeted within a 30-mile radius of Norwich. After the war, a large American force remained in East Anglia under the control of the US Strategic Air Command to counter the perceived military threat from Soviet Russia, and was based at the Lakenheath, Mildenhall and Sculthorpe airbases. In 1956, the government agreed to build 1,500 extra houses for US airmen and their families living in East Anglia, 210 at Sculthorpe, in return for £5,300,000 worth of tobacco; 1,500 more houses were planned to be built sometime in the future.

Being out of range of German aircraft during World War II, America did not suffer the destruction to businesses and property as had occurred in the UK from the intense enemy bombing. Therefore, America was able to recover more quickly from the consequences of a major war. Bomb sites were still a common feature in many English cities well into the mid-1950s and early 1960s. In America, the entertainment industry was undamaged and in full swing during and immediately after the war, while in the UK it functioned with difficulty. British cinemas were filled with movies from Hollywood, while, at home, film making was only slowly recovering. There is little doubt that ideas and fashions emanating from America via the cinema were the source and inspiration for many of the exciting changes that were taking place in the culture of Britain's youth, especially in music, at the cinema, on the radio and, eventually, on television, American society was shown to be more affluent and exciting than a British society that was still slowly emerging from a decade of dull post-war austerity. America's young men and women were seen to have far more money, independence and fun than their British counterparts. A view reinforced by the attitudes and behaviour of the many American servicemen who made use of the entertainment facilities

American GI and girlfriend on part of South Norfolk golf course where the American hospital was built at Wymondham.

The Gable Gaitors, named after Col. Gable the Commanding Officer at the American hospital at Wymondham during World War II, were typical of American influence on the music scene in Norfolk. They often played there and at other venues.

available in Norwich, Lowestoft and Great Yarmouth. Local youths were attracted by the colourful and well-cut clothes worn by the off-duty US soldiers and airmen who visited Great Yarmouth and Norwich to drink and relax in the seafront and city bars. Many teenagers tried to imitate them by buying brightly coloured jumpers, baseball jackets and canvas boots for their casual wear, and cut their hair crew-cut style. Even American cigarettes were longer than their British counterparts.

The substantial number of American servicemen based in Norfolk was undoubtedly responsible for Norwich's early involvement in the jazz music scene, second only to London. It is also likely that it was American servicemen who popularised jive dancing among the young people of Britain, by nature a toned-down version of the energetic Lindy Hop but with less aerial acrobatics. On 19 March 1956, an American Branch of the Norwich Industries Club opened in Spencer House on Lobster Lane replacing RAFA[1] as tenants, forcing the nomadic Norwich Jazz Club to seek new premises for a third time.[2] Meanwhile, at Lobster Lane, club facilities were created for the sole use of US servicemen and their guests, with central heating set at a higher level than before, food and drinks bars equipped with refrigerated shelves, a restaurant and a dance floor with an obligatory jukebox.

The presence of young American servicemen in Norfolk was not without difficulties, despite sharing a common language. Local youths often resented the sight of extravagantly spending brash Americans driving fast cars embellished with wings and ornamental chrome wheel trims, their well-tailored clothes and their ability to attract the attention of local young women; a resentment that often led to violent clashes. A reporter from the *Eastern Daily Press* commented that:

The young unattached American servicemen, of whom perhaps the Norfolk man is most aware, are not lonely! "They get around" I was gravely informed. More often than not, English people would regard this phrase in its rather more undesirable application having in their minds eye a picture either of the young men who are besieged by teenage girls or the fraternity who appear in courts for driving offences.[3]

Their lively and often irresponsible off-duty behaviour frequently resulted in undesirable outcomes.

Four American airmen were given first-aid at Low Road Corner, Drayton early yesterday after their car collided with a telegraph pole and snapped it in half ... the impact not only broke the telegraph pole but moved the foot of it about 12 inches through an asphalt path.[4]

Columnists in the Norfolk press consistently offered advice to parents whose daughters were dating Americans. A liberal attitude to pre-marital sex gave rise to an increase in illegitimacy. Nearly half the children born to single mothers in Norwich during 1955 were fathered by American servicemen. The Norwich Deanery Moral Welfare Committee was wont to comment that:

Nowadays parental control and home discipline are somewhat conspicuous by their absence. This means that some of the girls are lacking in self-control. They have never been taught to exercise restraint.[5]

Inevitably, marriages were commonplace between American servicemen and local women. A liaison officer from Lakenheath stated that:

Out of each batch of young, unmarried Americans who settle in Norfolk for the usual period of three years, about one third of them will return to the States with Norfolk brides.[6]

Unfortunately, the Americans were in East Anglia for a reason. War with Russia was a definite possibility and thought by some British residents to be imminent. Life was lived with the constant fear of the 'four-minute warning'[7] that would herald large-scale atomic annihilation. A civil defence exercise throughout all East Anglia held on 7 May 1956 simulated the effects locally of hydrogen bomb attacks on London and Birmingham, together with an atom bomb falling on the mouth of the Yare destroying all Gorleston and most of Great Yarmouth. The suggested consequence of such an attack was for massive casualties as well as an extensive radio-active cloud contaminating all East Anglia except for the extreme north of Norfolk and the south of Suffolk. As part of this exercise, civil defence volunteers were taught how to build soup kitchens and temporary shelters from the debris of buildings that would be destroyed in the attack. A follow up exercise on 23 May rehearsed the effect of a further atom bomb dropping on Mousehold Heath. The fear of a nuclear war undoubtedly had a defining influence on the opinions and actions of Britain's young people everywhere. A 'live for today, because tomorrow may never come' attitude was prevalent among a substantial portion of Britain's youth. Dr Lincoln Ralphs, Chief Education Officer for Norfolk, commenting on the situation confronting young people, said that:

> It was a wonder that they were not all neurotic for they grew up hearing, seeing and reading of possible annihilation.[8]

Notes

1. Royal Air Forces Association.
2. The upstairs accommodation at Spencer House was extended in 1978 by knocking through into the adjoining Conservative Association premises on Dove Street. Currently (2022) it is the location of the Platinum Lace Gentlemen's Club.
3. *Eastern Evening News*, Thursday 10 May 1956.
4. *Eastern Evening News*, Saturday 9 June 1956.
5. *Eastern Evening News*, Thursday 8 March 1956.
6. *Eastern Evening News*, Tuesday 8 July 1958.
7. It was estimated that it would take four minutes for rockets armed with atomic warheads to travel from Russia to the UK.
8. *Eastern Evening News*, Thursday 20 March 1958.

Ken Colyer at the Lads' Club

Having been displaced from Spencer House by the creation of the American Club, the Norwich Jazz Club was forced to move into temporary accommodation at the St Giles Parish Hall on Cow Hill. Nevertheless, a measure of the club's developing status in jazz circles was manifested in its ability to attract into the city big-named bands from London, the first of which was the Cy Laurie Band who performed at the newly occupied St Giles Parish Hall on Monday 16 May 1955.

> London's Cy Laurie and his Jazz Band certainly drew the crowds to Norwich's St Giles Hall this week. There were three hundred enthusiasts there including airmen from all RAF stations in the county.[1]

Following on from the success of Laurie's visit, the club organised a jazz band ball to be held at the hall on Monday 11 July. The *Eastern Evening News* advertised that:

> In the austere and definitely highly unjazz-like interior of St Giles Hall in Cow Hill, the Norwich Jazz Club is holding a Jamboree.[2]

Bands scheduled to appear at the Jamboree were the Mustard City Stompers, the resident club band; the Collegians with singer Colin Burleigh; Ted Ramm, a jazz pianist formerly with the Cy Laurie Band; the Anglo Dukes of Rhythm, a Dixieland Band from the USAAF base at Lakenheath; and singer Anna Hannant, landlady of the *Jolly Butchers*, who was billed in the press as 'Norfolk's Queen of Jazz.' Commenting on Anna's proposed appearance, the *Eastern Evening News* stated that:

> She's sure of a rip-roaring welcome for the jazz club boys and girls will be greeting her collectively for the first time since the Orford Arms days, quite a few moons ago.[3]

Unfortunately, the Anglo Dukes of Rhythm were forced to cancel due to commitments at the airbase and were replaced on the night by a newly formed Norwich-based jazz band, the Dixielanders, led by trumpeter Brian Green, a former member of the Les Hague Orchestra.[4] The Dixielanders were invited by the club to substitute for the Anglo Dukes after having impressed locally with a dynamic debut performance a week earlier at the Coltishall Village Hall on Thursday 30 June. The ball at St Giles was deemed to have been an enormous success despite the hall lights failing for part of the show. Following their performance at St Giles, the Dixielanders were given a regular Friday night booking at the Cottage in Thorpe and an appearance at the Phoenix Club in London in October. On 7 November 1955, the Norwich Jazz Club moved premises yet again, relocating from their temporary base at St Giles to a regular Monday evening club night in the Boulton and Paul Sports and Social Club at Rosary Corner on Thorpe Road.

The continued ability of the Norwich Jazz Club to attract nationally known bands to the city was undoubtedly instrumental in expanding the growing interest locally in jazz, especially among Norwich's young people. To cope with the extra demand caused by visiting bands, performances were often held in larger premises, notably those that were available for hire at the Lads' Club on King Street.[5] Guesting at the Lads' Club on Monday 5 September was the Chris Barber Jazz Band. The function was a sell-out. All one thousand tickets were sold long before the event. On the night, three hundred disappointed jazz fans queued outside the club hoping to be the first in line to purchase any tickets that might have been returned. Appearing in Norwich for the first time, the Barber Band was supported by the Collegians. The concert received rave reviews in the local press. Steve James of the *Eastern Evening News* reported that:

> This Trad Jazz, with the rough edges off, was good to hear. I have room to mention only a few numbers, a fine 'Saratoga Swing,' a lively New Orleans 'Up Jumps the Devil' and the final 'Ramble'.[6]

Singing with the band was a 23-year-old ex-art teacher, Ottile Patterson, who had recently been introduced to Chris Barber as a potential world-class jazz singer by Norwich's own Beryl Bryden. Playing during the interval between sets was the Lonnie Donegan Skiffle Group, the first time that skiffle music was performed live anywhere in Norwich.

> The band-within-a-band, the Lonnie Donegan Skiffle Group, must be heard to be appreciated. It gives a wonderful rendering of spirituals and ring-shouts peculiar to true Negro 'race' music.[7]

The *Eastern Evening News'* record reviewer, Peter Phillips, was not so complimentary about the introduction of skiffle. Commenting on the release of a long-play recording entitled *Traditional Jazz at the Royal Festival Hall*, he wrote in his column that:

> If the (Alex)Welsh Dixielanders surprised me with the power and feeling of their 'Panama Rag,' their 'Memphis Blues' left me gasping … The Ken Colyer and Chris Barber jazzmen also do well. Especially good is the Barber Band's 'Its Tight Like That.' But the Lonnie Donegan Skiffle Group strikes

me as little more than an excuse for three members of the Barber Band to demonstrate their versatility (Don't ask me what skiffle is).[8]

Despite the icy weather and a thick fog that was covering most of East Anglia, over one thousand fans queued once again outside the Lads' Club on Thursday 5 January 1956 to see a performance by Ken Colyer's Jazzmen. Steve James commented that;

The only British band-leader ever to have seen the inside of an American gaol drew a full house of nearly a thousand at the Norwich Lads' Club last night when he and his jazzmen gave a concert there under the auspices of the Norwich Jazz Club.[9]

Supporting Colyer's Jazzmen was the club's resident band, the Mustard City Stompers.[10] A mostly seated audience stamped their feet to a succession of jazz classics including *Walking with the King*, *Dippermouth Blues*, *The World is Waiting for the Sunrise* and *The Old Rugged Cross*. Ken Colyer was born at Great Yarmouth on 18 April 1928 and became a jazz enthusiast and performer after being introduced to this genre of music by his elder brother, Bill. In 1949, Colyer joined the Crane River Jazz Band in London performing as their leader and trumpet player. After a brief period in the Merchant Navy, he spent time in New Orleans studying and playing jazz in its traditional style. A white man learning from and playing with black jazz musicians was regarded as unacceptable behaviour by America's deep-south separatist white population. Having overstayed the period of his visa, he was sentenced to a short term in prison before being expelled from the USA; a harsh sentence undoubtedly imposed because of his fraternisation with the black community in New Orleans. On his return to England in 1953, Colyer formed the Ken Colyer Jazzmen with Chris Barber on trombone, Monty Sunshine on clarinet, Ron Bowden on bass, Lonnie Donegan on banjo and Jim Bray on drums. The release in late 1953 of the Jazzmen's long play recording *New Orleans to London* is regarded by jazz historians as marking the start of the movement that led to the universal popularity of British-style Traditional Jazz among young people in the late 1950s.

Ken Colyer was not an easy man to work with and his intransigent views on how jazz should be played led to an acrimonious split with his band in 1954. Following Colyer's departure, Chris Barber, assisted by Lonnie Donegan, reorganised the remnants of the band to form what became known thereafter as the Chris Barber Jazz Band. Eventually, Colyer established a new Colyer's Jazzmen in what was a classic formation playing jazz in a fluid traditional New Orleans ensemble style,[11] and it was this band that performed at the Lads' Club in Norwich. The evening's line-up consisted of Ken Colyer on trumpet, Ian Wheeler on clarinet, Mac Duncan on trombone, Dick Smith on bass, Colin Bowden on drums and John Barnstable on banjo. Soon after the concert, columnist Steve James commented in the *Eastern Evening News* that:

> Interest in jazz music is certainly spreading. Recently I have seen learned dissertations on it in 'The Times,' the 'Daily Telegraph' and the 'Observer,' not to mention having heard the art of Louis Armstrong discussed on the Third programme of all the unlikely spots. Seemingly, the wide Norwich interest shown in the subject reflects the general trend. Monday saw no fewer than three local sessions going on — the Norwich Jazz Club at Boulton & Paul's Social Club, the 59 Jazz Club at the Herbert Frazer Hall in Bethel Street and the Norwich Modernists at the Cottage in Thunder Lane.[12]

On Saturday 19 May 1956, 800 young people attended another Norwich Jazz Club production at the Lads' Club entitled *Jazz Waggon* which featured Mick Mulligan and his Band with the singer George Melly. Supporting Mulligan and Melly were once again the Norwich based Mustard City Stompers[13] and solo singer, Anna Hannant, with Lowestoft Jazz Club's pianist Colin Bates as her accompanist.

Ken Colyer's influence on the evolution of British beat music in the 1950s should not be underestimated. During his stay in America, he had developed a keen interest in the music of both the black and white working communities of the southern states, especially the songs made popular by the guitar-playing folk musicians Woody Guthrie, Huddie Ledbetter (Leadbelly) and Big Bill Broonzy. On his return from America, Colyer, on guitar, assisted by Lonnie Donegan and Alexis Korner, also playing guitars, Chris Barber on bass and brother Bill on washboard, introduced impromptu performances of American folk songs during the intervals between jazz sessions. Songs that they sang with a jazzy beat in which the voice and guitar were the dominant instruments rather than the traditional trumpet, clarinet and trombone. Playing jazz was exhausting for the three lead wind instrumentalists and these sessions were introduced simply to entertain and occupy a potentially lively and drink enthused audience while the frontline musicians rested. Nevertheless, these sessions became extremely popular with jazz audiences and developed into a new and, in time, a much-copied style of music, uniquely British, which Bill Colyer had christened as 'skiffle,' borrowing a term formerly used in America for impromptu jam sessions at parties. It also elevated the guitar in the minds of British musicians from being simply a part of the rhythm section of a jazz band, an alternative to the banjo, to the role of a lead instrument.

Although initially appealing to an enthusiastic minority of the over-eighteens, thanks to its association with public houses, jazz and its spin off skiffle were rapidly becoming the music of choice for many young people and were especially popular among students and young men and women from the urban professional and middle classes. This was a trend that accelerated when jazz moved from the public houses into larger clubs and dance halls where promenading and jiving were possible on dedicated dance floors. As a result, age ceased to be an insurmountable barrier for the younger jazz fan. Jazz's increasing popularity among Britain's young people also stemmed from its link with jive, a link that was not always appreciated by the more serious among the traditional jazz enthusiasts. The fact that jazz was mostly instrumental had enhanced the notion among many new converts that jazz was primarily music for dancing, while, for the connoisseur, it was mood music to listen to and appreciate.

> The Teenagers today seem to grow up with a latent talent for jiving which simply wants to be released. ... Jiving depends upon rhythm and upon the enthusiasm and vitality of the jazz band. It is a sort of primitive abandon; you have to get into a form of trance and let the rhythm get hold of you. ... Most youngsters who attend dances at the Lido, Samson and Hercules or Norwich Industries Club regularly sooner or later start to jive.[14]

To cater for this new demand by young dancers, weekly jazz and jive sessions were introduced by the management in most of Norwich's dance halls. The Samson & Hercules introduced occasional jazz and jive nights in between its regular modern and 'old tyme' dances. On Monday 3 May 1954, the Samson & Hercules

The 'Samson and Hercules' doorway photographed in 2011.

held its first Jazz Band Ball featuring Ken Colyer, the Collegians and Beryl Bryden. On Wed 12 May 1954, the Lowestoft Palais followed suit with its own Jazz Band Ball. Jiving was encouraged at the Balls and jive competitions were held by the organisers.

> Jivers whirled and twirled in frantic competition at the Samson and Hercules ballroom last night when the area heat and final of the national Free Style Jive Championship was held there. The majority of those taking part in this strenuous exercise were 'teenagers' but the winning couple were in their early twenties.[15]

Every Friday was jazz and jive night at the Norwich Industries Club. On 28 October 1955, the club held its first Jazz Band Ball, and on 9 December a Grand Jazz Band Jamboree and Jive Contest.

On 16 April 1956, Brian Green opened a jazz club at the Herbert Frazer Hall, a large single-storey wooden building behind the Labour Party Offices on Bethel Street, called the 59 Jazz Club after the number on the Labour Party Offices' door.

> Opening night of Norwich's 59 Jazz Club at the Herbert Fraser Hall in Bethel Street this week saw 180 fans sign on for membership. The club band, Brian Green and his Dixielanders, played to a capacity crowd with standing room only for late comers. The programme ranged from that old 'Tiger Rag' to the bands own rhythmic 'Midnight Blues'.[16]

Interest in jazz continued to grow, especially among large sections of Norwich's youth. Five hundred or more followers of jazz attended two performances by Cy Laurie and his Band at the Gala Ballroom on Monday 9 July and Thursday 26 July 1956. The Norwich Jazz Club went from strength to strength, and on Monday 10 September 1956, the club organised a jazz festival during Battle of Britain Week on behalf of the RAF Benevolent Fund called *'Jazz in the Air'* featuring five local jazz and skiffle bands. In November, the club enrolled its 2000th member, Audrey Tipple of Britannia Road, Norwich, who received a special cake to celebrate the occasion. The 59 Club signed up its 500th member in the same month. The resident band, Brian Green and the Dixielanders, spent an eventful summertime break in Skegness.

> The Dixielanders took their holiday this year en masse…they all went to a holiday camp at Skegness. They took their instruments with them and, unlike the case of the girl who took her harp, someone asked them to play… for a week the Dixielanders' brand of jazz attracted dancers numbering two thousand. They also played at a jazz concert that had a 5000-strong audience.[17]

In 1956, the restrictions on American musicians performing in Britain was partially lifted and a scheme was begun that arranged for a one-for-one-exchange of a swing band from America with a dance band from the UK. The first exchange involved a tour of the UK by the Stan Kenton Orchestra and by Ted Heath and his Band to the USA, organised by the impresario Harold Davidson. Due to the efforts of the Samson & Hercules' owner, entrepreneur Geoffrey Watling, the UK tour of the Stan Kenton Orchestra included a concert at the St Andrews Hall in Norwich on Thursday 15 March 1956. Billed as the 'the King of Progressive Jazz,' a well-attended concert saw Kenton, on piano, with his 20-piece orchestra blast out old classics like *Stomping at the Savoy* and *Cherokee* together with selections from his soon to be released album, *Cuban Fire*. Whiffler reported that he:

> Went along to St Andrews Hall to watch the crowds going in. They were not the typical youngsters one sees in the dance halls but a mixed crowd of all ages.[18]

Further exchanges resulted in a visit to St Andrews Hall on Monday 3 September by Sidney Bechet and the André Reoweliotty Band, supported by Humphrey Littleton, and on Tuesday 30 October by the Lionel Hampton Orchestra. Whiffler again:

> Enjoyed the performance of the Lionel Hampton band—not so much for the music, for the only recognisable tune was "God Save the Queen"—but the manner of presentation, instrumental skill, the showmanship and the sheer exuberance of performance.[19]

Other than the Kenton concert, the performances were not fully attended and suffered a financial loss, indicating perhaps that the preference among Norwich's youth was not for big bands playing Progressive Jazz and Swing but for the British exponents of Traditional Jazz as exemplified nationally by the smaller bands of Ken Colyer and Chris Barber, and locally by the Collegians, the Mustard City Stompers and Brian Green's Dixielanders. Modern jazz was for listening. It did not lend itself to dancing. Traditional jazz provided the beat for dancing and in the 1950s, young people wanted to dance.

Notes

1. *Eastern Evening News*, Saturday 21 May 1955.
2. *Eastern Evening News*, Wednesday 6 July 1955.
3. *Eastern Evening News*, Saturday 9 July 1955.
4. Brian Green and his Dixielanders, 1955 line-up; Brian Green (trumpet), Ian Bell (trombone), Peter Oxburgh (clarinet), Jack Wilkinson (tenor-sax), Denis Howe (banjo), Tony Powell (piano), Denis Payne (bass), Dick Pearce or Joe Eden (drums).
5. The Lads' Club was founded in 1918 by Chief Constable John Dain to provide useful and

interesting activities for young men to keep them from idleness and unsocial behaviour. From 1924, the club was located at the premises on King Street, now the site of the King's Centre.

6. *Eastern Evening News*, Friday 21 October 1955.
7. *Eastern Evening News*, Saturday 15 October 1955. Music produced and recorded for the African American community in the USA was initially described as 'Race music.' Over time, the description was dropped and replaced by the more acceptable and all-embracing term, 'Rhythm & Blues.'
8. *Eastern Evening News*, Friday 11 May 1956.
9. *Eastern Evening News*, Friday 6 January 1956.
10. The Mustard City Stompers in 1955: Al Garnet (trumpet), Jack Farrer (trombone), Ted Hook (clarinet), Joe Dade (piano), Jim Beaumont (banjo), John Thaxton/Pete Brandish (bass), Albert Redgrave (drums).
11. In an ensemble style there are no individual instrumental solos, but all the frontline instruments become engaged in a collective improvisation around the basic theme.
12. *Eastern Evening News*, Thursday 24 May 1956.
13. A biro sketch of the Mustard City Stompers at the Norwich Jazz Club signed and dated 'George Melly/1956' sold for £500 at Christie's of London in 2011.
14. *Eastern Evening News*, Thursday 1 December 1955.
15. *Eastern Evening News*, Friday 8 June 1956.
16. *Eastern Evening News*, Saturday 21 April 1956.
17. *Eastern Evening News*, Saturday, 22 September 1956.
18. *Eastern Evening News*, Friday 16 March 1956.
19. *Eastern Evening News*, Thursday 1 November 1956.

In the Beginning

The summer of 1956 was mostly cold, dull, and very wet; a depressing time for everybody. In Great Yarmouth, Ronnie Ronalde at the Wellington Pier, Eddie Calvert at the Windmill and Jimmy Jewel and Ben Warris at the Royal Aquarium tried hard to lift the spirits of the holidaymakers who were pale from a lack of sun. In Norwich, the promise of a more exciting future was suggested by a variety show at the Hippodrome entitled *Rock-N-Roll*, a hint of things to come in its title rather than what was implied by its content.

> The sort of show which can help to put the music hall back in the good grace of the people who like their entertainment without the need to apologise to discerning friends for stage indiscretions.[1]

The star of the show was comedian Roy Rolland appearing as 'Old Mother Kelly.' In his earlier days, Roy was an understudy for Arthur Lucan, the original 'Old Mother Riley'[2], a much-loved family favourite. Roy's audience was encouraged to rock and roll with laughter. It was certainly not a rock 'n' roll music show.

Dancing in one form or another remained the main form of entertainment for most young people. Not only was jive becoming popular, particularly in urban Norwich where jazz clubs were now a well-established feature, but also traditional dance styles had their youthful adherents. Old and new in music and dance existed happily side-by-side. The weekly programme at most of Norwich's major dance halls catered for all styles of dancing.

> Why is it that more and more people—young and old—are taking up old-time dancing as their chief source of recreation? Since its revival in this country immediately after the 1939/45 war, it has steadily gained and held its amazing popularity against all competitive types of entertainment. ... There is no disputing the fact that the 'Empress Tango' and the 'Waltz Marie' are going to have far more adherents than ever the Mambo or the Creep had.[3]

The dance hall was still the main location for young men and women to meet socially and to form romantic relationships, not without a major concern for their parents.

> When teenage John took teenage Margaret to a dance in pre-war days, she danced at least once with Tom, Dick and Harry, and every other lad in her

group. Etiquette demanded it. At a similar party today, however, it is most likely that Margaret will dance the whole night with John. Eighteen months ago, parents were dismissing sole dancing complacently as a passing fad. Today they are neither so sure nor so happy about it. And if a girl dances with one boy all night, lights turned down low and goes home together cosily in a car, it may place a moral strain on the couple. Those who crystallise their association around their mid-teens are in danger of being sorry and disillusioned after marriage.[4]

In Norwich, as in most other major urban areas, jiving was not restricted solely to its jazz clubs but was also becoming a feature in most dance halls throughout the city. One evening a week was designated at many ballrooms for jiving although the management of most were still reluctant to let jiving and ballroom dancing take place at the same time. At the Norwich Industries Club, weekly jive nights had become a regular feature. The city's dancing schools were quick to respond. In September, the Eileen Page School of Dancing introduced jive classes for beginners.

Being one of those simple souls who always believed that jiving was a natural rhythmic movement done, so to speak, from the hips, I was surprised to notice advertisements for jive classes at the Gala Ballroom in Norwich. Miss Eileen Page put me right. "There is," she explained, "the standard technique for Latin American jive which we, and the other teachers of dancing, have taught for some time in private lessons. I have found, however, that youngsters who have learnt this find it is not the jive danced in the ballroom," So the jive as she is done is what students are learning at the Gala, but it will still be banned at the Saturday dances there. "Jive needs lots of room" says Miss Page.[5]

Without the influence of jazz clubs, jiving was not a regular feature in any of the dance halls of Great Yarmouth or in the village halls of Norfolk's rural districts. Once a link had been established in the minds of most dance hall management between Teddy Boys, rock 'n' roll and jive dancing, the ballrooms along Great Yarmouth's seafront and at the Floral Hall in Gorleston displayed large banners stating that jiving was not allowed.

Sir, why are the older generation so dead set against jiving? When they complain of it, do they ever stop to think of how some of them went crazy over the Charleston in the twenties which, in our opinion, must have been equally as bad or even worse? In Yarmouth and Gorleston there is no dance hall in which we can jive. In a previous letter we were told to go to Lowestoft. Why should we go there when we have dance halls in our own town? Lowestoft has both a jazz club and a dance hall where jiving is allowed. Why doesn't Yarmouth keep up with the time? The old days are over; this is the modern world where jiving is gradually taking the place of the more sedate type of dancing.[6]

For many people out on a Saturday night, the ban on jiving seemed to be a wise move. To capitalise on the success of Bill Haley's recording of *Rock Around the Clock* that had been featured in the film *Blackboard Jungle*, American producer Sam Katzman and director Fred Sears quickly put together another low-budget film promoting Haley's rock 'n' roll music, which they also called *Rock Around the Clock*. A ground-breaking film in that it was targeted specifically, if not exclusively, at young people. The film was released in America in March 1956, where it was screened in cinemas to large noisy audiences and was a major box-office attraction. When it became available on the British cinema circuit in August 1956, disturbances in London and Manchester resulted when couples, identified as Teddy Boys and Girls by the press, were forcibly restrained by the cinema's management from jiving to the music during performances of the film. Over one thousand dancing and singing youths held up traffic in Manchester's city centre after seeing the film. Reports in most national newspapers claimed that bottles, lightbulbs and fireworks had been thrown at the police, and inflamed the situation even more by suggesting that mini riots inside cinemas were commonplace. Inspired by reports of these events in national newspapers, London youths battled with police outside the Gaumont Cinema in Lewisham and at the Trocadero on the New Kent Road. The expectation of trouble resulted in the film being banned in many towns and cities, and even prompted the Bishop of Woolwich to comment that the film, in particular, and rock 'n roll, in general, represented an attack on the moral and spiritual wellbeing of young people. Even the Rev Gilbert Thurlow, Vicar of Great Yarmouth, was forced by public opinion to suggest that:

It was rather remarkable that young peoples' characters were so weak as to be affected by a passing influence of this kind.[7]

The concerns expressed by those like the Bishop of Woolwich and the Rev Thurlow made it inevitable that most young people would want to see the film as soon as it became available, while, at the same time, encouraging a fear among the older generations that the increasing popularity of jive at Saturday night dances was a retrograde step.

Notes

1. *Eastern Evening News*, Monday 9 July 1956.
2. When Arthur Lucan died in 1954, Roy Rolland assumed the on-stage character of 'Old Mother Riley'. After a disagreement with Kitty McShane, Lucan's widow, he renamed the character as 'Old Mother Kelly'.
3. *Eastern Evening News*, Thursday 30 August 1956. Music historians claim the Waltz Marie to be the oldest of the so-called modern sequence dances. The Royal Empress Tango is another sequence dance that was first choreographed by HA Clifton in 1922. The Mambo is a Latin American dance that became popular in the dance halls of the 1940s and 50s, due to the music of Perez Prado and his Orchestra. The dance moves for the Mambo were created in the 1930s by the Cuban composer Arsenio Rodriguez. The Creep is a slow shuffling dance that was extremely popular with Teddy Boys and their partners.
4. *Eastern Evening News*, Friday 31 August 1956.
5. *Eastern Evening News*, Saturday 8 September 1956.
6. Letters to the Editor, *Great Yarmouth Mercury*, Friday 8 July 1955.
7. *Eastern Evening News*, Saturday 15 September 1956.

Rock Around the Clock Tonight

Norwich was one of the first cities outside of London to show the film *Rock Around the Clock* in its cinemas. On Monday 20 August 1956, the film featured in a week-long double bill at the Gaumont Cinema[1] on Norwich's Haymarket together with the comedy *Doctor at Sea*. Its showing passed almost unnoticed. There was no rioting or disturbances of any kind. The audiences were mostly quiet and restrained.

> During odd phases of the film music, young patrons occasionally resorted to hand-clapping in the way it is encouraged in some jazz music sessions, and, so far as it was necessary, quiet appeals were made by the staff to exuberant groups—apparently without resentment—to respect the comfort of less impressed patrons.[2]

Even the revues in the local press were downbeat.

> Several top-line American orchestras and singers are to be seen and heard in 'Rock around the Clock,' a musical with a lively story, starring Johnny Johnson, Alix Talton and Bill Haley and his Comets. The story concerns rivalry in hot rhythm circles on one hand between two women who both fancy the same man and on the other between business interests. Some of the tunes featured have already reached hit parade status and the film introduces the 'rock n roll' dance. This should be attractive fare for many besides the bobby-soxers.[3]

Screaming audiences were not a new phenomenon, even in Norwich. In America, many singers and crooners had their fanatical teenage followers. Rock 'n' roll singers were not the only ones to have screaming fans. Frank Sinatra and Johnny Ray were said to present a moral danger to young women. In Britain, it was Dickie Valentine who was the focus for attention. Everywhere he went he was mobbed by his young female fans and his performances were greeted by cheers, screams and whistles, despite him being a happily married man. One of his more fanatical admirers was Suzanne Crowley of Brighton who followed him around the country wearing one of his records as a hat. His fan club was so large that annual meetings were held in the Royal Albert Hall. He was without doubt the most popular of all the contemporary home-grown artists because he was not only a good singer with a gentle laid-back voice and handsome to boot, but also a fine impersonator of other performers. In 1949, Valentine had joined the Ted Heath Band as its lead singer and was subsequently voted the top male vocalist of 1952. As a solo artist he was voted the *New Musical Express'* Best British Male Singer for every year from 1953 until 1957. In 1955 he had five songs in the UK record charts, *The Finger of Suspicion* and *A Christmas Alphabet* reaching the top spot of number one. From 21 February 1955, Dickie Valentine appeared in a week-long variety show at the Carlton Cinema in Norwich. His performances were greeted with the obligatory screams and shouts.

> Mr Valentine is obviously a talented artist with a pleasant stage personality and seems to have the power of captivating certain sections of the audience to judge by their almost hysterical reaction to his singing.[4]

CARLTON THEATRE

NORWICH.

General Manager, H. WHYSALL.   Phone : NORWICH 24194

Dickie Valentine

Week commencing   SOUVENIR PROGRAMME
MONDAY, FEB. 21st _____ 6d. _____

Dickie Valentine at the Carlton, February 1955.

Inevitably, the reports in the press of bad behaviour by young people that had become associated with the film *Rock Around the Clock* caused a number of councils to question the showing of the film in their locality, concerns that eventually spread into East Anglia.

> The Mayor of Lowestoft (Mr W F Pretty) declared last night that he hoped no cinema in Lowestoft would show the film 'Rock around the Clock' which, he said, causes certain groups of teenagers to act nothing more than African natives.[5]

He went on to say that Teddy Boys and jiving to rock 'n' roll music were unacceptable in Lowestoft. His words elicited a flood of condemnatory responses.

> If his worship has any deep-seated contempt for the African native, we would have expected him to come out into the open and not hide under the 'Rock Around the Clock' film controversy.[6]

As in America, prejudice and racial stereotyping was an issue for a few in mid-1950s Britain. Yet, Teddy Boys had not posed a serious problem in either Great Yarmouth or Norwich. Some minor disturbances had occurred but nothing too serious. Two police constables in Great Yarmouth reported that they had followed

A gang of about seven youths dressed in Edwardian clothing down Regent Road towards the seafront. The youths behaved in a disorderly manner by shouting, singing, stepping in front of oncoming traffic and trying to swing on two hanging signs.[7]

They also reported that they had seen them jumping on and off garden walls, dancing on the pavement and that they had played a rock 'n' roll record in the British Home Stores.

Unfortunately, the film's second three-day showing from Thursday 18 October until Saturday 20 October at Norwich's Regal Cinema in a double bill with *Apache Ambush*, a classic American Western, did not pass without incident.

Norwich had its second visit from the now notorious film 'Rock around the Clock.' The first time, before nation-wide publicity had given some almost sinister significance to the rock 'n' roll theme, passed off without it being noticed. Last week's visitation contributed some mild excitement inside and outside the cinema concerned. The performances seem to have been enjoyed by the younger element of the population, particularly on Saturday, when the film drew patrons from a radius of forty miles around. A little liveliness in the street afterwards soon dispersed and if some would-be street dancers got hustled in the process no one was any the worse for it. There is a certain satisfaction in the fact that the authorities refused to be panicked into banning a harmless entertainment and that their faith in the good sense of the majority of young people attending was justified.[8]

After the Saturday night show, a hundred or more teenagers made their way up St Benedict's, singing and jiving as they went, causing chaos by walking in the road, holding up the traffic and hitting the sides of cars and buses. A few arrests were made and later, at the local Magistrates court, one youth was fined five shillings (25p) for throwing a firework at the police.

On Monday 19 November *Rock Around the Clock* began a week-long stay at the Regal Cinema in Great Yarmouth, despite vociferous local opposition. It was now a must-see film for most young people. Despite the best efforts of the usherettes and the cinema management to control the teenage audience, screams and shouts greeted the appearance of the various rock 'n' roll stars on the screen and many couples attempted to dance to the music on the stairs and in the gangways. Despite the weak storyline that charted the rise of a rock 'n' roll group from obscurity to fame, the music of Bill Haley and his Comets, Freddie Bell and his Bellboys, and the Platters was greeted with wild enthusiasm. One rock 'n' roll standard followed another, including *Rock Around the Clock, See You Later Alligator, Razzle Dazzle* and *R-O-C-K Rock* from Bill Haley, *Giddy Up a Ding Dong* from Freddie Bell and *Only You* and *The Great Pretender* from the Platters, most of which had already appeared in the UK record charts.[9] Not that the music could be heard over the noise from the overly exuberant audience. Those who were not screaming, or dancing, were clapping in time with the musical beat. After the show was over, large gangs of singing youngsters spilled onto Great Yarmouth's Regent Road to dance on the pavements and in the adjoining park. Some of the more audible and raucous Bill Haley imitators were surprised when the police warned them that singing and dancing in a public place was an offence late at night. Much to the disappointment of some, there was no rioting, seat slashing or violence. The Tuesday edition of the *Eastern Evening News* reported that:

> Shouting, jiving, jostling teenagers crowded in front of the Regal Cinema Yarmouth last night after the first showing in the town of the rock 'n' roll film 'Rock Around the Clock.' They blocked the pavement and spilled out onto the road slowing down traffic. The crowd was dispersed by the police. As the last performance at the cinema came to a close the back of the circle in the cinema became a mass of jiving couples. The noise drowned much of the soundtrack. Extra attendants were on duty at the cinema.[10]

For most young people, the film was exciting, unlike anything they had ever seen before. *Rock Around the Clock* was markedly different from previous musicals such as *Seven Brides for Seven Brothers, Calamity Jane* and their like, because it was aimed specifically at the young. As a result, most of its audiences were exclusively drawn from the teen and twenty age range. Normal theatre etiquette was often abandoned and shouting, screaming, clapping and stamping of feet were tolerated during performances of the film. Neither was the music relevant to the film's plot as the storyline was merely being used as a convenient vehicle for promoting the sounds of rock 'n' roll. As with *Blackboard Jungle*, it was the sight of couples jiving on the screen that excited most young people, that energetic form of dancing far removed from the normal sedate Waltz, Foxtrot and Quickstep of the Saturday night dance hall. A dance that, once seen, everyone under thirty immediately wanted to learn. For many hopefuls it proved to be an impossible dream because the dancers in the film were professionals demonstrating the more extreme moves of the Lindy Hop rather than the less gymnastic moves of the rock 'n' roll dance being developed in British dance halls.

Unfortunately, opportunities to learn how to jive were distinctly limited for rock 'n' roll enthusiasts. Although there was little difference between jiving to jazz

The fashionable dance was the Jive.

and jiving to rock 'n' roll music, not everybody in 1956 went to a jazz club, and not every jazz club encouraged jiving. At the time jazz was very much becoming the music of sweater-clad college students and young left-wing inclined urban middle-class professionals, while rock 'n' roll was evolving as the music of ordinary working-class young men and women. Jazz records were frequently reviewed in the columns of the *Eastern Daily Press*, but rock 'n' roll records barely warranted a mention. For most, watching those who could jive and imitating their movements was the only way to learn. Norwich's dance schools refused to teach jiving to rock 'n' roll music. Following an interview with Laurie Singer (the husband of Eileen Page, the dance tutor at the Gala Ballroom), Whiffler of the *EDP* reported that Eileen would not be teaching jiving to rock 'n' roll music.

> Reason? "There isn't such a dance" Laurie assured me, "the name relates only to a particular kind of music." Laurie had a moment of anxiety the other evening over rock 'n' roll. He heard his band-leader announce a rock 'n' roll number and wondered fleetingly whether the Gala would escape unscathed.[11]

Inevitably, as the demand for jive tuition from the fans of rock 'n' roll increased, the dance school instructors changed their minds and introduced dance classes for teenage rock 'n' rollers. However, most dance halls continued to ban rock 'n' roll music and jive. A few couples would try jiving to the music for a quickstep, but they were normally dissuaded from doing so by the ballroom management; afraid that the jiving couples would hinder the progression around the dance floor of the quickstep dancers and that their energetic gyrations made collisions and stamping on toes inevitable. Despite its energy, jiving rock 'n' roll fashion was a static dance while the quickstep was progressive and the two did not mix.

Notes

1. The Gaumont Cinema on the Haymarket closed in 1959 and was demolished. The Carlton Cinema on All Saints Green was renamed as the Gaumont Cinema after 1959.
2. *Eastern Evening News*, Wednesday 12 September 1956.
3. *Eastern Evening News*, Monday 20 August 1956. A bobby-soxer was a term originating in the USA for certain female fans of popular music between the ages of 13 and 25. The term derived from the fashion among many teenagers for wearing ankle length socks or longer socks rolled down (bobbed down) to the ankles.
4. *Eastern Evening News*, Tuesday 22 February 1955.
5. *Eastern Evening News*, Tuesday 11 September 1956.
6. *Eastern Evening News*, Friday 14 September 1956.
7. *Eastern Evening News*, Thursday 4 October 1956.
8. *Eastern Daily Press*, Monday 22 October 1956.
9. Freddie Bell & the Bellboys was a white American Group in the style of Bill Haley & his Comets. Despite being one of the first white groups to capitalise on the growing interest in R&B music, their success in America was limited. Their biggest hit was the Freddie Bell composition *Giddy up a Ding Dong* which went to number four in the UK singles chart. The Platters were one of the earliest black harmony groups of the rock 'n' roll era singing in a Doo Wop style, often a cappella, melding African American Gospel and R&B.
10. *Eastern Evening News*, Tuesday 20 November 1956.
11. *Eastern Evening News*, Saturday 15 September 1956.

The Author Remembers
1957-58

In January 1957, when the main Tacolneston transmitter was operational and television had become readily available throughout Norfolk, my parents rented a television set from an electrical shop in Great Yarmouth, a Bush 14-inch TV which took pride of place in our living room, usurping the radio as the family's main source of entertainment. For a while it was the only form of entertainment for my parents, especially in the evening, replacing going out to dances and whist drives, and trips to the cinema. I still preferred 'going out' to 'staying in.' I soon found that few of the programmes on the BBC's lone television channel were of interest to me, that is except for one programme that became essential viewing for all young people, a one-hour Saturday early evening programme of music and dance called *The Six-Five Special*. A programme that not only promoted the music and fashions of young people but also legitimized jive dancing.

Dancing was an essential skill for most young people. Many relationships were forged on the dance floor. Even my parents met at a dance in Potter Heigham. My parents were good dancers and had taught me the basic steps to most modern ballroom dances in our living room. A great achievement in such a small space. I was a competent dancer of the waltz, quickstep and foxtrot, and had little difficulty in finding female dancing partners. My first attempt at jiving was at a Saturday dance in a local village hall:

> ... my first introduction to rock 'n' roll was a demonstration during the interval at a Saturday dance in Martham. I watched the twirling couple with amazement, excited by the dance and the brief glimpses of stocking top, knickers and suspender. When the demonstration was over, we were all given an introductory lesson in jive as part of the evening's entertainment.[1]

My jiving skills were honed during the summer of 1957 in the tearoom of the Eels Foot public house, an establishment on the shores of Ormesby's Trinity Broad, a mile from my home. In the evening, the tearoom was used as a dance hall, mostly for entertaining visiting coach parties from Great Yarmouth. Dancing was usually to records played on an overly large radiogram. In the early evening, the tearoom was often empty for a time before the coaches arrived, providing local teenagers with an opportunity to play their own records on the radiogram and to learn the energetic twirling movements of jive. I learnt to jive at the Eels Foot to the rhythmic beat of Elvis' *Teddy Bear, Bye Bye Love* by the Everly Brothers and Paul Anka's *Diana*.

My education in rock 'n' roll was complete when I bought my first record player. I had insufficient resources to be able to buy a new machine so, like my bedroom radio, it was acquired through the second-hand market.

Purchased in 1957, this first record player was a beige and red Dansette electric single play model with three speeds to accommodate 78, 45 and 33 rpm records, which I acquired second-hand for £2. The plastic playing arm contained a rotating cartridge with two needles, one for 78 records and the other for 45 and 33s. Up to that time I had no means of playing records. My Rollesby grandparents had an old-fashioned wind-up gramophone which used steel needles to play their collection of 78 rpm records, mostly of dance music from the 1930s. However, by the early 1950s it had obviously lost its appeal as it had been consigned to an outside shed together with their collection of records, relegated to become a plaything for the grandchildren.[2]

The first record that I bought was of a song called *Love is Strange* by Mickey and Sylvia. Why I bought it I am not sure as it hardly fell into the category of rock 'n' roll. Thereafter, records were added at a rate of about one every fortnight, mostly skiffle or rock 'n' roll numbers, especially any recordings by my favourite performers Lonnie Donegan, the Everly Brothers and Buddy Holly and the Crickets. As yet, jazz had not become part of my musical culture. The sound of jazz was rarely heard among the working folk of Norfolk's rural regions.

My repertoire with the ukulele-banjo improved immensely when, in 1957, I met a retired sailor who was an expert with the instrument, the father of a girlfriend at the time. Under his tuition my songs expanded from the usual George Formby comic pieces to include numerous sea shanties and other folk songs. My parents were so impressed that they bought me a new ukulele-banjo in a shiny black carrying case for my seventeenth birthday which I embossed with my initials in yellow gloss paint from a tin that I found in my father's tool shed. My ukulele skills must have become locally well known, because, soon after, I was invited by another village teenager, Lenny, to join him in forming a skiffle band. Lenny had bought a guitar and was becoming quite accomplished at playing chords and chord sequences. Together, with a few friends we formed Rollesby's first village-based skiffle band, although our abilities were quite limited and neither of us could sing in tune. Nevertheless, with me on my ukulele-banjo, Lenny on guitar, his best friend performing with a paper and comb, a tea-chest bassist and a washboard player we made an acceptable rhythmic noise and occasionally provided the music for dancing at the newly formed village youth club.

Eddie Bates and his Accordion Band, a typical village dance band.

Most Saturday nights I went out dancing with my friends at a village hall somewhere in the Fleggs, where the music was usually provided by a locally based accordion band, often Rollesby's own Eddie Bates' Accordion Band. As soon as I was eighteen, I regularly ventured into Great Yarmouth to join my sixth-form school classmates at one of the larger dance halls in Gorleston or Great Yarmouth, staying overnight with my grandmother in Yarmouth. My preferred venue was the Floral Hall in Gorleston where dancing was to music from the newly appointed Bert Galey's Orchestra. A pint in a pub beforehand, to give me the courage to ask a young woman to dance, and then the pleasure of a waltz, foxtrot or quickstep with a female in my arms. At the time, jiving was discouraged. The craze of the moment was for the cha-cha-cha, a simple Latin American dance that, if necessary, could be performed without a partner. Lines of dancers frequently snaked across the Floral Hall's dance floor stepping out the moves of the cha-cha-cha in unison.

In September 1958, I invested all the money I had saved from fruit picking and harvesting beans during the summer vacation in the purchase of the instrument of the moment, a guitar. With the help of a Bert Weedon instruction book I was soon quite proficient at playing the chords for numerous popular songs of the day. The move from a ukulele-banjo to a guitar was quite easy as the fingering for the top four strings of the chords on the guitar was the same as the fingering for those on the ukulele. I had only to learn what to do with the bottom two strings. By the end of the year, my skills were sufficient for me to be asked to sing at our family's Christmas Day party. My mother's often requested favourite was my version of Harry Belafonte's *Scarlet Ribbons*.

Notes

1. Colin Miller (2008), *The Fifties Replayed* p52.
2. Colin Miller (2005), *Country Boy* p162.

From Jazz to Rock

The honour of being the first Norwich based rock 'n' roll group belongs to Bob Barbour and his band, the Rockets. An experienced musician, Bob was yet another former member of the influential Les Hague Orchestra. As with many of Britain's early rock 'n' roll groups, the Rockets were a clone of Bill Haley's Comets. The initial line-up comprised Bob Barbour on electric guitar, Len Barker on double bass, Roger Vickers on alto-saxophone and Freddy Marrison on drums. The Rockets were billed to make their premier performance at the Cottage ballroom on Thursday 25 October 1956, but this appearance was cancelled. The band finally made its debut on Thursday 1 November at the Industries Club which was quickly followed by an appearance on Friday 2 November at the Boulton and Paul Social Club where they were advertised as the latest rock 'n' roll sensation. On Monday 12 November, the Rockets took part in a competition with the Mustard City Stompers called *Jazz versus Rock* at the Boulton and Paul Social Club, to determine which style of music was the most popular and which the best music for jiving. Before his venture into rock 'n' roll music, Bob Barbour was primarily a jazz musician. As well as performing with many local dance bands, he co-formed and played bass in a modern jazz group known as Bob Barbour's Modern Seven, later to be known as the extremely popular Norwich Modernists. Like many jazz musicians, Bob Barbour jumped on the rock 'n' roll bandwagon seeking a quick financial return, assuming that it would be a short-lived phenomenon.

Bob Barbour's other claim to fame was that he was one of the first musicians in the country to play a shoulder slung electric bass guitar. While guesting with the John Rogers' Band it was reported that:

> Norwich bassist Bob Barbour got tired when he played standing up — and that's how the first instrument of its kind in the world came to have its debut at the city's Samson and Hercules ballroom recently…Lionel Hampton has a deep-toned electric guitar; but it doesn't make a double-bass noise. The secret of the Barbour instrument is that the string length is the same as on a bass…Bob's instrument is now being manufactured by the well-known London firm of Grimshaw's. The one he is using now in John Rogers' resident band at the Samson and Hercules is the first.[1]

During the late 1950s, Grimshaw's produced a line of bass guitars under the SS (Short Scale) brand featuring their patent pick-ups hidden under the fretboard, but its development was never connected to Bob Barbour. The *Eastern Evening*

News correspondent later commented that:

> Twenty-six-year-old Bob, whose new line in electric basses I reported some time ago, tells me that the new instrument was developed in America. He had one made for him over here—the first of its kind in the country.[2]

On 21 March 1957, a reformed Bob Barbour and his Rockets replaced his mentor, Les Hague and his Orchestra, as the resident band at the Gala Ballroom playing a mix of rock 'n' roll, traditional and modern jazz. After a brief time as the resident rock 'n' roll band at the Gala, Bob Barbour rebranded the Rockets as the Bob Barbour Orchestra and resumed playing a mixture of dance music and jazz, with the inclusion of a very occasional rock 'n' roll number.

Bob Barbour was not the only jazz musician to convert briefly to rock 'n' roll. In a musical revue at the Hippodrome on 3 November 1956, singer Lee Lawrence was supported by a so-called original rock 'n' roll trumpeter, Nat Gonella. At forty-eight years of age, jazz trumpeter Nathaniel Charles Gonella was hardly a teenage rock 'n' roll idol. After a lengthy career playing the trumpet in various jazz and dance bands, including with Billy Cotton and his Band in the 1930s, Gonella was touring in a revue performing as a solo act. It was reported in the press that many pensioners enjoyed his performance. To reverse falling audience numbers, the management at the Hippodrome were quick to feature rock 'n' roll in its revues. On 10 December, recording artist Ronnie Harris[3] starred in a revue called *Rockin' n' Rollin'*.

> Youthful enthusiasts vigorously clapped out the rhythm of the newest crazes in dance time at the Hippodrome last night as a musical combination, styled the Rock 'n' Roll Rockets, blazed their way through a spirited programme. Not much could be heard of the vocalists, Ronnie Harris and his vivacious wife Terry Blayne, above the crash of the drums and the staccato double forte of electric guitar and saxophone but words seemed to matter nothing at all.[4]

Inevitably, as young people wanted not only to listen to rock 'n' roll but also to jive to the music, it soon became an attractive commercial proposition to organise dances specifically aimed at meeting that demand. The first rock 'n' roll dance in Norwich was held on Monday 29 October 1956 from 8.00pm until 11.00pm at the club room in the Ailwyn Hall on Lower Clarence Road, close to Thorpe Station. Dancing was to the latest rock 'n' roll recordings played on a gramophone and the entry fee was a mere 1/6 (7.5p). The *Eastern Evening News* recorded the occasion:

> They were dancing jive fashion, but the music was the rock 'n' roll kind played on gramophone records at the Ailwyn Hall on Lower Clarence Road.[5]

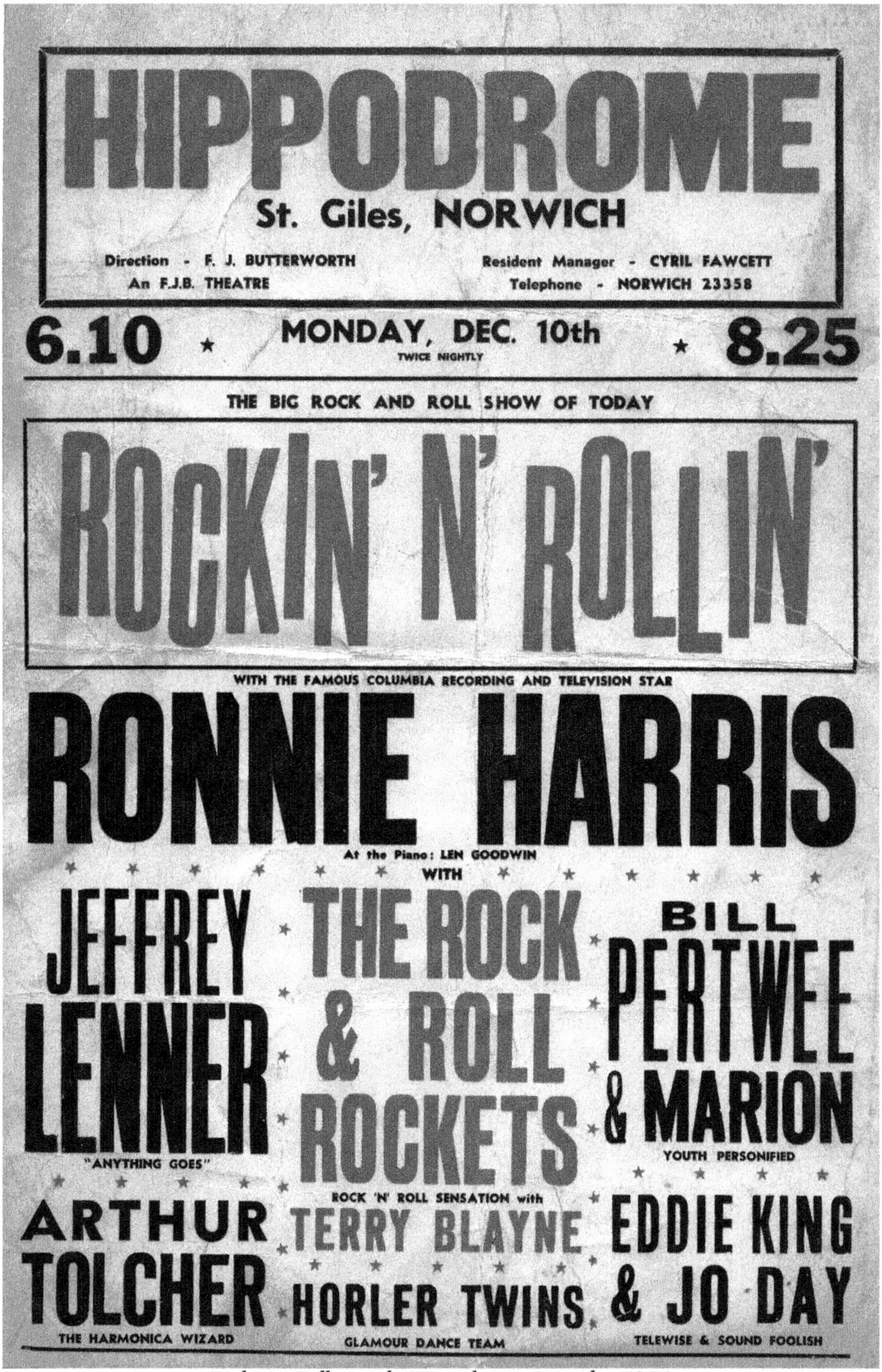

Rockin' n Rollin' at the Hippodrome, December 1956.

The Grosvenor Rooms Ballroom, Prince of Wales Road.

The event was so popular that the sessions became a regular event every Monday evening. On Thursday 20 December 1956, a new dance hall opened in buildings formerly used as a cinema close to the bridge on Prince of Wales Road called the Grosvenor Rooms. On the opening night, a full house danced to music from Neville Bishop and his Band. Rock 'n' roll was not discouraged by the management.

> Rock 'n' roll on a bigger scale is to come. One evening a week will be devoted to that alone, said Mr Cloudesley, but on those evenings the licenced bars would be closed he added.[6]

The first ever rock 'n' roll evening in Great Yarmouth was at the Queen's Hotel on Tuesday 11 December 1956.

> The Pink Room of the Queen's Hotel was filled by teenage couples doing the rock 'n' roll dance from the musical 'Rock around the Clock' on Tuesday evening when Yarmouth's first rock 'n' roll evening was organised by the Gorleston dancing teacher, Mr Douglas Hall. Posters advertising the session had the comment 'not for squares.' For nearly three hours 150 teenagers jived and rocked to the latest records of Elvis Presley, Bill Haley and other rock 'n' roll stars. To the exciting rhythm of current hits such as 'Rudy's Rock' and 'Rip it up' girls were thrown over their partners' shoulders and between their legs.[7]

The Queen's Hotel, Great Yarmouth c1950.

Thereafter, regular rock 'n' roll sessions were held not only at the Queen's Hotel but also at other venues in Great Yarmouth especially at the Goode's Hotel and the Yare Hotel Ballroom. Every Wednesday at the Goode's Hotel was Juke Box Jamboree Night, where pop fans could rock 'n' roll to amplified records, an early version of a disco.

On 19 April 1956, Elvis Presley made his debut in the UK music charts with his recording of *Heartbreak Hotel*; composed by Tommy Durden and Mae Boren Axton. The song was inspired by a newspaper article reporting the suicide of a jilted male who killed himself by jumping from a hotel window in Miami. It was recorded by Presley at the McGavock Street Studios in Nashville, backed by the Blue Moon Boys with Chet Atkins on guitar and Floyd Cramer on piano, and was released on 27 January 1956 as a single on the RCA Victor label. It reached number one in the US Billboard music charts and became America's biggest selling single of 1956, giving Presley his first million-selling record. Following the success of *Heartbreak Hotel*, Presley achieved six other Top Twenty hits by the end of the year including the exceedingly popular *Blue Suede Shoes*. In Britain, the BBC's restricted play policy combined with a general antagonism against rock 'n' roll music meant that his songs were rarely heard. His popularity was entirely due to Radio Luxembourg, an expanding record industry, an appearance in the film *Love Me Tender* and word of mouth. His antics on stage had become legendary. *Heartbreak Hotel* spent 22 weeks in the UK Top 20 singles charts during the summer months, peaking at number two in June. As far as the record reviewers in Norfolk's local newspapers were concerned, Elvis Presley did not exist.

Equally as influential as his single play records was his long play recording *Elvis Presley: Rock 'n' Roll Volume I* that was released in November 1956. Prominent on the front of its sleeve was a black and white photograph of a young singer, Elvis, with slicked back black hair, his mouth wide open in song, strumming a very large acoustic guitar. The name of Elvis Presley was written in large pink and green letters along two of its sides. The songs, which included *Blue Suede Shoes, Tutti-Frutti, That's All Right, Money Honey* and *Lawdy Miss Clawdy*, presented a vastly different

Elvis Presley: Rock 'n' Roll Volume I.

and distinctive style of rock 'n roll to that of Bill Haley; one with a distinctly country element but still one appropriate for jive dancing. On Saturday 8 December, Presley's recording of *Love Me Tender*, from the film of the same name, appeared for the first time in the UK music charts. While it was a massive hit in the USA, the song only made a minor impact in the UK charts, its highest position being at number twelve. It was a ballad and not eminently suitable for dancing. A rock 'n' roll singer singing ballads was briefly confusing, but it was Elvis, so it sold, nevertheless.

As 1956 came to end, it was clear that the year had witnessed many changes. The fear of war with Russia was ever present, growing even more threatening. The tension was not eased in any way by the ruthless suppression by invading Soviet forces of the 23 October Hungarian Uprising. Britain was also enduring popular uprisings in many parts of its Commonwealth: the Mau Mau in Kenya, EOKA in Cyprus and the MNLA in Malaya. Closer to home, on 12 December 1956, the Northern Irish police were engaged in a lengthy gun battle with members of the IRA. Ordinary National Servicemen were not immune from danger. The biggest problem for the British government was when the Egyptian President Gamal Abdel Nasser nationalised the Anglo-French company that managed and controlled the Suez Canal, a vital trade route from Europe to India and the Pacific region. His army then occupied the canal. After negotiations failed, British and French forces forcibly re-took the canal back into Anglo-French control on 5 November 1956 in an ill-conceived invasion of Egypt that had little chance of success. The ultimate humiliating withdrawal of all the British and French forces showed clearly that they no longer possessed the influence that they once had and that the prominent power in the world was the United States of America. Without the backing of America, any aggressive action in the Middle East, such as the Suez invasion, was doomed to fail. Not only was America dominating world politics of the day but was also considered by most to be the ascendant culture, a position promoted by the continual outpouring of glossy films from Hollywood and the example set by the many American servicemen stationed in England and elsewhere all over the world.

The films *Blackboard Jungle* and *Rock Around the Clock* had fuelled a growing interest in rock 'n' roll and jive dancing, particularly among Britain's working-class youth. By the end of 1956 it had developed from obscurity into a craze and had even spread into rural Norfolk. Yet what it was and who started it was a question left unanswered.

What is rock 'n' roll? Few people seem to know musically. It has been defined as a 'watered down jump blues with hillbilly overtones' and a hand-clapping style of off-beat music reminiscent of swinging gospel songs.[8]

For most ordinary youngsters it was music from America, and it began with Bill Haley, his Comets and *Rock Around the Clock*. For a while, Bill Haley and his Comets became the stereotypical rock group, and their music defined the sound of rock 'n' roll; music with a definite beat ideal for jiving but different in many ways from jazz. Elvis emphasised that it was music for young people performed by young people. Bill Haley defined the sound while Elvis created the look.

Notes

1. *Eastern Evening News*, Saturday 11 August 1956.
2. *Eastern Evening News*, 16 March 1957. The reformed Bob Barbour and his Rockets at the Gala; Bob Barbour (guitar), Bob Sheldrake (saxophone), Pete Voisey (saxophone), Len Barbour (trumpet), Freddie Marrison (percussion), Ivor Dunne (piano).
3. Ronnie Harris was originally a dance band singer, spending some time with Ray Martin and his Orchestra. He is credited with one hit record 'The Story of Tina' in 1954. Ronnie Harris and the Coronets also recorded 'Don't Talk to Strangers' in 1956.
4. *Eastern Evening News*, Tuesday 11 December 1956.
5. *Eastern Evening News*, Tuesday 30 October 1956.
6. *Eastern Evening News*, Thursday 20 December 1956. The Grosvenor was built early in 20th century as a set of general function rooms called the New Assembly Rooms. These were converted into a cinema in 1912 and to a dance hall in 1956. Gene Vincent played at the Grosvenor Rooms on 21 July 1961 and, more famously, the Beatles made their only appearance in Norwich at the Grosvenor on 17 May 1963. The dance hall was closed in 1964 and the buildings were demolished to make way for an office block.
7. *Yarmouth Mercury*, Friday 14 December 1956.
8. *Eastern Daily Press*, Wednesday 12 September 1956.

The Six-Five Special

Because of the policies imposed by the BBC, most Norfolk teenagers found it necessary to tune in to Continental radio stations such as Radio Luxembourg to hear popular music from America, particularly rock 'n' roll. Radio Luxembourg was an American style English language commercial radio station transmitted from the Grand Duchy of Luxembourg every evening from 7.00pm at 208 metres on the medium wave; a station that was normally introduced as 'Your Station of the Stars'. Its programmes were a mixture of popular music played on records, game shows and variety, interspersed with commercial advertising. Listeners were encouraged to drink Horlicks and Ovaltine, use Horace Batchelor's method for winning the football pools, follow the adventures of Dan Dare, Pilot of the Future, marvel at the sporting knowledge of Leslie Welsh the 'Memory Man' and listen intently to the contestants competing in *Opportunity Knocks*, *Take Your Pick* and *Double Your Money*. But the biggest attraction of Radio Luxembourg for the younger listener was its focus on all forms of popular music, including the latest recorded music from America.

Nevertheless, even on Radio Luxembourg, opportunities were limited for the teenage listener to hear music from Bill Haley, Elvis, or any of the other recognised rock 'n' roll artists until late 1956. Before that time, most early evening music programmes featured middle-of-the-road singers and dance bands. Pete Murray's highly influential *21 Record Show* and Jack Jackson's *Record Roundabout* were late night programmes, starting long after most teenagers were in bed, and the highly influential Saturday night *Jamboree* did not start broadcasting until the end of May 1956. The most popular programme of all was the 11.00pm Sunday night *Top Twenty*. In the mid-1950s, this was usually preceded by Bing Crosby in *Bing Sings* and music from Frank Chacksfield and his Orchestra, not exactly recognisable as popular figures among the rock 'n' roll fraternity. But Radio Luxembourg still held a greater appeal for the younger listener than did the BBC. 'Reflector' in the *Eastern Evening News* recorded that on the BBC:

> Variety for tomorrow night comes under the title 'Calling the Stars' featuring Tony Fayne and David Evans, the new singing success Ronnie Carroll, Joan Turner, Semprini, Geoff Mitchell Choir and Max Wall as guest artist. It will pass an hour away quite pleasantly, no doubt, but I wonder if it will win back a single listener who has tuned to Radio Luxembourg for his Sunday evening entertainment. This is a typical example of the sort of competition

the BBC has to face from that station; the Glenn Miller Orchestra, Billy Cotton and his Band, Frankie Laine, Winifred Atwell, Vera Lynn, the Smith Brothers, Jo Stafford, Bing Crosby—all in one evening. Obviously, the BBC couldn't hope to present a star line-up like that.[1]

To complement listening to the radio, improved reception thanks to the newly operational second transmitter at Tacolneston had, at last, enabled television viewing to be widely available throughout all of Norfolk. On 9 October 1956, a new 560ft tall transmitter began in service replacing the temporary 230ft tower that had been operating since February 1955. As a result, by November, upward of 24,055 new TV licenses had been issued in Norfolk alone. Yet, despite the new transmitter, the black and white picture was often unclear because the reception was still variable and susceptible to interference from poor atmospheric conditions, passing traffic and electronic machinery.

Until the arrival of Anglia Television in the autumn of 1959, it was only possible to receive broadcasts from one BBC channel and, consequently, there was no choice in the programmes that were available to view. Nevertheless, once it had been installed, older people preferred to stay at home and watch the flickering images on their newly acquired television sets than to venture out to the dance hall, cinema or public house for their entertainment in the evenings, especially cold and wet winter evenings. Attendance at whist drives dwindled, the drama groups and concert parties of Norwich, Great Yarmouth and their surrounding districts struggled to continue, and many dance halls, cinemas and theatres lost customers to the convenience of watching television in the comfort of home. An evening out became an activity mainly for the young. Even the Saturday night dances that were once popular with the whole family became a marriage market for the under-thirties.

The arrival of television in Norfolk coincided with the BBC's abandonment of the Toddler's Truce on Saturday 16 February 1957. The so-called Toddler's Truce was an interval of one hour between televised programmes from 6.00pm until 7.00pm every evening, designed to give families sufficient time to have tea at the table or to prepare the younger members of the family for bed. Replacing the interval during the week was an early evening news programme called *Tonight*, introduced by a popular but middle-aged Cliff Mitchelmore. However, the BBC's response to the establishment of an independent television network in 1955 with its focus on providing popular entertainment for the whole family was a surprise to its teenage viewers. The *Six-Five Special* was a magazine programme for young people broadcast every Saturday evening at five-past-six immediately after the six o'clock news, an ideal time for attracting a younger audience, sandwiched as it was between the sporting opportunities of a Saturday afternoon and going to the dance hall or to the cinema in the evening. A programme planned not only to inform and educate but also to include all forms of music popular with a younger audience, including rock 'n' roll.

Broadcast for the first time on Saturday 16 February 1957, the very first day without the Toddler's Truce interval, the *Six-Five Special* was a new and exciting experience for young people. The creation of producer Jack Good, an Oxford graduate and rock 'n' roll enthusiast, the programme began with the image on the screen of a steam train hurtling along a railway track accompanied by the programme's up-beat signature tune, *Over the Points*, performed by the Bob Cort Skiffle Group. This was immediately followed by the appearance of a cheery Pete Murray who introduced the show with the words "Welcome aboard the Six-Five Special. We've got almost a hundred cats jumping here, some real cool characters to give us the gas, so just get on with it and have a ball." The show's other presenter, Josephine Douglas, provided a translation for those who did not yet understand the new teenage vocabulary. Having spent a lengthy period with Radio Luxembourg, twenty-nine-year-old Pete Murray was already a successful broadcaster and was recruited as the show's main presenter because of his extensive knowledge of the current trends in popular music. It was Murray who popularised the catchphrase "It's time to jive on the old six-five." Twenty-seven-year-old co-producer and presenter, Josephine Douglas, formerly an actress and model, represented the more serious side of the programme giving introductions and conducting formal interviews with guest celebrities in perfect BBC English. The former light heavy-weight champion boxer, Freddie Mills, was also recruited as a third presenter to introduce sporting features, which he did in an endearingly bumbling style.

The programme for the first show featured music from Kenny Baker, Michael Holliday, The King Brothers and Lev Pouishnoff, together with an interview with a guest movie star, Lisa Gastoni, a comedy sketch and a filmed report about mountain climbing. Kenny Baker was primarily a jazz trumpeter but, like other professional musicians, had responded to the fashion of the moment and formed a small band to play rock 'n' roll in the manner of Bill Haley. Michael Holliday, on the other hand, was a traditional crooner providing vocals in the style of Bing Crosby, and The King Brothers trio were a close harmony group, inappropriately billed on the day as Britain's rock 'n' roll kids. By contrast, Lev Pouishnoff was a sixty-six-year-old Russian pianist, a specialist in the works of Chopin, and Lisa Gastoni was a young up-and-coming twenty-one-year-old film actress from Italy who had recently featured in *Three Men in a Boat* and *The Baby and the Battleship*, the latter a British made comedy film starring John Mills and Richard Attenborough. While the show did not disappoint its young viewers, the press reaction was predictably lukewarm. The television critic of the *Eastern Daily Press* commented that:

The Six-Five Special on Saturday, the first of a new TV extra-time programme, was almost exclusively devoted to rock 'n' roll with one faint ray of what was no doubt intended to be culture. I thought it unkind to Pouishnoff to sandwich him somewhere between the rocking and rolling. ... That little bit of classical music was just about enough to irritate the rock 'n' rollers and not enough to gratify Chopin lovers.[2]

In later programmes, the theme music was performed in a style more jazz based than rock 'n' roll by the newly appointed resident band, Don Lang and his Frantic Five.

The original plan for just six Saturday programmes was quickly abandoned because of the resulting popularity of the show. For the next two years, the *Six-Five Special* became a weekly event watched enthusiastically by most of Britain's popular music-loving teenagers. The *Six-Five Special* had a major influence on the development of Britain's teenage culture because it was the first programme on television specifically aimed at young people containing a large element of popular music, albeit not exclusively rock 'n' roll. A limited budget and a programme made up entirely of live acts also ensured that the majority of the performers were British, giving a much-needed boost to their careers. Because of restrictions in place at the time, few American performers featured on the show and rock 'n' roll music was represented by cover versions of American songs sung by British artists; often cockneys singing with an American accent. To fill a programme of youth orientated live music lasting fifty-five minutes, its innovative producer, Jack Good, was forced to fall back on jazz, its spin-off, skiffle, and numerous stand-alone vocalists to compensate for the absence of American singers and the lack of good home-grown rock 'n' roll bands. Through the show, performers such as Terry Dene, Lonnie Donegan, Johnny Dankworth, Wee Willy Harris, Russ Hamilton, Jim Dale, the King Brothers and Don Lang became household names. Ronald Grant was forced to comment:

If you have a teenage daughter watching the Six-Five Special on Saturday (May 4) don't let her smoke, and it might be as well to see she isn't holding a cup of tea. The reason is a young jazzman who plays the alto-saxophone. He is Johnny Dankworth, leader of Britain's top jazz band. Teenagers have been known to be so enthralled by his music that they forget cigarettes they are smoking and burn themselves or their clothes.[3]

A regular performer in the early days of the show was ex-merchant seaman Tommy Steele with his band, the Steelmen. He was certainly the foremost British performer of rock 'n' roll at the time, having had a series of hit recordings during 1957 that included *Singing the Blues*, *Elevator Rock*, *Rock with the Cavemen* and *Knee Deep in the Blues*. No doubt at the behest of a BBC management not yet convinced of the durability of rock 'n' roll, conventional ballad singers and big-band vocalists, the likes of Dennis Lotis, Matt Monro, Michael Holliday, Rosemary Squires, Ann Shelton and Petula Clark were also included on the show to satisfy those young adults not yet wholly converted to rock 'n' roll and, potentially, their parents too.

As well as the music, the visual aspect of the *Six-Five Special* on home television sets played a key role in popularising rock 'n' roll as a musical genre and introduced new fashionable trends into the culture of the young. Through watching the *Six-Five Special*, young people not only developed their knowledge of the performers and their music but also became aware of the current fashions in clothing and hairstyles, the technicalities of rock 'n' roll dancing and the specialised language of the young. People were classified as 'hep cats,' 'cool dudes,' 'ace chicks' or 'squares,' they danced at a 'hop' where the 'joint' was often 'jumping' and said, 'See you later alligator' instead of goodbye to which the expected reply was 'In a while, crocodile.' The programme also did a great deal to legitimise teenage culture and allay the fears held by older people that rock 'n' roll and delinquent behaviour went hand in hand. To that end, the show's audience was carefully selected and controlled, anyone behaving in an unacceptable manner was quickly ejected, the stars were polite and well-groomed, and Teddy Boys were banned. On 5 March 1958, the invited audience included thirty-two teenagers from the Old Catton Methodist Youth Club in Norwich, twenty of whom were selected because of their dancing skills.

Notes

1. *Eastern Evening News*, Saturday 7 April 1956.
2. *Eastern Daily Press*, Monday 18 February 1957.
3. *Eastern Evening News*, Friday 26 April 1957.

On the Screen

A major contribution made by the *Six-Five Special* to the emerging teenage culture was that it introduced jazz and skiffle music to a wider audience, genres that were both related to rock 'n' roll because all three had common roots in African-American rhythm and blues as well as providing a strong pulsating beat ideal for jive dancing. Consequently, the broad genre of British 'beat' music may well have been formed thanks to the *Six-Five Special*. Nevertheless, in his column in the *Eastern Evening News*, 'Reflector' regretted what he considered to be a programme that had a limiting effect on young peoples' choices in music and advocated that their parents and teachers should compensate by promoting a love of classical music and opera among teenagers.

> If youngsters saw little else on television but Western films and the Six-Five Special they would probably grow up believing that they live in a world consisting only of scuffle and skiffle.[1]

The initial effort by the BBC's top management to insist on a classical music contribution in every programme had been quickly stifled by the producer, Jack Good.

The *Six-Five Special* was not the only televised show that had a defining influence on young peoples' musical tastes. On Monday evenings every fortnight from May 1955, viewers were treated to a thirty-minute programme called *Off the Record* presented by Jack Payne; a programme that was introduced by the BBC as its response to the growing market in sales of popular music on records and consisted of live performances of new record releases together with the latest news from the record industry. Initially, the show featured recordings by middle-of-the-road singers who were enjoyed by the whole family. Jack Payne made no secret of the fact that he was not a fan of rock 'n' roll and considered that it would be a short-lived fad. Shirley Bassey, David Whitfield, Michael Holliday, Lita Rosa, Ronnie Carroll, Vera Lynn and Alma Cogan made regular appearances on the show. Despite this, as with the *Six-Five Special*, *Off the Record* received disparaging reviews in Norfolk's local newspapers. Reflector commented:

> I confess I am sometimes baffled by the current list of 'top tunes.' So far as last night's recording artists are concerned - well I cannot say I ever wanted to turn the volume up.[2]

Among his weekly review of the current record releases, John Mitchell in the *Eastern Evening News* added that:

Of the dozens of popular discs that reach the market each month, how many could we say are really necessary? How many of today's hopefuls among the singers, for instance, will be known to us five years from now? Not many I fear.[3]

Inevitably Payne was unable to hold back the progress of rock 'n' roll despite his obvious dislike of the genre. By the end of 1957, by popular demand, *Off the Record* also included jazz and skiffle music from George Melly, Mick Mulligan and his Band, Nancy Whiskey, Lonnie Donegan and the Vipers; and rock 'n' roll from Don Lang, Tommy Steele and Bert Weedon. The BBC Concert Orchestra and the George Mitchell Singers normally provided support for solo vocalists. 'Reflector' in the *Eastern Evening News* was again forced to comment that the programme contained only music that was likely to feature in the UK record charts and failed to acknowledge other forms of popular music. Sarcastically, he commented that:

Nowhere is the popular song welcomed more warmly and enthusiastically than in 'Off the Record.' Pop vocalists pop up here at a rate of four, five or even six in every show.[4]

For most of 1957, *Off the Record* alternated every Monday with Victor Sylvester's *Dancing Club*. Despite Sylvester's image as the leader of a very traditional dance band, even he was forced to acknowledge the existence of rock 'n roll.

Sir, I was surprised to see rock 'n' roll the other night on TV in a dancing club — surprised because those taking part were not all teenagers. Quite a number of the women at any rate looked to be of "the older generation." This is the generation that is so down on teenagers and rock 'n' roll in general. But it seems that although quick to criticise the young, they are even quicker to copy them, given the chance.[5]

After changing to a Thursday night spot, *Off the Record* continued to be broadcast every fortnight until Thursday 27 March 1958. The final show featured Buddy Holly and the Crickets singing their latest release *Maybe Baby*, a rare live performance from an American artist. Another influential programme was the *Billy Cotton's Band Show*, despite not being targeted specifically at a younger audience. A fifty-minute radio programme that was broadcast at lunchtime every Sunday immediately after the equally popular *Two-Way Family Favourites*. In April 1957, the show was transferred from the radio to a peak viewing time on Saturday night BBC TV. Introduced by Cotton's call of "Wakey Wakey" and his signature tune *Somebody Stole My Gal*, it consisted of fifty minutes of popular music, comedy and dancing featuring resident singer Alan Breeze, piano player Russ Conway and the twelve dancers of the Lesley Roberts silhouettes. Kathy Kirby, Alma Cogan and The

High Lights regularly appeared on the show as guest singers. In yet another vain attempt to turn back the tide of rock 'n' roll, the BBC introduced the extravagant American *Perry Como Show* in a prime Saturday night position from 1 January 1958.

For the whole of 1958, the *Six-Five Special* continued to be the main purveyor of popular music for the young on BBC TV and the only choice for Norfolk's viewers.

The show that has had one of the most amazing television successes celebrates its first birthday on Saturday (February 22). It is that early evening show 'The Six-Five Special' which was put on initially as a 'filler' to use up extra viewing time. Now it has the biggest viewing figures of anything on the BBC.[6]

Commercial enterprises were not slow to capitalise on the show's popularity. Both Parlophone and Decca issued LP records under the banner of the *Six-Five Special*, usually compilations of songs by performers who regularly featured in the show. Pete Murray himself published a *Six-Five Special* songbook for aspiring rock 'n' roll musicians. In 1958, Insignia Films released the *Six-Five Special* film, with a fictional storyline based around a production of the show that included performances from Lonnie Donegan, Dickie Valentine, The King Brothers, Jim Dale and many others.

Despite the high audience figures, Jack Good resigned in early 1958 and left the BBC to produce a rival rock 'n' roll music programme called *Oh Boy!* for ABC, an independent commercial television company. Pete Murray and Josephine Douglas also departed soon after and the position of compere was transferred by the BBC to the singer Jim Dale, assisted by the manic comedians Mike and Bernie Winters. Without Jack Good in charge, the show lost its rock 'n' roll focus and regressed to featuring skiffle, big band singers and sentimental balladeers. Audience figures dropped dramatically while, at the same time, ABC's *Oh Boy!* gained in popularity. The *Six-Five Special* was finally axed on 27 December 1958. For most teenagers living in rural Norfolk, this was a disaster. There were no other popular music programmes being broadcast by BBC television as influential as the *Six-Five Special*. *Oh Boy!* was out of range for most of Norfolk's viewing population. They had to wait until the advent of independent television in Norfolk with the establishment of Anglia TV in October 1959 before other programmes with a dynamic teenage appeal became available.

The cinema also played a vital part in consolidating the popularity of American rock 'n' roll, especially during 1957. The restrictions on visits by American artists to the UK meant that it was only on the cinema screen where fans could see them perform. A plethora of films, good and not so good, cemented the reputations of many American rock 'n' roll stars. Most of the early rock 'n' roll films were available in Norwich's cinemas, usually with a U certificate allowing entry to younger cinema goers. Among those films appearing in the city during 1957 were *Don't Knock the Rock*, *Shake Rattle and Rock* and *Rock, Rock, Rock*. *Don't Knock the Rock*, a sequel to *Rock Around the Clock*, was shown in February at the Gaumont in Norwich and starred an unlikely Alan Dale, an ageing big-band vocalist, in the leading role of Arnie Haines, a misunderstood rock 'n' roll performer. Featured in the film were performances of rock 'n' roll from Bill Haley and his Comets, the Treniers and Dave Appell and the Applejacks. The film is best remembered for introducing Little Richard to an enthralled British audience. A dynamic introduction in which he excited viewing audiences with his manic renditions of *Long Tall Sally* and *Tutti-Frutti*. Fats Domino appeared in the film *Shake, Rattle and Rock* at the Ritz in April. In May, it was *Rock, Rock, Rock* at the Regent with Frankie Lymon and the Teenagers, and Chuck Berry. Elvis Presley had his female fans screaming in *Love me Tender* at the Essoldo in February and *Loving You* at the Gaumont in November. British interest was upheld by *The Tommy Steele Story* at the Norvic in September.

Notes

1. *Eastern Evening News*, Saturday 4 May 1957.
2. *Eastern Evening News*, Tuesday 6 December 1955.
3. *Eastern Evening News*, Thursday 8 December 1955.
4. *Eastern Evening News*, Thursday 15 February 1957.
5. *Eastern Evening News*, Tuesday 8 January 1957.
6. *Eastern Evening News*, Friday 14 February 1958.

The Rock Island Line

What Bill Haley and *Rock Around the Clock* did for rock 'n' roll, Lonnie Donegan and *The Rock Island Line* also did for skiffle. *The Rock Island Line* was a traditional American work song about a train driver smuggling iron on the Chicago, Rock Island and Pacific Railway. The song was discovered by folklorist and music collector, John Lomax, while on a visit to an Arkansas State prison in 1934 and was first recorded by Huddie Ledbetter (Leadbelly) in 1935. Lonnie Donegan's version of the song, featuring Donegan himself on vocals and guitar, Chris Barber on bass and Norwich-born Beryl Bryden on washboard, was played in the skiffle style that had been made popular by Ken Colyer. Formerly a track on the Barber Band's LP, *New Orleans Joy*, it was released as a single by Lonnie Donegan's Skiffle Group in 1955 and was paired with a version of *John Henry* on the obverse. The recording entered the UK Top 40 singles charts on 7 January 1956 where it remained for 22 weeks, reaching its highest position of Number 6 on 11 February.

Donegan's recording of *The Rock Island Line* did not owe its success totally to its links with jazz. Jazz was still music with a minority following. Whether by accident or design, its appeal for many teenagers lay in the fact that the Donegan Band had reproduced the same emphatic beat with *The Rock Island Line* as Bill Haley and his Comets achieved with *Rock Around the Clock*; a rhythmic beat ideal for dancing jive. It also tapped into the fashion of the moment for everything American. Programmes about American history dominated cinema and TV screens, particularly the history of the American west. On TV, *The Lone Ranger*, *The Cisco Kid*, *The Range Rider*, *Wagon Train* and *High Chaparral* entertained children and adults alike, while a succession of western films filled the cinema screens. In 1955, Norwich's cinema audiences were entertained by James Stewart in *The Far Country* and *The Man from Laramie*, Kirk Douglas in *The Indian Fighter* and Burt Lancaster in *The Kentuckian*. A western theme that also spilled over into the music charts with Jimmy Young's rendition of the theme song from *The Man from Laramie*, *The Yellow Rose of Texas* by Mitch Miller, Slim Whitman's *Indian Love Call* and *Sixteen Tons* by Tennessee Ernie Ford, to mention but a few.

But for most young people, the most influential film of 1955 was *Davy Crockett, King of the Wild Frontier*, a Walt Disney production starring Fes Parker in the title role. Based on three television programmes, the film depicted phases in the life of the legendary frontiersman: his early days on the wild-west frontier, his involvement in the Creek Indian wars, his time as a congressman in Washington and, finally, his death at the Alamo fighting for an independent Texas. Not only did it become a massive commercial success, but it also promoted certain moral values among the young as demonstrated by his concern for the rights of the Native American Indians and his death fighting for freedom from oppression. A call to 'stand up for what you believe in' that subconsciously permeated the thinking of teenagers and evolved as a basic principle of their emergent teenage culture. As a commercial success it had few equals and gave rise to a merchandising craze which included a fashion for coonskin hats with tails hanging down the back. Shoppers and holidaymakers in Norwich and Great Yarmouth were occasionally treated to the sight of American servicemen in Davy Crockett hats and Stetsons, with holsters and imitation six-guns, driving fast cars shooting cap guns at people as they passed by. Three versions of the film's theme tune, *The Ballad of Davy Crockett*, recorded separately by Bill Hayes, Tennessee Ernie Ford and Gary Miller, all entered the British record charts in January 1956, coincidentally or not at the same time as *The Rock Island Line*.

The producers at the BBC also appeared to have had fewer reservations about including British musicians playing skiffle in their programmes than they had to American artists playing 'subversive' rock 'n' roll. They were British and available, free from the restrictions that limited the ability of American artists to perform in the UK. Most were able to play their music live and did not rely on records for their music to be heard by the public. Consequently, *The Rock Island Line* was often featured on the radio, both in a live performance and on record, and, in the process, helped skiffle to assume a popularity which lifted it from being a brand of beat music with a minority following among the jazz fraternity into a national obsession for Britain's youth. Skiffle fast became the home-grown equivalent of America's rock 'n' roll, a convenient substitute when true rock 'n' roll was unavailable, especially when providing the music for jiving.

Because of his success with *The Rock Island Line*, Donegan immediately parted company with the Chris Barber Jazz Band to concentrate on performing skiffle rather than jazz and became skiffle's leading British exponent. As a result, Donegan was branded by the media as 'The King of Skiffle.' For the next few years, Lonnie Donegan and his Skiffle Group gave many live concerts throughout the country promoting skiffle, including an appearance in a variety show at the Theatre Royal in Norwich for the week beginning 18 February 1957, followed by two concerts on 27 July and 2 September at the Regal Cinema in Great Yarmouth.

But the things that give his group its particular character are a very full exploitation of two guitars, bass and drums, and all the current stage techniques, to say nothing of high-powered amplification. Mr Donegan must forgive us if those of us who have only heard his records come to see him with a little hesitancy. For his records convey only a half of his appeal. It is the incessant vitality, the relentless rhythm and the sheer noise of the show that must surely carry away everyone—except perhaps a completely unrepentant 'square'. [1]

Lonnie Donegan, King of Skiffle at the Regal Gt Yarmouth, 1957.

Elizabeth Cotton's composition Freight Train became a skiffle classic.

As well as the efforts and enthusiasm of Lonnie Donegan, the *Six-Five Special* had been equally influential in expanding the popularity of skiffle among its teenage viewers. Many of the newly established skiffle bands made their public debuts on its programmes. The BBC's collaboration with London promoter Stanley Dale in broadcasting rounds of his National Skiffle Contest during editions of the *Six-Five Special* enabled many amateur bands to showcase their music live on TV. Because of skiffle's success in the *Six-Five Special*, the BBC introduced a 30-minute radio show on its Light Programme at 10.00am every Saturday morning from 1 June 1957 called the *Saturday Skiffle Club* with a content that was aimed specifically at teenagers. Introduced by Brian Matthews and produced by Jimmy Grant, this highly influential programme highlighted the most popular skiffle bands of the time including Wally Whyton's Vipers, the Chas McDevitt Skiffle Group, Bob Cort, Johnny Duncan and the Blue Grass Boys, Russell Quaye's City Ramblers and jazzman George Melly with the Bubbling Over Four. The *Saturday Skiffle Club* became essential listening for Britain's teenagers. Nevertheless, the BBC made a significant effort to include European and other folk music in the programme's content to counter the obvious American biased song content of skiffle, especially British folk music. The inaugural show featured the Chas McDevitt Skiffle Group with Nancy Whiskey singing *Freight Train*, a song that was as influential in popularising skiffle as was *The Rock Island Line*. *Freight Train* was a traditional folk song written in 1904 by a young 12-year-old African-American woman, Elizabeth 'Libba' Cotton. The lyrics were inspired by the sound of trains passing along a track close to her home in North Carolina. The song was introduced into the UK by American folk singer Peggy Seeger who had discovered the song when Cotton worked as a house servant with the Seeger family. The version recorded by the Chas McDevitt Skiffle Group, featuring Nancy Whiskey as vocalist, spent 15 weeks in the British Top 20 music charts reaching its best position of number 5 on 8 June 1957. Its popularity was such that a version of the song was included in the repertoires of most British skiffle bands, not without controversy as the song was for a time wrongly credited to two British song writers before being correctly attributed to Elizabeth Cotton. Also, on the show was the Danny Levan Trio playing a selection of traditional British folk songs, with Danny Levan[2] on violin and Brian Dexter on accordion.

Notes

1. *Eastern Daily Press*, Tuesday 19 February 1957.
2. Violinist Danny Levan was formerly a member of the Ken Beaumont Band who, during the 1940s, included musical arrangements of traditional folk songs in their repertoire. Levan eventually joined Johnny Duncan & his Blue Grass Boys.

Skiffle in the City

As with most other cities, Norwich was quick to respond to the growing interest in skiffle music. A glut of small groups and bands were employed in the clubs and pubs of the city to satisfy the expanding local demand for live music. Initially, Norwich's jazz clubs followed the fashion set by Ken Colyer and Chris Barber by introducing skiffle sessions as a secondary fill-in attraction during the intervals between band sessions. As early as 1956, most of the city's jazz clubs were including skiffle interludes as a normal part of an evening's entertainment. Usually, the performers were competent musicians often drawn from the headline jazz band and, consequently, gave performances of a high musical standard. The Collegians teamed up with the Jock Bullen Skiffle Group and performed together in most of the city's jazz clubs. At the Cottage, the Derek Warne Skiffle Men regularly accompanied Lowestoft-based Colin Bates and his Jazzmen. Eventually, the demand from the jive dancing public was for skiffle alone and the jazz-skiffle combination evenings, where skiffle was normally secondary to jazz, were gradually replaced by skiffle only sessions. While the larger venues in the city, like the Hippodrome, were struggling to meet the expense involved in providing live entertainment with nationally recognised artists, the smaller clubs, dance halls and public houses were able to cope by using cheaper local musicians, fuelling a further growth in the number of Norwich based performers and bands, especially skiffle bands. At the same time, an expansion in the number of youth clubs within the city also provided an opportunity for the under eighteens to play, dance to or simply enjoy skiffle music.

The acoustic nature of skiffle compared to the louder amplified sound of rock 'n' roll made it ideal for the smaller function rooms and bars of Norwich's public houses, offering a commercial opportunity that few landlords could afford to overlook. Not only did the facilities of a public house provide a convenient venue for performances of skiffle and a base for individual groups to gather and practice, but also they provided the band's amateur musicians with the chance of a welcome income, however small, and an incentive to develop and improve in the hope of becoming famous. Which of Norwich's public houses was the first to feature skiffle evenings as an attraction is open to dispute but one of the first, if not the very first, was the Red Lion on St George's Street,[1] a small corner public house with two bars and a central passageway. Its location immediately opposite the Norwich Art School ensured that most of its patrons were free thinking young students who were aware of the current fashions in music and clothes. From 1955, the Red Lion was under the control of James and Beattie Beales who used the commercial opportunities provided by its unique location to good effect. In an article in the *Eastern Evening News* discussing the provision in 1957 of live music in the public houses of Norwich, R E Porter stated that among the first to feature skiffle music:

> ... is the Red Lion, St Gregory, where the host, Mr James Beales, introduced the J T Skiffle Quartet 18 months ago. Since then business has never looked back and the turnover has increased enormously. "We do not have rock 'n' roll," Mr Beales told me, "but folk songs of all nations and calypsos. They are popular with most customers of all ages from 18 to 80."[2]

The J T Skiffle Quartet, also known as the Jock Bullen Skiffle Group, was formed in 1956 by art student Jock Bullen and performed as the main band at the Red Lion. Later the same year, Bullen joined forces with ex-Serviceman Brian Lambert to form the highly successful Allez Katz.[3] Among the groups appearing regularly at the Red Lion was an extremely popular band, the Saints, from Thorpe St Andrew.

With its long tradition as a centre for jazz, it came as no surprise when the Jolly Butchers public house on Ber Street also became one of the earliest in the city to form its own skiffle group. The brainchild of one of the pub's regular singers, Albert Cooper,[4] the band was formed in 1956. Guitarists Albert Cooper, Norman Hedley and Bernard Rudden[5] provided the vocals accompanied by Dave Keeley on tea-chest bass and Vernon Alden scraping out a rhythm on the washboard. Singer Albert Cooper was a regular performer at the Jolly Butchers after his abilities as a jazz and blues vocalist were discovered during one of Anna Hannent's open sessions in which ordinary members of the pub's clientele were encouraged to perform and sing to a piano accompaniment. Having discovered Cooper's vocal talent, Anna frequently joined with him to sing duets and they appeared together for many years at jazz concerts and festivals throughout Norfolk as well as in sessions at the Jolly Butchers. Albert Cooper's signature song was *Hello Central Give Me Doctor Jazz*.[6] He bought his first guitar while on a trip to Italy in 1955 and was soon able to play well enough to accompany his own singing on stage. Albert Cooper's decision to form a

The Jolly Butchers Skiffle Band, 1957.

Black Anna and Albert Cooper, a popular jazz duo.

skiffle band based at the Jolly Butchers was made when his friend, Bernard Rudden, returned to Norwich after graduating from university. In time the Jolly Butchers Skiffle Group became one of the most popular bands in the city and featured at many city venues. Beryl Bryden occasionally guested with the band during her frequent returns to her hometown of Norwich.

Many other public houses with accommodation suitable for performances of live music quickly followed suit and capitalised on the commercial opportunity offered by the growing interest in skiffle music. One of Norwich's more popular skiffle groups had its headquarters at the Swan public house on King Street. Every Sunday was skiffle night at the Swan with music provided by the resident band, the aptly named Cygnets. The Swan was fortunate. The Park House public house on Catton Grove Road was only granted a music licence on the understanding that the resident three-piece band would not play rock 'n' roll or sing skiffle songs on a Sunday.[7] The Cygnets skiffle band was formed in 1956 by four young gymnasts from the Lads' Club which was located immediately opposite the Swan. The group comprised guitarists Jeff Dawson and Mick Holmes, who also provided the vocals, Barry Littleboy on bass and Stan Brown on drums. The landlords at the Swan, Jack and Doris Pye, were all too willing to provide the band with a venue in which to practice and perform, bringing the public house a much-needed boost to its income. When the band's leader, Jeff Dawson, approached the manager at the Norwich Industries Club seeking an engagement, they were reluctantly given a ten-minute fill-in slot during an interval at the club's weekly dance. "They were an immediate success and, in fact, could hardly get off the stand when their time was up."[8] The reaction to their performance was so enthusiastic that they were prevented from leaving the stage by an over-exuberant audience demanding numerous encores. As a result, many more engagements at the Industries Club followed as well as a regular Monday night booking at the Ailwyn Club's rock 'n' roll dance. When their following outgrew the capacity of the Swan to cope, the group reluctantly moved from the public house to become the resident skiffle band at the Cottage in Thorpe. Elsewhere, the Red Cap Skiffle Band performed every Tuesday and Saturday at the Fye Bridge Tavern[9] on Wensum Street. The historic Woolpack on Muspole Street in the Golden Triangle district of Norwich played host to the Kingfishers Skiffle Group, who were billed as East Anglia's youngest and best—presumably, they were drinking orange juice. Skiffle was also big business in the clubroom at The Manor House on Drayton Road where the Kingfishers, the Rebels and the Ronnie Hanton Skiffle Band were regular performers.

The first skiffle groups, locally and nationally, were composed of competent musicians, usually with a jazz background. However, by 1956, inspired by Donegan's version of *The Rock Island Line*, skiffle was adopted by many young people as their music of choice, not just for listening to but also to play. The popularity of skiffle and the subsequent proliferation of skiffle groups was because skiffle music was easy to play on an acoustic guitar, mandolin, ukulele or banjo. It also provided the rhythm for dancing jive. Most songs involved mastering a basic tune with few chord changes. Their lyrics were normally simple stories about the real-life experiences of working men and women, usually American, and told of their struggles, hardships, loves and achievements. Consequently, for some, skiffle was music of the working classes and a vehicle for protest against prejudice, inequality and injustice. For others it was simply an exciting form of music, another variation on the latest music from America, and a welcome change from the sugary sweet ballads and comedy songs of the 1940s and early 1950s. As well as recognisable skiffle numbers, the repertoires of most skiffle groups included the latest rock 'n' roll hits and other popular songs of the day.

Young musicians of all ages and at every level of musical ability found themselves able to produce an acceptable skiffle performance. Skiffle groups merely followed the long-held tradition of small local amateur bands providing the music for dances and social gatherings at community and village halls, usually playing with easily transportable instruments, often an accordion or a fiddle. However, accordions and fiddles were not the best instruments for producing an acceptable skiffle or rock 'n' roll sound and were replaced by most of the younger musicians by a ukulele or a guitar. While Colyer and Donegan had demonstrated the use of guitars, musicians such as Arthur Godfrey in the USA and George Formby in the UK had promoted the ukulele as a cheap-to-buy and easy-to-play instrument for ordinary people. It was a simple step up for ukulele players to progress towards performing with a guitar. A typical skiffle band consisted of a singer, or a group of singers, backed by two or more guitar, banjo or ukulele players, the more the merrier to make an acceptably big sound. The jazzy backing beat was often provided by a rhythm section consisting of homemade percussion instruments, a washboard or a tea-chest bass. To cater for the growing demand, inexpensive and often poorly made acoustic guitars became readily available in music shops, and sheet music included chord names and finger placement diagrams above the musical notation to show untutored musicians what to play. Acoustic guitars were on sale at Wilson & Ramshaw's in Norwich's Bridewell Alley and Woods Music Shop on Dove Street from as little as 87/6 (£4.37) and amplifiers with a tremolo for eighteen guineas (£18.90)[10] for those who preferred to play rock 'n' roll. As a result, skiffle groups were cheap to form because they did not necessarily require the expensive electric guitars, drum kits, amplification equipment and speaker systems needed by a successful rock 'n' roll band. Nor did they require the musicianship of a jazz ensemble, giving ordinary young men and women the ability to play and perform skiffle music both at home in private for fun or in public to provide the rhythm for dancing and, for some, the chance of fame and fortune. Consequently, skiffle groups grew up everywhere.

Some groups began life in the front room or parlour of a band member's home, encouraging and enabling the under eighteens to become involved in making music. The Jailbirds[11] were formed in a back room at the home of the Zagni brothers on Cecil Road in Norwich, when they were still in their early teens. The development of youth clubs in Norwich and elsewhere also provided opportunities for younger participants. Mrs M Robinson, adviser to National Association of Mixed and Girls Clubs, was reported to have said:

> If you want to make yourself popular with a youth club, unearth grandma's old metal washboard and take it along. Skiffle groups use them with thimbles to make music. Empty cigar boxes for turning into box fiddles, tea chests which are used with a broomstick as a bass, and clothes brushes which produce a swishing sound on an old suitcase are also welcome. Even combs with a piece of paper over them are used by the skiffle players.[12]

The locally popular Mireille Gray made her singing debut with the Jolly Butchers' Skiffle Group when only fifteen at a dance for teenagers held in the Hellesdon Community Centre at the Middleton Lane Secondary Modern School. The Downhomers were a product of the St. Thomas Youth Club in Earlham. The Blue Stars were pupils of the Hillside School in Thorpe, and the successful Saints Skiffle Band was formed by Tony McGinnity at the Thorpe St Andrew Teenage Club[13].

Mireille Gray and the Jolly Butchers Skiffle Band.

Perhaps one of the latest and most up-to-date organisations within the club is the formation of a skiffle group which is led by Tony McGinnity called the Saints Skiffle Group. Its members have fulfilled many outside engagements in Norwich and District and played recently at the Teenage Club's variety concert.[14]

McGinnity eventually achieved national fame as a professional rock musician, better known by his stage name of Tony Sheridan, later to become a mentor to the Beatles[15]. Mireille Gray frequently joined the Saints to sing her signature song, *Freight Train*. In Great Yarmouth, the Central Youth Club on Deneside had its own band while the Vampires were an accidental product of the Dereham Youth Centre.

> The notion of forming a skiffle group first came when rehearsals for a youth show were in progress. It was envisaged as a comedy act. [16]

In Cromer, students from the local Secondary Modern School combined as the Wild Four Skiffle Band.

As well as the youth clubs and public houses of Norwich, the larger dance halls and night clubs began to feature skiffle as an attraction, seeking to capitalise on the latest craze and employing mostly cheap local amateur skiffle bands rather than the better paid nationally recognised professionals. Regular skiffle nights were held by the Norwich Jazz Club at the Boulton and Paul Social Club's premises on Thorpe Road. Regular performers at the club were the Kestrels, the Jailbirds, the Rodents,[17] the Kingfishers and the Vampires, all locally based bands.[18] In November 1957, Earlham's Downhomers[19] formed a short-lived skiffle club at the Herbert Fraser Hall on Bethel Street when Brian Green's Dixielanders relocated the 59 Jazz Club to the Grosvenor Rooms on Prince of Wales Road. Following the success of the Cygnets, Wednesday nights at the Norwich Industries Club were designated skiffle nights; evenings of skiffle music for dancing that usually featured three different bands. At various times the Cygnets, the Saints, the Kestrels, the Vampires, the Rebels and the Jolly Butchers Skiffle Group made appearances at the club. When the Norwich Industries Club's premises on Oak Street were taken over by the Federation Club in September 1957, the nature of the organised entertainments changed, focussing on providing entertainment for the whole family rather than for one specific age range. The space allocated for music and dancing was reduced and skiffle nights ceased, ending their pro-active role in promoting live popular music from new local bands.

Belonging to a skiffle band was not so easy in the villages surrounding Norwich. Other than a front room at somebody's home, facilities for practice were limited. Many villages had neither a village hall nor a youth club. Nor was there a great demand for skiffle music. Conventional modern and old-time dancing with live music provided by local musicians and bands was still the preferred format at most village dances. When skiffle bands did appear, attendance was often low. Older residents stayed away, concerned not only by the perceived hazards posed by jiving couples but also by the fear that skiffle music would attract an undesirable section of society to the village dance. The small number of teenagers living in the immediate surrounding area meant that teenage only dances were not viable in most villages.

Like many groups in the more rural areas, the Reptiles, a skiffle group based at the Youth Centre in Fakenham, suffered from the lack of suitable performance spaces.

> Fakenham may be up to date in the matter of a skiffle group, but because of the lack of a suitable hall, dances are few and far between and so this teenage group has been somewhat limited in its attempts to show what it can do on its own territory.[20]

Furthermore, a folk tradition was alive and well in many of the Broadland and seaside villages of Norfolk and Suffolk. Some still retained their local singers and story tellers, including Harry Cox at The Crown in Catfield; Sam Larner in the Fisherman's Return, Winterton; Ben Baxter and Dick Hewitt at the Vernon Arms in Southrepps, and George Beech at the Bell in Hemsby. Consequently, folk singing was already well catered for in many rural public houses. *Birmingham Town*, a traditional song performed by George Locke from the Broadland village of Rollesby, was recorded in 1910 by the composer Ralph Vaughan Williams and incorporated into one of his musical compositions. In his book *The Fifties Replayed*, the author describes a visit he made in 1958 to a Norfolk public house while on an outing to Cromer with a party of senior citizens.

> ... the return journey involved a stop at a wayside public house where I was invited to play my ukulele. ... After I had sung my complete repertoire of George Formby songs, the landlord thanked me for my efforts and declared that it was now their turn to entertain. Immediately, an ancient weather-wizened man dressed in a khaki army greatcoat and brown floppy hat, produced a harmonica from his pocket and accompanied the landlord while he sang various traditional and local folk songs about fishing for herring and ploughing the soil. Eventually, he was replaced by a second man dressed in a striped shirt, brown trousers held up by a belt of binder twine, a red spotted handkerchief tied around his neck and black hobnailed boots, who danced jigs on a wooden board accompanied by the same harmonica player. Fortified by numerous jugs of beer, everyone enthusiastically joined in a communal sing-song, supported by an inharmonious harmonica and ukulele accompaniment, until it was time to leave for home.[21]

Because of its association with the folk songs of the black and white working communities of America, skiffle gave an extra impetus to an already growing interest in the traditional folk music of both Britain and America. Many skifflers used Carl Sandburg's *The American Songbag* as a source for new material. In the early 1950s, while escaping from the McCarthy purges in the USA, the American song collector Alan Lomax[22] toured the British Isles researching the origins of well-known folk songs. Similarly, the BBC sponsored Peter Kennedy[23] to tour various rural and seaside regions of the British Isles to seek out and collect traditional folk music for a series of radio programmes on the BBC's Home and Light Services. The most influential of these programmes was *As I Roved Out* which was broadcast in six separate series between September 1953 and September 1958, and featured folk music from the villages of East Norfolk in many of its programmes, especially the songs of Harry Cox. The inclusion of folk music in both the *Six-Five Special* and the *Saturday Skiffle Club* further stimulated the revival of interest in folk music and many traditional British folk songs found their way into the repertoires of numerous skiffle bands. On 27 July 1957, the English Folk Dance and Song Society[24] held a weekend of singing and dancing at Wymondham College to music from the Jolly Waggoner's' Square Dance Band. In November, the same society held a meeting for young people at the Bignold School on Essex Street in Norwich. Even that most traditional record reviewer of the *Eastern Evening News*, John Mitchell, acknowledged the growing interest in folk music with a rare appraisal of an EP of folk songs with a nautical flavour recorded by Petty Officer Bill McDermid, appropriately titled *Splice the Mainbrace*.[25]

Notes

1. The Red Lion closed in 2004 and re-opened in 2008 as the Doghouse.
2. *Eastern Evening News*, Saturday 17 August 1957.
3. In 1956, the members of the Allez Katz were Jock Bullen (guitar and vocals), Brian Lambert (washboard and vocals), Bob Bowley (guitar), Ginger Waller (tea-chest bass) and Frank Wienlie (banjo).
4. Albert Cooper was born at Norwich in 1933 and for most of his life was an active participant in the city's music scene. In the 1960s, he established the popular Jacquards Club at the Mischief Tavern on Fye Bridge with his brother Tony. An account of his life in music can be found in *A Chronicle of Norwich's King of the Blues* by Kingsley Harris.
5. Academic Bernard Rudden, a graduate in Russian studies, became Emeritus Professor of Comparative Law at Oriel College, Oxford.
6. In 1953, Albert Cooper and his brother Tony jointly bought an early version of a tape-recorder. Most of his vocal repertoire in 1955 consisted of jazz and blues songs that he recorded from the Dutch radio station Radio Hilversum, especially jazz classics performed by Neva Raphaello and the Dutch Swing College, including Raphaello's version of the King Oliver classic, *Hello Central Give Me Doctor Jazz*. (Interview with Albert Cooper, 15/08/2019.)
7. *Eastern Evening News*, Monday 10 March 1958. The Park House closed in 1996 and reopened in 1999 as the Crown and Magpie.
8. *Eastern Evening News*, Thursday 28 February 1957.
9. The Fye Bridge Tavern closed in 1959 and reopened as the Ribs of Beef in 1985.
10. *Eastern Evening News*, Saturday 26 November 1960.
11. The members of the Jailbirds were Larry Jordan and Henry Johnston (vocals), Mike Lorenz and John Zagni (guitars), Howard Platt (banjo), Dave Pennington (bass) and Frank Zagni (drums). Larry Jordan was one of the many stage names used by singer Clarence Pye, formerly lead singer with the Ace of Clubs Dance Band. He also performed at various times as Larry Pye or Clarence Jordan.
12. *Eastern Evening News*, Thursday 31 January 1957.
13. The founding members of the Saints were Tony McGinnity (vocals and guitar), Kenny Packwood (guitar), John Taylor (tea-chest bass) and Andy Kinley (drums).
14. *Eastern Evening News*, Saturday 23 March 1957.
15. For more details about the career of Tony McGinnity/Sheridan, see Chapter 23.
16. Eastern Evening News, Thursday 28 February 1957.
17. The Rodents Skiffle Group was formed by airmen based at RAF Coltishall. The line-up in November 1957 was Mick Huscraft (guitar), Dave Barnard (electric guitar) Ray Birt

(banjo), Mick Short (tea-chest bass), Ray Harvey (washboard). The original line-up also included Bill Blackburn and Bernard Hancock.

18. The members of the Dereham Vampires were Hilton Tait (guitar & vocals), Rodney Head (guitar), John Bloomfield (tea-chest bass), Dave Green (washboard), Nigel Wright (banjo) and John Bennett (banjo). The band was managed by Eddie Kitney from Dereham.

19. The Downhomers were formed by Morris Lang (vocals), Neville Cox (guitar), Keith May (tea-chest bass) and Brian Bates (drums); joined later by Lester Middleton (vocals), Pat Wood (guitar) and Peter Moore (drums).

20. *Eastern Evening News*, Thursday 17 April 1958; Performing with the Reptiles were Patrick Pearce, David Bell & Terry Pearce (guitars) Keith Meekin (tea-chest bass) and Roy Spratt (washboard).

21. Colin Miller (2008), *The Fifties Replayed* p144-5.

22. Alan Lomax's Anthology of American Folk Music, issued by Folkway Records in 1953 as 18 LP records, provided a convenient source of song material for British skiffle bands. While resident in Britain, Lomax's contribution to a BBC Home Service programme *A Ballad Hunter* gave an added stimulus to the growing interest in British and American folk music.

23. Peter Douglas Kennedy was an enthusiastic collector of folk music and song. In the 1950s he was co-presenter of the BBC's *As I Roved Out*. His archive of British Folk Music, including details of his 1950s tours, is currently held in the British Library.

24. The English Folk Dance & Song Society was founded in 1932 with the aim of preserving, promoting and developing the traditional English folk arts of song, dance and storytelling. Ralph Vaughan Williams was its first president.

25. *Eastern Evening News*, 15 January 1958.

Art Baxter and the Sinners

The arrival of television in Norfolk brought with it problems as well as benefits. Attendance at theatres and cinemas started to fall as many older people preferred to stay in and watch television than go out for their entertainment, and audiences at the cinema and theatre were drawn increasingly from the younger age groups. Boy still met girl in the dance hall and potential relationships were normally cemented by a follow-up date at the cinema or theatre. Consequently, the entertainment on offer in the dance hall, cinema and theatre began to be targeted more precisely at the young, and never more so than at the Hippodrome Theatre in Norwich. Not only were the audience figures at the Hippodrome dropping but also its traditional offering of a mixed variety show aimed primarily at the ordinary working-class family was becoming more expensive to mount, thanks to heavy local city centre business rates, an entertainment tax of a third of all takings and exorbitant artists' fees. Frequently, the resulting show was inferior in quality to that being offered at the same time on television, especially when compared with the many glitzy productions from America such as *The Perry Como Show*, *The Phil Silvers Show*, *Burns and Allen* and *Hey Jeannie*.

> Hostile as many of us are to American filmed television imported here to fill our screens cheaply, Sergeant Bilko has his admirers. It is hard not to like this wise-cracking quick-thinking man and his squad.[1]

Various strategies were adopted by the theatre's management to improve attendance figures. Initially, variety shows with French sounding titles were staged that included long lines of scantily clad leggy dancers and speciality acts performing in front of static nude tableaus in a format made popular by the Windmill Theatre in London during World War II. The *Eastern Evening News* commented that:

> A great deal of dancing punctuated in a surfeit of disrobing makes up most of the 'Follies Striptease' show at Norwich Hippodrome.[2]

Eventually, rock 'n' roll acts were added to the cast of performers to attract a younger audience.

Appearing for a week at the Hippodrome from 4 February 1957 as the final act of a mixed variety show was a little-known rock 'n' roll band called Art Baxter and his Sinners. Art Baxter (the stage name of Arthur Gomm from Canterbury in Kent) was formerly a singer with Billy Ternent's Orchestra and had capitalised on the opportunities offered by the emerging craze for rock 'n' roll and the lack of home-grown British talent by forming his own band playing in the rockabilly style of Bill Haley. Many jazz and dance band musicians, locally as well as nationally, had responded positively to the financial opportunities offered by the demand for rock 'n' roll music from young people and formed small groups to play rock 'n' roll mostly in the manner of Bill Haley and his Comets. In a conversation with the journalist Ronald Grant, jazz drummer Tony Crombie indicated that:

> For years, he said, I have played the sort of music I wanted to play and it didn't get me anywhere much. In future I'm going to do just one thing—give the public what they want whether I like it or not. At the moment they want rock 'n' roll so my new band will play just that. When they get tired of rock 'n' roll then I will change to whatever they do want.[3]

Tony Crombie formed a moderately successful rock 'n' roll band called Tony Crombie and his Rockets in September 1956.[4] John Mitchell of the *Eastern Evening News* was extremely scathing of jazz musicians who converted to rock 'n' roll.

> Jazz players who turn to rock …are like ageing fat boxers, rolling around the wrestling ring to help pay off tax arrears.[5]

Despite being advertised as Britain's first rock 'n' roll band, a title that was also attributed at various times to both Tony Crombie and his Rockets and Rory Blackwell and the Blackjacks, Art Baxter's 1956 recording of *Rock You Sinners* had made negligible impact on the popular music charts, mainly because it was banned by the BBC on religious grounds. In Norwich, Baxter was welcomed as the first genuine top-class professional rock 'n' roll band to visit the city. Nevertheless, he received lukewarm reviews from the press.

> A series of pleasant enough acts leads in the end to one of the noisiest of noisy modern quintets which Art Baxter, their leader, calls his Rock 'n' roll Sinners. Baxter ties himself in knots, almost, and works himself into a frenzy yelling into the microphone, but he could have saved his voice last night, for scarcely a word of it could be recognised above the bashing of the drums, the hubbub and the blare.[6]

However, Baxter's music was enjoyed by most of the younger members of the audience who had interrupted the preceding acts with clapping, stamping of feet and yelling for their newly discovered hero in their impatience to hear rock 'n' roll. On the final night of his appearance in Norwich, several teenagers, who were inevitably described as Teddy Boys, jumped onto the stage and danced among the band. The management had failed to realise that when music for dancing is played to young people, young people are likely to dance. When other couples followed suit by leaving their seats intending to jive in the aisles or to surge towards the stage, the management panicked, pulled the plug on the band and played the National Anthem as a signal that the show had finished.

Baxter's short-lived career as a rock 'n' roll star ended soon after he appeared in an obscure 1957 B category film called *Rock You Sinners*, the same title as his first recording, written and produced by Beatrice C Fancey, and starring Jackie Collins, the infamous slack-wearing sister of Joan Collins. The resulting rock movie was described by some critics as being monumentally inept and a clueless exercise in film making. Released in June 1957, the film, charted the exploits of a radio disc jockey in the early days of rock 'n' roll. Appearing with Baxter in the film, hailed by some as the first British made rock 'n' roll movie, were Tony Crombie and his Rockets, jazz drummer Don Solash and his Rockin' Horses, Rory Blackwell and the Blackjacks, Dickie Bennett and George 'Calypso' Browne. The film had more success in Denmark where it was released in January 1958 under the title *Ungdom Med Rytmer (Youth with Rhythms)*.

Notes

1. *Eastern Evening News*, Tuesday 29 July 1958.
2. *Eastern Evening News*, Saturday 5 October 1957.
3. *Eastern Evening News*, Friday 12 April 1956.
4. The founding members of Tony Crombie and his Rockets were Clyde Ray (vocals), Jimmie Currie (guitar), Rex Morris (sax), Ashley Kozak (bass), Red Mitchell (piano) and Tony Crombie (drums). All were experienced jazz musicians. Jet Harris (bass), later of The Shadows, also played with the band. As well as a disputed claim to be Britain's first rock 'n' roll band, Tony Crombie and his Rockets also claimed to have recorded the first British rock 'n' roll song to enter the popular music charts with their version of *Shortnin' Bread Rock*.
5. *Eastern Evening News*, Wednesday 14 May 1958.
6. *Eastern Daily Press*, Tuesday 5 February 1957.

Bill Haley Visits Norwich

By early 1957 rock 'n' roll in Norwich was starting to thrive despite some negativity from the public and especially from the press. Most clubs and dance halls were beginning to offer 'rock 'n' roll only' evenings although jiving was discouraged during regular modern ballroom and old-time dance nights. An absence of good local rock 'n' roll bands meant that music for the 'rock 'n' roll only' evenings was provided either by the resident all-purpose dance orchestra, a skiffle group, or pop records played through an amplified record player. The Grosvenor's first rock 'n' roll evening on Monday 10 January 1957 to music from Neville Bishop's Broadcasting Orchestra was not a success, mainly because the licenced bars at the Grosvenor were closed for the evening and alcohol was banned. Despite this precaution, disturbances still occurred because, undeterred, many of the dancers had sought alcoholic refreshment in the pubs and bars on Prince of Wales Road before coming to the Grosvenor. The dance planned for the following Monday 17 January was immediately cancelled and the experiment was not repeated for some time.

Elsewhere, Eddie Gates[1] on an electric organ provided dance music for the Monday evening rock 'n' roll club-nights at the Ailwyn Hall. Eddie Gates eventually moved on to become the resident organist at the Raven Public House and was replaced at the Ailwyn by the more appropriate and youthful Cygnets skiffle group. Ernest Cowell's Dance Band played rock 'n' roll at the Lido while Al Collins and his Band beat out the rhythm at the Cottage. Having failed to become the resident dance orchestra at the Floral Hall Ballroom in Gorleston, the Gordon Edwards Band played rock 'n' roll instead at the Queen's Hotel in Great Yarmouth. At the Norwich Industries Club, the resident band, featuring Chic Randall on vibraphone, played pop, standards and music for old time dancing on different nights of the week. The Industries Club also boasted that it possessed the largest jukebox in East Anglia playing the latest rock 'n' roll records from America. Brian Freeman joined the Bob Barbour Orchestra to sing rock 'n' roll songs at the Gala.

Appearing on stage at the Carlton Cinema in Norwich on Wednesday 6 March 1957 for two performances as part of his well-publicised tour of Great Britain was Bill Haley and his band, his Comets. That the venue was a cinema highlighted the absence in the city of a suitably large concert hall in which to stage major live musical events. While many teenagers were excited by the thought of a visit from their American rock 'n' roll hero, some were concerned at his appearance in the

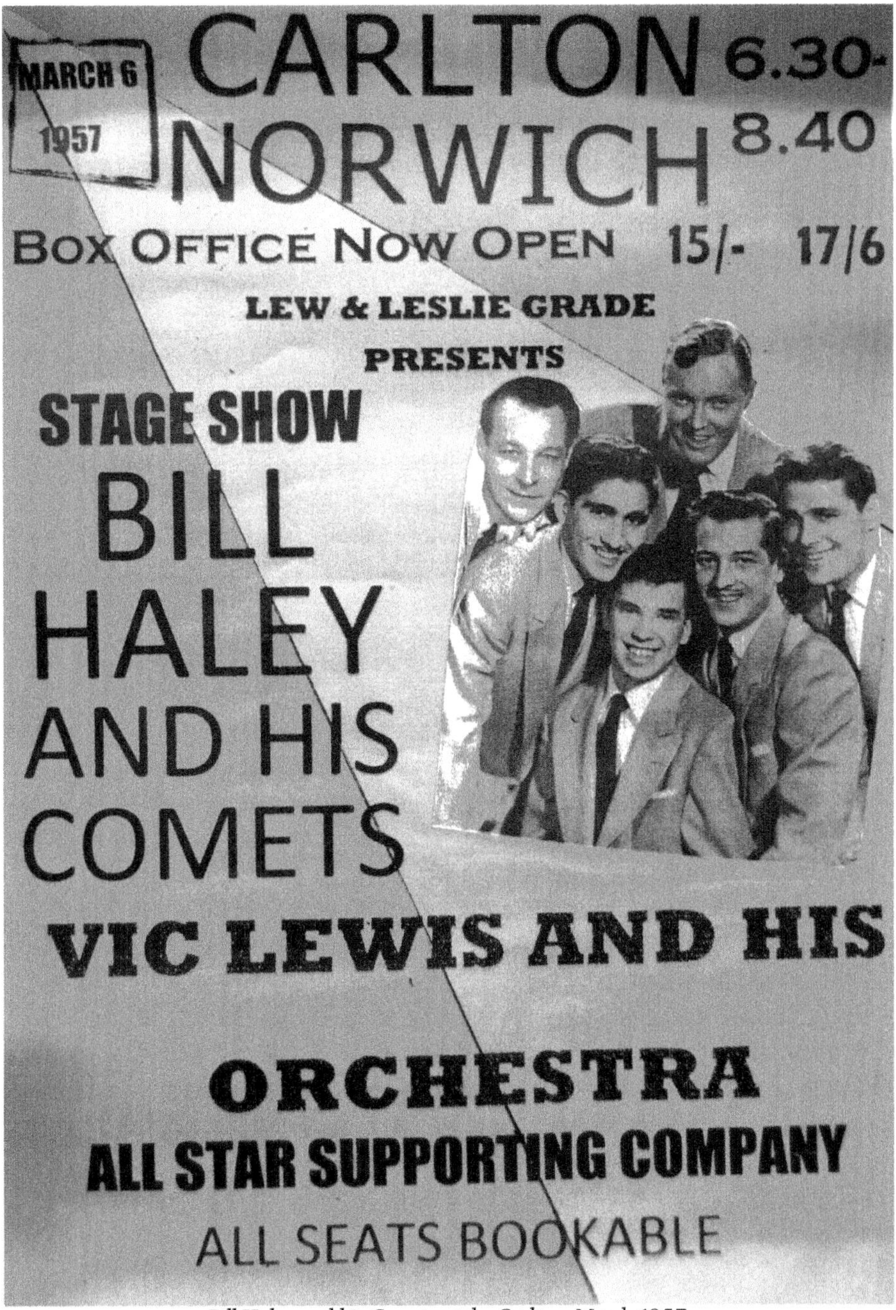

Bill Haley and his Comets at the Carlton, March 1957.

city. At an open discussion forum for young people entitled *We Beg to Differ*, held at their Dove Street Chambers, the Vice-Chairman of the Norfolk and Norwich Young Conservatives demanded that the Watch Committee should ban Haley's visit as he feared that it might encourage local Teddy Boys into violence. One speaker commented that Teddy Boys:

> had gained fresh impetus from rock 'n' roll and that their dress with its latest additions was disgusting.[2]

Unfazed by the opposition to his visit, many fans waited outside Thorpe Station from 6.30am on a cold, dismal morning, anticipating Haley's arrival in the city by train, but their wait was in vain. Bill Haley arrived from London by car and registered almost unnoticed for a night's stay at the Royal Hotel on Prince of Wales Road. A few lucky fans recognised the hotel's distinguished guest and were able to obtain autographs and signed photographs. One fan, Jennifer Potter, having missed seeing the star's arrival at the hotel, decided to leave her autograph book at the reception desk and was surprised to discover that the singer had signed it when she collected it the following morning.

When he did appear at the Carlton Cinema on All Saints Green, it was as the final act in yet another variety show. Performing in the show before Haley and his Comets were the Vic Lewis Orchestra, playing big band jazz in the style of Stan Kenton; Kenneth Earle and Malcolm Vaughan, a well-known comedy duo; and Desmond Lane, a penny-whistler. Their acts were not completed without difficulty. The teenage audience was there to see Bill Haley and they let the management know. When he finally appeared on the stage,

> Mr Haley's familiar figure complete with yellow fluorescent socks brought probably the biggest single yell of the evening, but his closing choice of three top favourites including 'Rock Around the Clock' was guaranteed to send the audience out at the same fever pitch as it came in.[3]

His rousing final three top favourites were *Shake, Rattle and Roll*, *See You Later, Alligator* and the inevitable classic, *Rock Around the Clock*. Despite repeated requests for the audience to keep their seats, a request reinforced by the presence of the chief constable and a cohort of heavy-weight bouncers in evening dress, Bill Haley performed accompanied by screams and shouts from his standing and gyrating fans. Whiffler commented that:

> without the infectious rhythm the performance of Mr Haley's Band would not be out of the ordinary, but it is the well-defined beat of the music which had ninety percent of the audience, some of the bus drivers included, clapping their hands and bouncing about in their seats.[4]

He further commented that:

> Nobody was badly behaved; the nearest I saw to any demonstration was a couple of young girls who stood up at the end of numbers, raised their hands above their heads and called out "Billy".[5]

At the end of the show emotions were calmed when the audience respectfully stood in silence while the National Anthem was played. After the final show, four thousand fans danced and sang outside the cinema until coaches and buses arrived to transport them home.

In a rare departure from his normal disapproving format, John Mitchell, the record reviewer of the *Eastern Evening News*, reluctantly acknowledged the existence of rock 'n' roll by a half-hearted appraisal of Tommy Sands' recording of *Teenage Crush*[6] but was forced to add:

> How much longer this craze will last is anybody's guess. I'm surprised myself it has gone on for eighteen months but still the record lists are as full of rock 'n' roll numbers as ever.[7]

From the tenor of his columns, it was clear that Mitchell was hoping that the craze for rock 'n' roll would soon subside and be replaced by a more acceptable form of music, far removed from any association with teenage rebelliousness. Like many, his hopes lay in calypso which he predicted would soon replace rock 'n' roll in teenagers' affections. The formation of the Norwich Spanish Guitar Club on Tuesday 23 April 1957 was greeted with a headline in the *Eastern Evening News* proclaiming "*Calypso ousts rock 'n' roll*". Singer Eric Connor added his voice to the argument, even if his facts were somewhat erroneous.

> Rock 'n' roll is just a crib—what's more it is out-of-date. After all rock 'n' roll is merely a by-product of the calypso, even the steps were taken from dance steps created in Trinidad between 1945 and 1950. ... Rock 'n roll rhythm is a slow calypso tempo.[8]

Even the Chief Education Officer for Norfolk was forced to voice an opinion.

> Although the calypso has commercially replaced rock 'n' roll, it is to the admirers of the Elvis Presley Cult that Chief Education Officer for Norfolk, Dr F Lincoln Ralphs, refers in the latest issue of the County Education Services Bulletin. "By 1967" says Dr Ralphs, "rock 'n' roll will be as antiquated as the minuet".[9]

The hope of some that calypso would soon replace rock 'n' roll was based on the success of the singer Harry Belafonte who had achieved a number three position in the UK record charts with *The Banana Boat Song* in April 1957, and number two the following August with *Island in the Sun*. Despite their best efforts, rock 'n' roll survived, and the calypso waned in popularity. 'Trawlerman,' reporting from Lowestoft, provided a more accurate description of the prevailing state of popular music.

> If anybody in Lowestoft hoped that rock 'n' roll is on its way out, a peep into the Kensington Ballroom on a Tuesday evening would get a great shock. I was there the other evening and saw roughly three hundred teenagers enjoying themselves to their hearts' content, a crowd so well behaved that they would have done credit to a religious gathering or a class in a technical school.[10]

He went on to say that the rock 'n' roll club at the Kensington had over five hundred members and that their fashion in clothing is of a modern style.

> Too many adults were anxious to see the end of rock 'n' roll because they were afraid of Teddy Boys. But where people go wrong is in thinking that Teddy Boys are thugs. The vast majority are nothing of the kind; they are just young men who desire to have a different dress to most of us in this generation.[11]

Notes

1. Despite being blind, Eddie Gates was a highly competent organist and began his career as the theatre organist at the Carlton Cinema in Norwich. Eddie Gates' Orchestra was for a time the resident dance band at the Floral Hall in Gorleston. The band's signature tune was 'Lisa.'
2. *Eastern Evening News*, Wednesday 27 February 1957.
3. *Eastern Evening News*, Thursday 7 March 1957.
4. *Eastern Evening News*, Thursday 7 March 1957.
5. Ibid.
6. Tommy Sands was an American actor and singer. Sands played a rock 'n' roll star in an episode of the drama series *Kraft Television Theatre* on American TV, in which he sang *Teenage Crush*. His recording of *Teenage Crush* reached number two in the US Billboard charts but failed to make any impression on the UK charts.
7. *Eastern Evening News*, Thursday 7 March 1957.
8. *Eastern Evening News*, Friday 3 May 1957.
9. *Eastern Evening News*, Thursday 12 September 1957.
10. *Eastern Evening News*, Friday 27 September 1957.
11. Ibid.

Competitions Galore

By the end of 1957, live bands that were providing music exclusively for the young in Norwich were mostly playing a mixture of jazz, skiffle and rock 'n' roll numbers on unamplified instruments. Few could afford the instrumentation needed to play electronically amplified rock 'n' roll. Furthermore, the amateur nature of most local groups limited their opportunities for gaining national recognition. Bands usually performed in the locality where they were formed because performance fees were often small and travelling costs were high. One opportunity for wider recognition lay in the numerous skiffle competitions that were being organised nationally and locally, usually for money prizes or occasionally for a recording contract, as in the larger national competitions. On Whit Monday, 10 June 1957, Sam Benjamin of the International Jazz Club organised a skiffle competition as part of the Bury St Edmunds Round Table's Annual Charity Fete in a park on the outskirts of the town for the prize of a recording contract with Esquire Records. On a cold, wet day, thirty-four groups from all over the country took part. One band was said to have walked the seventy-five miles from London to compete. Each group was allowed six minutes to perform two numbers. The competition was judged by skiffle performer Johnny Duncan, blues expert Paul Oliver and jazz critic Graham Boatfield. The competition was won by the 2.19 Skiffle Group from Rochester in Kent with their versions of *This Little Light of Mine* and *Trouble in Mind*. Second was the Station Skiffle Group from Fulham and third the Delta Skiffle Group from Glasgow. All three were offered recording contracts by Esquire. Only three Norfolk based groups took part, the Five-Sided Squares from Thetford, the Ramblers from Sheringham and the Vampires from Dereham, all of them unplaced.

In the autumn, the BBC sponsored the grandly named World Skiffle Championships, despite all the contestants being British. The country was divided into six geographic regions and competitive rounds held in each. The winners of each regional competition were invited to compete in a grand-final at the Locarno Ballroom in Streatham on Thursday 14 November. Taking part in the final were the Creole Skiffle Group from Glasgow, the Roach River Band from Littleborough near Manchester, the Trentside Five from Nottingham, Vince Ogley and the Moonshiners from Barnsley, Vince Eager and the Vagabonds from Grantham and the Lumberjacks from London. After an initial audition, a final three were selected who were introduced to a watching audience by Paul Carpenter and competed

97

live as part of the televised programme *Come Dancing* on that evening's BBC TV. Reflector in the *Eastern Evening News* wrote:

> We are it seems a nation of skifflers. Six thousand skiffle groups spread all over the country are trying to get into show business. Lured by visions of overnight success and a £250 prize, they entered for the World Skiffle Championships and after stoic souls had whittled them down, three finalists appeared in the 'Come Dancing' programme on television last night … Young men of talent must be allowed every opportunity to get to the top but I am quite certain there are not 6000 Lonnie Donegans waiting to be discovered; after last night I am certain these are not even three. This craze for imitating is widespread nowadays; it is not often that stars arise from the midst of it. Imitators are always too late. There is of course, a bright side to this mass skiffle movement—if you make washboards, guitars or check shirts.[1]

The £250 first prize went to the Creole Skiffle Group. Despite coming second and winning a £150 consolation prize, the only group destined for eventual musical success was Vince Eager with the Vagabonds who were given a regular booking at the famous 2is coffee bar in Soho based on their success in the competition.

On Wednesday 12 June 1957, the Norwich Industries Club held a skiffle competition for Norfolk based bands. Despite the local popularity of skiffle, only seven bands took part; the Angels, the Cygnets, the Jailbirds, the Kestrels, the Ramblers, the Saints and the Dereham based Vampires. The £15 first prize went to the Saints from Thorpe despite the band having been in existence for only a few weeks. Joint second and a prize of £5 each was awarded to the Cygnets and the Vampires. Under the leadership of Tony McGinnity, the Saints quickly assumed the mantle of the most popular skiffle group in Norwich. McGinnity, a rebellious youth, had channelled his energies into guitar playing and was quickly recognised as one of the best lead guitarists in the city. By October, McGinnity had changed his name to Sheridan, adopting his grandmother's maiden name, and, in November, accompanied by the rest of the band, hiked to London in search of a musical career. Having failed an audition for Soho's iconic Skiffle Cellar at 49 Greek Street, run by Russell Quaye and Hylda Syms, two of the band returned to Norwich. Tony Sheridan and his friend Kenny Packwood, remained in London and, in no time at all, became regular performers at the 2is coffee bar.[2] In January 1958, Steve James reported that:

> On TV tonight in the "6-5 Special" will be seen 16-year-old Kenny Packwood of 81 Gawdy Road, Norwich. He'll be guitaring as one of singer Marty Wilde's Wildcats. Kenny was a member of the Saints Skiffle Group in Norwich before he went to London. He soon got a professional job when he arrived there — a week's engagement at the Chiswick Empire.[3]

Inspired by the success of Sheridan and Packwood, 16-year-old Mireille Gray, a former singer with the Saints, also decamped to London in search of a musical career. Her greatest success was in coming third in the British Queen of Light beauty competition, open to blondes only, at the Lyceum Ballroom in London before being persuaded to return to Norwich by her worried parents.

Although the fashion for skiffle was to be short lived and destined not to endure, it did leave a lasting legacy, particularly on the culture of the young. Skiffle provided young people with the opportunity to perform in public and to enjoy making music. It also perpetuated the long tradition of ordinary people making music for themselves rather than relying on the radio, record players and professional bands to do it for them. It did not need any expensive equipment, and most popular music was not too difficult to play. It was music for ordinary working people performed by ordinary young men and women. It also vitalised the emerging interest in British folk music. Initially, most newly formed skiffle bands simply replicated the songs that were already made popular by more well-established groups; songs such as Lonnie Donegan's *Rock Island Line, Cumberland Gap* and *Gambling Man*; Nancy Whiskey and Chas McDevitt's version of *Freight Train*, Johnny Duncan's *Last Train to San Fernando* and the Vipers rendition of *Don't You Rock Me Daddy-O*. Many bands turned to British folk tunes to expand on their American biased repertoires. Others included selections from popular music, rock 'n roll and even old standards from the forties and early fifties.

Local and national skiffle competitions continued to be popular and were seen by many amateur bands as a potential pathway to success. A paying audience guaranteed that they were extremely lucrative ventures for the competition organisers and sponsors. More so because the participating bands normally performed for free, covered their own travelling expenses and brought along a large following of supporters. The best known of the national competitions was Stanley Dale's National Skiffle Contest. Heats for the competition were held as part of a touring variety show making week-long Monday to Saturday appearances at various theatres throughout the country. The first of the weekly shows began on 19 August 1957 at the Metropolitan Theatre in London and, after visiting twenty or more venues, ended on 28 April 1958 at the Hippodrome Theatre in Bristol. Each show featured singer Jim Dale and Wally Whyton's Vipers Skiffle Group as well as a comedian, a traditional music hall duo, a high-kicking troupe of female dancers and a knife thrower. In addition, four different local amateur skiffle groups were invited to compete in a mini competition as the last act in each show during the week. Each night's winning band was judged to be the one whose performance received the loudest applause, usually the group with the largest number of supporters. The five weekday winners competed again in a grand final during the Saturday show for a prize of £15 and the promise of an entry into a national final in London competing for a prize of £100. The promised London-based final failed to materialise but, instead, Stanley Dale entered into an arrangement with the BBC for the Saturday winners from each venue to appear in a mini-competition to be broadcast live on television during editions of the *Six-Five Special* from May to July 1958. The ten best of these groups, as judged by the programme's invited audience, appeared again in three semi-finals. The first was televised on 12 July and featured the Rebels from Leeds, Double Three from Colchester and the Southerners from Reading. The second on 19 July was a competition between the Dark Town from Liverpool, the Vikings from London, the Woodlanders from Plymouth and the Teenage Vipers from Glasgow. The third held on 9 August featured the Station Group and the Saxons from London, and the Moonshiners from Sheffield. The grand final of the competition was held during the edition of the *Six-Five Special* that was televised on 23 August 1958 in which the Woodlanders were declared the winners, with the Saxons second and the Rebels third.

Over nine hundred groups took part in a Daily Sketch National Skiffle Contest during February and March 1958, another highly publicised competition organised by the Daily Sketch newspaper and sponsored by Ingram's Shaving Cream. Heats for the competition were held in most large towns and each heat winner became eligible to compete in a more prestigious district final. The winners of each of the district finals were entered into an 'ultimate final' held in London. The Norwich heat was surprisingly won by a newly formed skiffle group called the Neptunes.[4]

> The Neptunes have got through to the district final in a skiffle contest organised by a National Newspaper. If they win this final—it is being held in Ipswich—they'll play in the 'ultimate final' in London. If they win that, there'll be a TV audition for them, a recording date and a week's variety appearance.[5]

Unfortunately, in the district final that was held at the St Matthew's Baths' Hall in Ipswich, the Neptunes were unplaced. The 'ultimate final' was held in April in front of an audience of 3500 screaming youngsters at the Commodore Cinema in Hammersmith and was won by the Apex Rhythm & Blues All Stars from Northampton. Their reward was a guest appearance for a week in July in the show *Pot Luck* at the Regal Theatre in Great Yarmouth, starring Charlie Chester, and a record contract with Star Sound Studios where they recorded their version of *My Dixie Darling*.

Norwich's most successful skiffle group of 1958 was the Zagni brothers' band, the Jailbirds. In April, Norwich was chosen as one of eight regional centres for a competition sponsored by the Rank Organisation in conjunction with the BBC's

Six-Five Special to discover the *Teenage Entertainer of 1958*. Local teenagers from all forms of entertainment took part in three competitive heats held at the Gaumont Cinema on the Haymarket in Norwich on Tuesday 8, Wednesday 9 and Thursday 10 April. The winners and runners-up of each heat competed against each other at the same cinema on Friday 11 April for the right to become the champion act and to represent the region in a national final. The adopted practice of selecting the winning act by audience applause also guaranteed that each entertainer brought large numbers of supporters and that the competition was held in front of a sell-out audience. The Jailbirds won the Wednesday heat, with singers Mireille Gray and Sylvia Stebbings tying for second place. The Jailbirds went on to win the Friday-night final and gained entry to the National Final that was held at the Gaumont State Theatre in Kilburn, London, where they competed against the other seven centre winners for the grand prize of £100, a guest appearance on the *Six-Five Special* and a record contract with EMI. In what was at the time the largest auditorium in Europe and in front of a cheering audience of four thousand teenagers, the Jailbirds came second to the Weavers, a skiffle group made up of sixth formers from Canton High School in Cardiff.

Opportunities for local bands continued to evolve in the city. On Tuesday 18 February 1958, another new jazz club was opened in the cellar of the Orford Arms public house on Red Lion Street, formerly used by the Norwich Jazz Club.[6] Not for the first time nor for the last was the Orford Cellar to become a centre for popular music in Norwich. President of the newly formed club was entrepreneur and promotor Norman Guest, himself a former chairman of the Norwich Jazz Club, in the guise of Guest Star Entertainments.[7] The club did not open without opposition and controversy. Members of the Norwich Jazz Club expressed some concern that the new club merely duplicated already existing facilities and could make both clubs non-viable. An agreement was reached where the clubs would avoid competing against each other for custom by opening on different nights of the week. Norman Guest also resigned his membership of the Norwich Jazz Club's Committee. Initially Tuesday evenings at the cellar were assigned to traditional jazz and Fridays to modern. Regular performers at the Tuesday sessions were vocalist Colin Burleigh and the Collegians Jazz Band, and Brenda Bear with the Billy Roy Band. Fridays featured be-bop style music from the Rex Cooper Quartet and the Freddie Marrison Four.

For the Jailbirds, coming second became an unfortunate habit. In the final of a one-off competition to discover the 'East Anglian Skiffle Group of the Year' organised by Guest Star Entertainments and held in the Cellar at the Orford Arms on Monday 30 June 1958, the Jailbirds came second to the Sidewinders from Coltishall. Heats for the competition took place in the cellar on Monday 9 and 16 June 1958 with the final on the 30 June. Six bands—the Sidewinders, Larry

The Orford Arms, Red Lion Street.

Jordan and the Jailbirds, Jack O'Diamonds, the 8T8 Band, the Rebels and the Downhomers—competed in the final in an over-crowded and stiflingly hot cellar during which Lester Middleton of the Downhomers collapsed on stage due to heat exhaustion.[8] Despite their disappointment, the Jailbirds' singer, Larry Jordan, was voted 'Best Singer of 1958'. Following the success of the competition, Norman Guest augmented the entertainment already on offer at the cellar by establishing a weekly skiffle club as a Monday night attraction.

> Skiffle is on its way out—but, in the immortal words of Nell Gwyn, "It's an unconscionable time a-dying." In fact, in the opinion of Norwich's Norman Guest, it's still got enough life in it to merit a new club for the fans and the jivers.[9]

The Orford Arms public house was extremely popular with the American servicemen who were visiting the city for rest and relaxation, many of whom frequently supplied the jukebox in one of the street-level bars with imported records from America. The cellar at the Orford Arms was a dark, smoke-filled space with a low ceiling and mural covered walls that, at best, could accommodate a listening audience of three hundred people. On the skiffle club's opening night, a packed cellar was entertained by the Ronnie Hanton Skiffle Group[10] and singer Mireille Gray. Following the sudden death of Ronnie Hanton the following month, the Jack O'Diamonds was installed as the club's resident band.

Another clubroom much favoured by visiting American servicemen was the riverside Blue Room attached to the Norfolk Railway House (now the Compleat Angler) on Prince of Wales Road, particularly by black GIs. While few places in Norwich imposed a colour-bar or banned black customers, the American's themselves defined venues and even towns in East Anglia where black servicemen were not welcome. The Blue Room, advertised as Britain's brightest bar, imposed no colour-bar on its customers and, as a result, became the Norwich headquarters for visiting African-American servicemen.

The Blue Plaque at the entrance to the Orford Arms Cellar.

Whether justified or not, the Blue Room also developed an unsavoury reputation as a centre for the sex trade in Norwich. As well as the inevitable jukebox, live music was an attraction every evening from Monday to Friday. Local bands and musicians normally provided music, and in 1957 these were mainly skiffle groups. The Saints, the Cygnets and the Jailbirds were regular performers at the Blue Room.

Non-competitive festivals of music also became commonplace and were not only a means of raising money for a venue or charitable cause, but also for advertising a band's existence and, hopefully, its musical skills. A festival of skiffle held on Wednesday 11 June 1958 that was organised on behalf of the Dereham Memorial Hall funds by Hilton Tait, a member of the Dereham Vampires skiffle group, attracted an audience of over two hundred to listen and dance to ten local bands.[11] Performing at the festival were the Vampires and Riversiders[12] from Dereham, the Sputniks[13] from Downham Market, the Sinners[14], the Allez Katz, Kingfishers and Jack O'Diamonds from Norwich, the Marshlanders from Poringland, the Thunderbolts from North Walsham and Plumstead's Yare Valley Skiffle Band.[15]

Notes

1. *Eastern Daily Press*, Tuesday 12 November 1957.
2. Tony Sheridan's career in music is well documented in print and on the internet. Of his highly colourful career, a few instances are worth mentioning here. He is claimed to have been the first person to play an electric guitar on TV during an edition of *Oh Boy!* He was considered as the first choice for the position of lead guitarist in Cliff Richards' backing group the Shadows, but he failed to turn up for an interview and the position was given to Hank Marvin instead. In 1960, he was on tour with Gene Vincent and Eddie Cochran and, by a lucky chance, did not travel in the car that was involved in an accident near

Chippenham in which Eddie Cochran was killed and Gene Vincent seriously injured. At Hamburg in 1961, the Beatles were Sheridan's backing group for his recording of 'My Bonnie'. Paul McCartney regarded Sheridan as a role model and called him 'The Teacher.' He was falsely declared as missing presumed killed while entertaining troops in Vietnam. He was born in Norwich 21 May 1940 and died in Germany 18 February 2013. Kenny Packwood joined Marty Wilde's backing group, the Wildcats, in December 1957. At various times he played guitar with Georgie Fame, Billy Fury, Vince Eager and Johnny Duncan and the Blue Grass Boys.

3. *Eastern Evening News*, Saturday 1 January 1958.

4. The members of the Neptunes were Peter Read (guitar & vocals), Jimmy Jewel and Arthur Ellis (guitars), Barry Gray (drums) and David Merton (bass).

5. *Eastern Evening News*, Saturday 15 March 1958.

6. The Orford Jazz Club was established by three committee members of the Norwich Jazz Club, Norman and Jean Guest, and Pat Elmes. Their continued membership of the Norwich Jazz Club's Committee was considered by many to be prejudicial to the interests of the older club. All three subsequently resigned from the committee but remained club members.

7. *Eastern Evening News*, Saturday 15 February 1958.

8. Larry Jordan was one of many stage names used by singer Clarence Pye. He eventually became a well-known singer and personality in the Norwich music scene under his own name.

9. *Eastern Evening News*, Saturday 12 July 1958.

10. The personnel of the short-lived Ronnie Hanton Skiffle Group were John & Barry Campling (guitarists), Micky Large (guitar), Barry Butcher (bass) and Ronnie Hanton (vocals and drums). Hanton's signature song was Momma don't allow. Hanton, Large and Butcher joined the Jack O'Diamonds in July 1958. Ronnie Hanton tragically died on 14 August 1958 from an asthma attack while still in his twenties.

11. The Grade 2 listed Dereham Memorial Hall was established in 1815 as a carriage building coachworks. Purchased in 1908 as a public hall, it served as a cinema before being converted into a swimming pool. The pool was subsequently covered and used as a dance hall. After World War Two, the hall was purchased by the Dereham Urban District Council for use as an entertainments centre and renamed the Dereham Memorial Hall in memory of the service personnel who gave their lives in both World wars.

12. The Riversiders skiffle band were formed in January 1958 and based at the Bull public house in Dereham. The founder members of the band were Johnny Webb (guitar and vocals), Terry Purple and Jack Frosdick (guitars), Timothy Smith (Tea-chest bass) and Cecil Baxter (washboard).

13. The members of the 1958 Sputniks band were Terry Hewitt, Don Hewitt and Tom Chamberlin (guitars and vocals), Andy Newdeck (washboard), David Welling (tea-chest bass) and Melvyn Harnwell (drums).

14. Due to a change of personnel the Sinners were renamed the 8T8 immediately after the Dereham festival, just in time for the skiffle competition in the Orford Arms Cellar.

15. The Dereham Vampires appear to have disbanded sometime before the end of 1958. Hilton Tait continued his involvement with organising music concerts at Dereham's Memorial Hall.

The Beat Goes On

As late as 1958, live music in the city continued to be dominated by dance band music, skiffle and jazz. Local rock 'n' roll bands were still very rare. New skiffle bands continued to be formed even though the skiffle boom had passed; the Woodchoppers, the Rebels, the East Landers, the Footprints, the Cobras, the Dices and numerous others, although few achieved lasting success. Many of these were manned by musicians from previously disbanded groups and combos. In February, a reorganised Five-Sided Square from Thetford, newly renamed the Thetford Sideliners[1], appeared on BBC radio's topical magazine programme *East Anglian Highlights*.

Generally, the great proliferation of bands formed in both the city and county during the early days of skiffle was being reduced into a smaller number of more proficient units as band members either retired from playing, moved on to join a better band, were called up for National Service in the forces, or work and marriage assumed a far greater importance. A major loss occurred in April when the Cygnets disbanded and the Monday night rock 'n' roll sessions at the Ailwyn ceased, only to be replaced by a more sedate form of music from blind musician Eddie Gates on his electric organ. Only Mick Holmes of the Cygnets continued his involvement in music; the remainder of the band moved on to pursue other interests. Those groups that remained mostly followed the trend that was developing nationally of gradually evolving from their skiffle roots into either a conventional rock 'n' roll band, a rhythm and blues combo or a folk group, especially when the addition of amplification increased the musical potential and adaptability of the band.

The Sinners Skiffle Group was a typical example. Initially, the group was formed by guitarists Terry Wickham and Mike Woodcock, drummer Albert Woolridge and washboard player Brian Bates, previously a member of the Downhomers. Following the example set by the Downhomers at the Herbert Fraser Hall on Bethel Street, the Sinners established a club of their own in a function room at the Sportsman public house on Barrack Street. At the Grand Opening on Friday 18 April 1958, the aptly named Sinners Rhythm Club was advertised as a club for young people that aimed to provide a mix of jazz, skiffle & rock 'n' roll every Friday night from 7.00pm for a listening and dancing audience, suggesting a growing versatility among the newer more competent groups. The club's stay at the Sportsman was short lived as by the end of May it had relocated to the larger premises offered by the Spread Eagle on Sussex Street.[2] A subsequent change in the personnel of the Sinners saw Wickham and Woodcock team up with vocalist Malcolm Hooper, guitarists Ivan Zagni and Mel Fuller, and bass player David Hobbs. At the same time, it was decided to change the name of the group to the 8T8 Band in time for the Orford Cellar skiffle competition that July. By the end of November, a further change in personnel saw Wickham and Woodcock combine with guitarists Terry Read and Alan Callf, and vocalist and drummer, Stewart (Stewy) McIntosh, to form a beat band which was known thereafter as the Zodiacs, allegedly the first band based in Norwich specialising in the sound of rock 'n' roll. Most groups had included at least one rock'n'roll number in their skiffle-based repertoires, but the Zodiacs were predominantly a rock group. A month earlier, McIntosh, formerly a member of the Allez Katz, had taken part in, and won, the final of the *'Find the Voice'* competition at the Dereham Memorial Hall singing a selection of rock 'n' roll songs. His reward was £2 and two professional engagements at the hall. The club at the Spread Eagle was such a success that the management of the Ailwyn Club invited the Zodiacs to relocate their weekly meetings from the Spread Eagle to their dance hall on Lower Clarence Road. As a result, on 1 December 1958, the Ailwyn's Monday rock 'n' roll evening was resurrected and renamed as the 8T8 Rhythm Club with the Zodiacs as the resident performers.

Similarly, the Jack O'Diamonds Four, the resident band at Norman Guest's Monday night Orford Cellar Skiffle Club, was a collaboration between vocalist Mick Holmes from the disbanded Cygnets and three former members of the Ronnie Hanton Skiffle Group—Micky Large on guitar, Barrie Butcher on bass and Ronnie Hanton himself on drums. When Hanton tragically died from a fatal asthma attack on 14 August, his place in the band was filled by drummer, Ron Lee, from the Mark Preston Trio. Singer and guitarist Don Ingram, previously a member of the Sidewinders Skiffle Group, eventually joined the band giving it also a conventional rock 'n' roll line-up in the style of Cliff Richard's Shadows. The skiffle club at the Orford proved to be a short-lived venture. At the end of August, Norman Guest was appointed to the post of assistant entertainments manager at the Samson & Hercules dance hall. As a result, he moved both his jazz and skiffle clubs from the Orford Arms to a temporary location at the Herbert Frazer Hall on Bethel Street before moving them permanently to the newly refurbished snack bar and café in the cellars beneath the Samson's dance hall.

A consequence of the skiffle craze was that it generated a general interest in folk music of all kinds. The English Folk Dance Society was particularly active in Norwich. On Saturday 3 May 1958, the Society held a Festival of Folk Song and Dance at the Lads' Club, organised by Miss Marjorie Shepherd, the Society's East Anglian representative. Performers from the four counties of Norfolk, Suffolk, Essex and Cambridgeshire gave an exhibition of traditional song and dance to a packed audience. The varied performances included fiddle music from Kay

Graham; sea shanties from Bob Roberts of Pin Mill in Suffolk; a medley of folk songs from the Wisbech Little Theatre Group; an exhibition of Norfolk Step dancing by Dick Hewitt from Southrepps; Morris dancing from the Cambridge and Colchester Morris Men, including a spectacular version of the Flamborough Sword Dance; and Scottish dancing by the Norwich branch of the Scottish Dance Society. Skiffle was represented by the Jolly Butchers Skiffle Group led by Albert Cooper. However, to the folk purists, skiffle was a modern construct and did not truly represent traditional folk music. The *Eastern Evening News* correspondent commented that the Wisbech Theatre Group's contribution:

> illustrated the essential spontaneity and plasticity of folk song performance. By comparison with this unaccompanied singing, skiffle—presented by the Jolly Butchers Group of Norwich—pinned down the expression to a too rigid beat and swathed the words blurringly (sic) in amplification.[3]

The mood of the evening was greatly lifted when a packet of 'energy' tablets fell from the pocket of one of the dancers.

Unlike skiffle, jazz was growing even more popular by reaching out to a wider audience, particularly among the young, but not without some resentment among its traditional followers. For most of its new converts, jazz was regarded as dance music, music with a rhythmic beat suitable for jiving, while its traditional audience regarded it as music to listen to and appreciate, and even, for some, an historic expression of defiance though the medium of music by the oppressed Black population of America. Its association with middle class students, liberal thinkers and left-wing politicians inevitably established a strong link between jazz and protest movements. The protesters on the first Aldermaston March of 5 April 1958 walked the route from London to Aldermaston accompanied by music from numerous jazz bands. Jazz was the music of the CND movement.[4] Jazz bands were a regular feature on all its subsequent annual marches. Over nine thousand people took part in the second march from Aldermaston to Trafalgar Square. The *Eastern Evening News* correspondent reported that:

> In bright sunshine and with a band playing jazz, the anti-H Bomb marchers moved on from Turnham Green Chiswick this morning on the last stage of their four-day 53-mile trek from Aldermaston (Berkshire) to Trafalgar Square.[5]

Notes

1. *Eastern Evening News*, Saturday 8 February 1958.
2. The Sportsman, Barrack Street is closed and has been used at various times as a solicitors' office and a dental surgery. The Spread Eagle, Barrack Street closed in November 2008.
3. *Eastern Evening News*, Monday 5 May 1958.

4. CND, Campaign for Nuclear Disarmament. 'Ban the Bomb' was its slogan.
5. *Eastern Evening News*, Wednesday 30 March 1959.

City of Jazz

Despite the advent of rock 'n' roll, jazz in all its forms continued to broaden its appeal both nationally and in Norfolk, especially among those middle-class young people in the urban areas of Norwich, Lowestoft and Bungay who were not attracted by rock 'n' roll. The *Six-Five Special*, together with an increasing number of weekly jazz programmes on the BBC Radio's Light and Home Services, including the ever-popular *Jazz Club* as well as *At the Jazz Band Ball*, *The World of Jazz*, *Dixieland Jazz* and *A Break for Jazz*, brought jazz music to a younger audience. Despite this, the youth of Great Yarmouth and the rural districts of Norfolk still lagged behind in their appreciation for jazz music. In Norwich, however, the demand for jazz was on the increase and the preference continued to be for traditional jazz. On 4 January 1957 over seven hundred young people danced to the Chris Barber Band at the Samson & Hercules and, a few weeks later, it was jazz again from Cy Laurie's Band, also at the Samson. Chris Barber returned to Norwich on 14 April 1957 and played to a seated audience at the Carlton Cinema. Progressive big band jazz was not so popular despite many top-quality visitors to the city.

> The great William 'Count' Basie and his Orchestra came to the Samson and Hercules last night (Monday 28 October 1957). With twenty-six numbers in two hours, he gave Norwich jazz fans an unforgettable night. ... It was a fabulous concert of blues and ragtime turned into commercial jazz by a swinging, jumping, happy band of Negro musicians at the very top of the jazz tree and as artistic in their own right as Ben Hogan or Picasso or Eileen Joyce.[1] One sad note — in spite of the six o'clock start, the hall was only half filled for the first part of the evening.[2]

Inevitably, once jazz had been established in Norfolk's urban centres as an entertainment primarily for the young, its influence began to percolate into Great Yarmouth and the more rural areas of the county, albeit slowly and patchily. Jazz clubs were established at the Pavilion in West Runton[3] on the North Norfolk coast and at the Memorial Hall in Dereham where the Mid-Norfolk Jazz Club hosted national as well as local bands. On 15 November 1957, over 350 young fans from Dereham and the surrounding villages crowded into the Memorial Hall to listen and dance to Cy Laurie and his Band. Although Great Yarmouth's first ever jazz and jive dance was held in November 1955 as a fund-raising event for the Far East Prisoner of War Association, the town's jazz fans had to wait until May 1957 for its first weekly jazz club to open at the Sandringham Hotel on the promenade, followed by another in the Queen's Hotel at the seaside end of Regent Road. In 1958, a jazz club opened in premises at the Old Hall behind the police station on West Road in Caister-on-Sea and provided the youth of the Fleggs with an opportunity to hear jazz locally without the need to travel into far off Norwich. Their cliental were in the first instance drawn from the middle classes, working class youth still preferred rock 'n' roll. However, the proliferation of new clubs provided Norfolk's local bands with a choice of locations at which to perform. The Collegians, the Mustard City Stompers and Brian Green's Dixielanders regularly appeared at venues all over East Anglia. Brenda Dury and the Tailgate Jazz Band from Bungay made guest appearances at the Cottage in Thorpe and at the Norwich Jazz Club.

On Sunday 17 February 1957, the Speedway Jazz Club opened its doors for the first time at the Firs Stadium in the city and provided jazz every Sunday from the Collegians and other guest bands. The Norwich Jazz Club continued to thrive in its new location at the Boulton and Paul Sports and Social Club. On 15 July, George Melly entertained a lively audience on club night with his signature versions of *Send Me to the Electric Chair* and *Frankie and Johnny*. Having backed away for the time being from hosting rock 'n' roll sessions, the newly opened Grosvenor also turned its attention to jazz. Its larger and more comfortable premises in a prime position on Prince of Wales Road had enticed Brian Green to relocate the 59 Club from Bethel Street to the 'jazz cellar' at the Grosvenor where it opened as a members' only Sunday Club. When Brian Green left the Dixielanders to join the Jack 'Tubby' Rogers Orchestra for a summer season at the Skegness Holiday Camp, the remaining band members, Pete Oxborough, Dick le Grice, Barbara Gay and Brian French, concentrated on playing jazz under the leadership of Pete Bell. The band was such a successful exponent of its genre that it participated in three auditions on the same day for appearances on BBC radio, BBC television and ITV. As well as concerts, jazz dances were also held in the cellar at the Grosvenor on Monday evenings with the music provided by guest artists. In his column in the *Eastern Evening News*, Steve James described the facilities of the cellar at the Grosvenor.

> The basement room behind the main hall stage lit with red shaded lamps is a place with plenty of atmosphere when the mainstream boys get playing their instruments. There is room to jive for those who want to, but the majority seem more than ready to sit and listen.[4]

Every Saturday night, the focus at the Cottage was on traditional jazz from the Collegians and other local bands. Also at the Cottage, the Norwich Modernists continued to play modern jazz every Sunday to a small but enthusiastic following, frequently featuring guest soloists. On one occasion, Tubby Hayes joined the band for the evening playing jazz solos on his tenor saxophone. The Norwich Modernists,

Jazz on the Queen of the Broads, 1957.

led by Peter Fenn[5] at the piano, comprised Rex Cooper on drums, Pete Brandish on bass (replacing Bob Barbour), Brian Whittle alto saxophone, Johnny Byles tenor saxophone and Clifford Aldred on trumpet. In an interview, Peter Fenn explained that:

> The Modernists had their real beginnings about two years ago (1955) when a group of musicians, including Jack Hornsby, Rex Cooper, Brian Green and Peter Fenn himself decided that there was not enough modern jazz in Norwich and went each month to play at the Gibraltar Gardens, Heigham Street.[6]

Monday evening entertainment at the Cottage was provided by the Peter Fenn Quartet, led again by Peter Fenn supported by Johnny Byles, Rex Cooper and Peter Brandish. Having just returned from a season in Casablanca, Mike Capocci[7] eventually replaced Peter Fenn on piano when Fenn accepted the offer of a summer season playing with the Leslie Douglas Band at Weston-Super-Mare in Somerset. Rex Cooper assumed the leadership of the band. By the summer of 1957, the Modernists had left the Cottage to become the resident band at the Grosvenor's jazz cellar and were replaced in turn at the Cottage by Barbara Gaye's Band Show, the Brian Roy Band, featuring the return of Brian Green on trumpet, and by the Ray

Stratton Quintet, with Mike Capocci on piano and the young Mireille 'Freight Train' Gray as their lead singer.

On 9 June 1957, the Bungay and District Jazz Club organised the first Broadland Riverboat Shuffle, an event that was to become an annual fixture in the Norfolk and Suffolk jazz calendar. At Great Yarmouth, 180 enthusiastic jazz fans boarded the leisure boat *Queen of the Broads* for a trip along the river to Wroxham, to be entertained on the way by jazz from the Collegians, the Dixielanders and the resident bands of the Bungay and Lowestoft Jazz Clubs. Not everyone was as enthusiastic as those who took part in the Shuffle.

The Bungay Jazz Club must be prevented at any cost from sailing again through Broadland infecting the air with its tainted music. Let its members and fans join the Salvation Army and, as one dear old friend of mine suggested, "Blow for God and not the Devil".[8]

Notes

1. Ben Hogan (1912-97) was an American who became one of the greatest golfers of all time. Pablo Picasso (1881-1973); a Spanish artist considered to be the most dominant and influential artist of the C20. Eileen Joyce (1908-91) born in Tasmania, Australia, rose from obscurity to become a well-known and highly regarded classical pianist. Her life story was portrayed in the 1950s film *Wherever She Goes*.
2. *Eastern Evening News*, Tuesday 29 October 1957.
3. The Pavilion at West Runton was a popular music venue on the North Norfolk coast. Originally a sports hall, it was converted for music and dancing during World War II as an entertainment venue for locally based troops. Because of its excellent acoustics, it developed as a performance centre for local and national popular music groups playing jazz, skiffle and rock 'n' roll. It was demolished in 1986. A commemorative plaque is located on the adjacent village inn.
4. *Eastern Evening News*, Saturday 31 August 1957.
5. Peter Fenn (born 1 April 1932 at Great Yarmouth, died May 2011 in Norwich), formerly a music teacher at the Henderson School in Norwich; became a professional musician playing the piano with the Leslie Douglas Band in Weston-Super-Mare. Returned to Norwich in 1959 when he became Musical Director for Anglia TV and, among his many achievements, he composed the signature tune for the programme *Sale of the Century*. Played regularly at the Orford Cellar and led the resident band at the La Tudor Rosa in the 1970s.
6. *Eastern Evening News*, Saturday 2 February 1957.
7. Mike Capocci (1929-2011) was a jazz pianist; better known as 'Norwich's King of Jazz'. In 1956, he played piano in Casablanca, Morocco with the Johnny Hawkins Band. In 1958, after a brief time back in the city, he joined the Ken Mackintosh Orchestra and then formed his own band playing for a number of years at venues in Jersey. He returned to Norwich in 1980. Over time he took over and ran jazz clubs at the Jolly Butchers on Ber Street, The Santana Club (formerly The Jaquards) on Magdalen Street, the Red Lion in Thorpe and the Green Man in Rackheath. He was instrumental in reforming the Norwich Jazz Club in 1998 where he performed regularly with his band, the Mike Capocci Trio.
8. *Eastern Evening News*, Thursday 13 June 1957.

The Author Remembers
1959-60

In 1959 my life changed radically; some might say for the better. In June, I obtained three good passes at Advanced Level in the GCE examinations, much to the surprise of my grammar school masters, and was accepted for a place to study mathematics at the university in Leicester. From that September, I lived two separate and quite different lives. For seven months of the year, I was a student at university, away from the security of life at home in Rollesby and very much out of my depth. For the remaining five months, I resumed a normal life in Norfolk with my village friends and former grammar school colleagues. In both, my time was fully occupied by a hectic combination of work and play, with an unfortunate emphasis on the latter.

Enticing recreational activities were becoming more readily available to me and my contemporaries, partly due to the personal independence that comes with maturity—I was now in my late teens—and partly due to the economic upturn of the late 1950s. We had never had it so good. New entertainment venues of all kinds were being established to encourage young people in particular to spend any surplus money languishing in their pockets. At weekends when at home I went dancing. Sometimes at a local village hall but more often at the larger dance halls of Great Yarmouth and Gorleston, staying overnight with my grandmother in Great Yarmouth. As well as the Floral Hall, a new major entertainments centre was opened in Great Yarmouth when the Garibaldi 'hotel' was converted into a night club and dance hall in 1958. Dancing most nights at the 'Gari' was to music from the resident Gordon Edwards Band, with my one-time next-door neighbour, Linda Taylor, as their vocalist. I had also discovered jazz. My liking for skiffle and the singer Lonnie Donegan had inevitably led to a connection with jazz, and I was soon adding recordings from that genre to my growing record collection. The first jazz record that I bought was a long play recording by the Chris Barber Jazz Band, *Chris Barber Plays*, and I soon developed an enthusiasm for the bouncy rhythm of the music which was ideal for jive dancing. My enthusiasm for jazz was consolidated when I discovered recordings by the charismatic Acker Bilk and his Paramount Jazz Band. Not only was his music enjoyably rhythmic but he also promoted a fashionable 1920 s look in his on-stage attire, which I tried to copy.

In 1959, opportunities locally to hear live jazz were limited. My first experience of jazz was from records. The established jazz clubs of Norwich were not easily accessed by young people living at a distance from the city. However, I discovered by chance that on most weekends numerous jazz fans gathered in Diver's wine bar on Regent Road in Great Yarmouth before driving to the clubs in Norwich. Any spare places in their vehicles were usually made available to those without transport. My first visit to a jazz club was made in this way, although I am still unsure which venue it was that we arrived at. Whenever possible, I joined the weekend trek from Great Yarmouth to the Norwich jazz clubs, dressed in a uniform made up from one of my grandfather's collarless striped shirts, a lose-fitting grey waistcoat (also my grandfather's), corduroy brown trousers and suede boots. A grey duffle coat with a CND badge attached completed the ensemble. I considered myself to be dressed in the style of a trendy Beatnik.

Until 1960, live rock 'n' roll was rarely heard in rural Norfolk. Even in urban Norwich, most bands still played skiffle rather than rock 'n' roll. Listening to rock 'n' roll music was restricted to songs heard on the radio, on television, the record player or on one of the many jukeboxes appearing in the coffee bars, public houses and amusement arcades of Norwich and Great Yarmouth. Therefore, it came as a great surprise to me and to my village friends when, in 1960, a regular mid-week rock 'n' roll dance with a live band, usually from Norwich, was established at the village hall in Hemsby, a thirty-minute cycle ride from my home. I joined many of my friends at the hall in Hemsby to demonstrate the dance skills I had learned earlier to records at the Eel's Foot tea rooms in Ormesby.

On Friday 25 September 1959, I bade a tearful goodbye to my parents and boarded the train at Great Yarmouth's Vauxhall Station for Leicester and my new life as a university student. It was the first time that I had been away from my home in Rollesby for any length of time. I had been warned by friends, who had already started their studies at university, that my life would be different from then on. And so it was. For my first year in Leicester I lived at Beaumont Hall, a students' hall of residence, where my breakfast and evening meals were provided in the hall's main restaurant as part of the service, and two housekeepers made my bed, cleaned my room and organised my weekly laundry. The university's culture and most of its students were middle-class. Students with a working-class background were still in a minority, although the opportunities offered by the 1944 Education Act were beginning to take effect. In addition to lectures, entertainment on the main campus was organised by the Leicester Students Union. Live music consisted of classical music recitals at lunchtime and a conventional dance orchestra at the Saturday night dance. Jazz was tolerated—a newly established Friday night jazz club was popular with a minority of students—but rock 'n' roll was considered beyond the pale.

Fortunately, I had brought my guitar with me to Leicester because I soon discovered that a fellow student, Dave Cousins[1], another Beaumont Hall resident, was a folk singer and guitarist of some reputation. His abilities were well-known within and outside of the university. His reputation acted as a magnet, attracting many able student musicians to join his circle of friends. Impromptu sessions of folk song were commonplace, and I joined in whenever possible, learning new songs and improving my playing technique. Included in Dave's circle was a clarinettist called Bob Gordon-Walker. At weekends and during the long vacations, Bob, played clarinet for the Original Downtown Syncopators (the ODS), an Original Dixieland Jazz Band (ODJB) tribute band. In August 1960, I met with Bob and the ODS in Norfolk when they were on a nationwide tour that included performances in Norwich and at the newly established United Jazz Club in Caister:

> My obvious acquaintance with members of the band ensured that I was not without a dance partner for most of the evening. ... I was delighted to notice that another of Bob's friends and myself were both continually surrounded by the best looking females in the room and a couple of sullen looking gentlemen. ... I suddenly realised that my companion was in fact Billy Fury who was starring in 'Meet the Beat' at Yarmouth's Britannia Pier at the time, and it was he and not me that was attracting the females. The sullen six-footers were undoubtedly his minders.[2]

A major event during the spring term for the university and Leicester's other colleges was Rag Week—a week when students engaged in various activities aimed at raising money for local charities. Among the many organised events open to the public during the 1960 Rag Week was a music hall style revue in the Corn Exchange on Leicester's Market Square. As their contribution to the entertainment, members of the university's folk and jazz clubs produced a comedy sketch entitled *Crumbeat*, allegedly a parody of BBC television's popular rock 'n' roll show, *Drumbeat*. My part in the sketch required me to sing a risqué version of Cliff Richard's *Voice in the Wilderness* backed by acoustic guitars enhanced by home-made amplification equipment. The standard of our performance was so good that we were immediately inundated with requests for bookings, displaying a desire among some elements of the student population to hear rock 'n' roll music. As a result, in the following September, a folk singer, two jazz musicians, a skiffler and me, all fans of the rock 'n' roll genre, formed Leicester University's first rock 'n' roll band. Thereafter, rock 'n' roll was accepted as an integral part of the university student's music scene, even if grudgingly by some.

Notes

1. After completing his course at university, Dave Cousins pursued a career in music, founding and leading a band called the Strawbs. Their most successful recording, *Part of the Union*, reached the number 2 spot in the UK Top Twenty charts during February 1973.
2. Colin Miller (2008), *The Fifties Replayed* p86.

Into the Night Club Age

By the late 1950s, the possibility of a nuclear war with Russia was still a major concern for the residents of Norfolk as well as for the rest of the UK, particularly among young people. This was exacerbated by the presence in East Anglia of a US air-force, armed with nuclear weapons and seemingly ready and willing to wage war, which guaranteed Norfolk would be a prime target for any first strike by Russia. This fear was heightened when Thor rockets armed with H-bomb warheads were stationed at Feltwell in Norfolk. The Federation of American Scientists added to that fear by announcing that stockpiles of nuclear weapons had the capability to wipe out the whole human race. Inevitably, protests took place at Feltwell and elsewhere, organised by CND. A large 'Ban the Bomb' rally took place in Norwich during the week 13-19 September 1959, culminating in a march through the city on Saturday 19 September led by a local jazz band. The Archdeacon of Norwich was quoted as saying:

> The sin of our modern age might well mean not only the death of millions of individuals but the death of the whole human race—of which danger the Sputnik was the warning symbol.[1]

A civil defence recruitment pamphlet, discussing the possibility of an H-Bomb being dropped on Norwich, was more optimistic:

> On the principal that you do not use a steam-hammer to crack a nut, such a bomb might never be used against Norwich. And if it was—well, a direct hit on the centre of the city would clearly put Norwich beyond help.[2]

Despite these reassurances, a Civil Defence exercise code-named 'Exercise Maybe' took place on Monday 2 May 1960 to assess the ability of Norfolk's emergency services to deal with the dropping of an H-bomb on Norwich followed immediately by a county-wide chemical attack, the largest exercise ever to be held in the county.

As jazz grew in popularity it inevitably became an attractive commercial proposition for promoters and record companies. The raw edge of Ken Colyer's traditional brand of jazz was challenged by a cleaner and more marketable style of jazz produced by the likes of Chris Barber, Acker Bilk and Kenny Ball, a style of jazz that also appealed to the rock 'n' roll fans, late to appreciate jazz. Gimmicks became the order of the day. Acker Bilk and his band performed dressed in striped

117

waistcoats and bowler hats. In his review of the Temperance Seven's first 1957 record release *One Over the Eight*, John Mitchell described the band as something between a music hall act and a jazz band:

It's an absurd record really but I can't stop playing it.[3]

Formed in 1955 by students at the Royal College of Art, their comedic performances and gimmicky 1920s style of jazz were applied in a theatrical way to a wide variety of classic compositions ranging from *Tiger Rag, Hard Hearted Hannah* and *The Eaton Boating Song* to *Yes Sir, That's My Baby*.

In Norwich, 'Trad' jazz continued to dominate, performed by the city-based Collegians and the Mustard City Stompers. On his return to Norwich after spending the 1957 summer season in Skegness with the John Tubby Rogers Band, trumpeter Brian Green combined commitments at the Samson & Hercules with brief appearances with the Brian Roy Band before joining the Bungay based Tailgate jazz band as its leader and trumpeter. Managed by Guest Star Entertainments, Brian Green and the Tailgate Band became regular performers in Norwich's growing number of dance venues and jazz clubs. Towards the end of 1958, Brian Green parted company with the Tailgate Band to re-join his original jazz band, the Dixielanders. After a visit to Norwich in August 1960 by the Original Downtown Syncopators, an ODJB tribute band[4], Brian Green added an alto and a baritone saxophone to the normal six-piece line-up of the Dixielanders and replaced the bass with a sousaphone to recreate a 1920s jazz sound in an ensemble he called his new Oom-cha Jazz Band.[5] Also managed by Guest Star Entertainments was the East Anglian Jazz Band, a band brought together in January 1959 by the efforts of trombonist Ian Bell, himself a former member of Brian Green's Dixielanders.[6]

To cope with the growing number of competent bands and an increasing demand for popular music for dancing from the younger members of the public, Norwich saw a comparable rise in the number of clubs and other live music venues. Tiger Tim was forced to comment in the *Eastern Evening News* that:

Neon lights are flashing above our somnolent streets. The deep throated boom of a jukebox echoes through the darkness. Our night life is no longer limited to pub crawling, and fish and chips; and quiet petting in the one-and-nines. All of a sudden we're in the night club age.[7]

Due to the impending closure of the Boulton & Paul Social Club at Rosary Corner, the Norwich Jazz Club was again forced to move to a new location in a function room to the rear of the Bedford Arms public house on Bedford Street, formerly used as a bowling alley. The jazz club's first night at the Bedford was on Monday 20 January 1958 when the Mustard City Stompers played jazz to a listening audience. Thereafter Monday nights were designated as listening sessions while every Tuesday jiving was allowed. Brenda Bear, formerly of the Brian Roy Band, joined the Stompers as their resident singer and during the intervals between band sessions the audience was entertained by skiffle from Albert Cooper and the Jolly Butchers Skiffle Group. In time, as skiffle gave way to rhythm and blues music, the Jolly Butchers Skiffle Group was rebranded as the Albert Cooper Blues and Boogie Band. Every Monday the band returned to its musical roots and played jam session jazz while Cooper sang the blues to a listening audience. Albert Cooper's views about dancing were clearly expressed in a Jazz Club publication:

Norwich's own Albert Cooper, Blues singer.

> I do not like to see jivers in a club because I always get the impression that they are only using the place as a glorified form of matrimonial agency.[8]

Despite the restricted premises at the Bedford, the club enrolled Miss Shirley Miller as its 500th member in 1959, and the active membership was sufficiently large for special events to be held in the main ballroom at the Grosvenor Rooms, including the club's annual Christmas party. The entertainment at the jazz club's ball on 25 March included music from the Tom Collins jazzmen from Colchester, the Mustard City Stompers, Anna from the Jolly Butchers, Sid Miles, a female impersonator and Andy Anderson and his accordion. Also, at the 1960 Christmas party:

> A special cabaret act by Anne, Norfolk's Queen of the Blues, was the highlight of the evening when Norwich Jazz Club held its annual party at the Grosvenor Ballroom, Norwich. Over six hundred members of the club took part in the programme which included jiving to their own band, The Mustard City Stompers. Early next morning members were at Thorpe Station to see their blues queen off to London where she is taking part in a cabaret show at a night club.[9]

To complement the jazz club, a Jazz Record Appreciation Society was set up at the Bedford Arms with the aim of increasing its members' knowledge and appreciation of jazz in all its forms through listening to original recordings. The establishment of similar societies nationwide had given rise to the establishment of record shops specialising in new and second-hand jazz recordings. The Record Shop on Lancaster Road in Great Yarmouth was advertised in the press as an essential destination for the jazz record collector. By 1960, the record society had

The Bedford Arms, a location for jazz in the city.

moved to a quieter location at the Wellington public house:

> Norwich Jazz Record Society meets at the Wellington, Muspole Street on alternate Tuesdays. Real Jazz stands in the same relationship to 'popular music' as 'classical music' does to the 'Palm Curt' and the efforts of this group of enthusiasts to raise popular interest from the spineless and ephemeral 'Hit Parade' to a virile folk music with its own lasting beauty are most commendable.[10]

Following its move from the Orford Cellar, Norman Guest's jazz club finally reopened on Monday 8 September 1958 as one of the many attractions in the café and snack bar located in the medieval cellars under the Sixteenth Century Augustine Steward House adjacent to the Samson & Hercules. By the end of the first night in its new premises, seven hundred members had been registered at the club.

> Here Norwich boys and girls are able to enjoy jazz music in the atmosphere of a London club, with soft lights, snug alcoves, whitewashed walls, low beams and the small dance floor or jive space.[11]

Under Guest's stewardship, a comprehensive week-long programme of popular music was on offer including sessions at lunchtime as well as in the evening. In addition to live music, a large modern jukebox was installed in the cellar to provide music from the latest recordings in the 'hit parade.' Monday nights were devoted to modern jazz with the Rex Cooper Modernists as the resident band. On Wednesday evenings it was 'Trad' jazz from 'guest star' managed bands, including the Dixielanders and the East Anglian Jazz Band. Friday nights featured rock 'n' roll from the Zodiacs and other local 'rhythm' groups.[12] Every day except for Sunday, the cellar was open from 10.30am until 2.00pm for sandwiches and light lunches with music available on the jukebox. Tuesday and Thursday evenings from 8.00 until 11.00pm and all day every Saturday were advertised as *Juke Box Jive*, when club members could jive to music from the jukebox. The jukebox was financed by members paying for record plays. For a time, the cellar club at the Samson was a major attraction for the youth of Norwich.

Following the departure of Norman Guest from the Orford Cellar, activities there temporarily ceased. However, following the formation of an Orford Cellar Management Company, musical entertainment was re-established at the Cellar with the creation of new jazz and skiffle clubs. Opening night for the skiffle club was Wednesday 15 October 1958 when the Allez Katz from the Red Lion, was appointed as the resident band. A new weekly jazz club was opened on the following Tuesday featuring traditional jazz from various local bands including

Beryl Bryden at the Orford Cellar, 1959.

the Tailgate Band and the Collegians. Jiving was banned. On Fridays, the Ivan Tooes Quartet and the Neuwe Quintet, featuring Rex Cooper on drums, provided music in a modern manner. Despite the lack of dancing the club quickly acquired a membership of over 850. The skiffle club was short-lived as the public interest in skiffle was waning, but jazz continued to be played every Tuesday and Friday. In January 1960, Beryl Bryden accepted an invitation to become the club's President.

> "No skiffle, no rock, no Teddy Boys and no members under eighteen," the Cellar Club "is being run by a group of Norwich pro- and semi-pro musicians who are interested in jazz and not primarily for money."[13]

Correspondence between the club's secretary and various jazz clubs in New Orleans resulted in an exchange of colourful posters which thereafter adorned the walls of the cellar. The club's policy was to encourage members and musicians to take an active role in the club's activities.

> Like other jazz clubs, the Orford Cellar Organisation encourages musicians in the audience to 'play-in' with its regular bands. The other evening no fewer than twenty-five took up the invitation. The club caters for both the 'Trad' fans and the modernists. Tuesdays are Trad nights and Fridays are for moderns.[14]

Regular impromptu sit-ins by visiting musicians insured that most jazz club programmes included regular musical numbers known by most musicians, professional and amateur. The ability to sit-in depended upon knowing the musical piece being played by the resident band.

Following a change of landlord at the Orford Arms, the Orford Cellar Jazz Club also ceased its attachment to the Orford and, on Friday 1 July 1960, moved its club nights temporarily to the Cat and Fiddle on Magdalen Street before relocating in November to a permanent venue at the Lamb public house in the centre of Norwich, immediately opposite to the Orford. Nevertheless, the facilities at the Orford did not remain unused for long as, on Tuesday 22 November 1960, saxophonist Johnny Byles opened an all-modern jazz club at the cellar featuring the Rex Cooper Combo each Tuesday and the Peter Fenn Band every Friday.[15] To avoid confusion, the former Orford Cellar Jazz Club was renamed as the Green Turtle Jazz Club in its new location at the Lamb.

By the late 1950s, clubs were opening everywhere. The Norwich City Supporters Club was established in the premises vacated by the Boulton and Paul Social Club at Rosary Corner, providing a six-day mixed programme of jazz and pop music, dancing and other entertainments. At the club's opening night on 26 November 1958, a packed audience was entertained by 14-year-old popstar Laurie London, known primarily for his hit record *He's Got the Whole World in his Hands*. On Tuesday 20 January 1959, the Great Yarmouth Jazz Club relocated from the Queen's Hotel to the Penrice Arms along King Street. Jazz also became a regular Saturday night attraction in the town when promoters New Jazz Incorporated introduced Jiving at the Gari in the newly opened Garibaldi Ballroom. At the first night on 3 November 1960, dancers jived the night away to music from the Andy Fairweather Brown All Stars. Elsewhere, new jazz clubs were opened in Lowestoft and Wymondham, and the United Jazz Club at the Old Hall in Caister went from strength to strength. In the autumn of 1960, the United Jazz Club too was forced to move to new premises, relocating its activities from Caister to the ballroom of the Goode's Hotel on the Promenade in Great Yarmouth. The Claremont Pier Jazz Club in Lowestoft opened its doors for the first time on Tuesday 24 May 1960.

Encouraged by landlords Wilf and Jessie Brooke, a new jazz club was also established at the Rushcutters public house in Thorpe, formerly known as the riverside Thorpe Gardens. The entertainment at the first night of the Riverside Club on Monday 4 January 1960 was provided by the Collegians, singer Anna Hannant and the Riverside's newly formed jazz band featuring vocalist Vivienne. The Riverside Jazz Band, led by Jack Farrer on trombone, was established by Bill White, formerly treasurer of the Norwich Jazz Club. Within a week the club had enlisted over one thousand members. Seeking a more convenient location, the

Riverside Club eventually moved from Thorpe Gardens to a large upstairs function room at the Cock Tavern, affectionately known as Studio 4, on the junction of Crown Road and King Street in the centre of Norwich, adjacent to Anglia House, home to the new regional commercial television channel, Anglia TV. At the club's opening night on Saturday 18 June 1960, the musical entertainment was provided by the club's own Riverside Jazz Band. The Cock Tavern was regularly used by the staff of Anglia TV and, because Anglia House only had three studios, going to Studio 4 implied a visit to the public house by the station's employees.[16] A month earlier in May, seeking a closer

The Cock Tavern, also known as Studio 4.

cooperation between local jazz clubs, Tony Cooper, secretary of the Riverside Club, was instrumental in forming the Federation of East Anglian Jazz Clubs with the aim of coordinating activities for the benefit of all the participating clubs and societies.

Notes

1. *Eastern Evening News*, Thursday 1 May 1958.
2. *Eastern Evening News*, Friday 13 March 1959.
3. *Eastern Evening News*, Wednesday 22 January 1958.
4. ODJB; the Original Dixieland Jazz Band from New Orleans was formed in 1916 by five white musicians from different ethnic backgrounds led by Sicilian born cornetist Nick LaRocca. Following the trend of the time, the group moved to Chicago in 1917 and were an immediate sensation. While Buddy Bolden is credited with the creation of jazz, or jass as it was then called, the ODJB were allegedly the first to consolidate that style of music and call it jazz. They are credited with the first ever jazz recording with the release in 1917 of Dixieland Jass One-Step and Livery Stable Blues on the Victor label. Victims of inverse-racism, their contributions to the development of jazz have been largely ignored and the band was often described as the five white guys who had stolen African-American music.
5. Brian Green's Oom-cha Jazz Band members were Tony Jukings (clarinet) Robin Burgess (sousaphone) Derek Kenyon (drums) Ian Bell (trombone) Cyril Richmond (alto sax) Eric Hudson (baritone sax) Brian Green (trumpet) and Barbara Green (banjo); music arrangers were Stan Jennings and Ginger Green.
6. The East Anglian Jazz Band consisted of members Roy Copping (piano), Joe Thoroughgood (drums), John Harrison (clarinet), Ian Bell (trombone), Ron George (trumpet) and Jack Farrow (bass).

7. *Eastern Evening News*, Friday 21 November 1958.
8. Norwich Jazz Club; News & Views, February 1957.
9. *Eastern Evening News*, Tuesday 20 December 1960.
10. *Eastern Evening News*, Friday 1 July 1960.
11. *Eastern Evening News*, Tuesday 9 September 1958.
12. Rhythm Group; another name for a group playing rock 'n' roll.
13. *Eastern Evening News*, Saturday 17 January 1959.
14. *Eastern Evening News*, Saturday 24 October 1959.
15. The Peter Fenn Band comprised Peter Fenn (piano) Johnny Byles (tenor sax) Peter Brandish (bass) Peter Hague (drums) Geoff Keeley (trombone) Kerrell Garner (violin) and Jackie Guard (trumpet).
16. In the late 1960s, the Cock Tavern became the headquarters of the Norwich Folk Club. Closed in 1983, the building is currently being used as offices.

Record Charts

By the autumn of 1958, live music in Norwich was still mainly music for dancing. Dancing remained the major free-time activity for most people, young and old. Every dance hall had its resident orchestra, most of which catered for all types of dancing, old time, modern and the occasional session of jive. However, the great local upsurge in the number of live bands caused by the popularity of skiffle was slowly abating. The best bands survived and prospered while the less competent gradually faded away. With so many to choose from, Norwich's dance venues became more selective in the bands that they employed. At the same time, competent musicians were inevitably enticed away from poorer groups to join the members of the best. New bands were often simply a re-grouping of the better musicians from the less able or defunct bands. The result was that, by the end of 1958, live music in Norwich was provided by a smaller number of more accomplished local ensembles, supplemented occasionally by visits from nationally recognised professional orchestras, singers and bands. The music they provided was mainly jazz and skiffle in the clubs and pubs, and dance band music in the larger ballrooms and dance halls; the former aimed at a younger audience newly addicted to jiving and the latter at people of all ages out on the town for an evening of mostly modern or old-time dancing. Other than a few popular hit songs that had found their way into the repertoires of some skiffle bands, the sound of rock 'n' roll was virtually absent from the live music scene although things were soon to change. To hear rock 'n' roll music in the mid- to late-1950s often meant watching TV or listening to gramophone records and the radio, rather than attending performances by local or national live bands. Had it not been for innovations in record production, cheaper record players, Radio Luxembourg, the Six-Five Special and the gradual dissemination of jukeboxes, the initial impetus given to rock 'n' roll music by the films *Blackboard Jungle* and *Rock Around the Clock* could have easily fizzled out.

By the mid-1950s, technological developments had made record players and music recorded onto disc cheaper, more durable and readily available to the music loving public. Before 1957, most music was recorded on 12-inch shellac double-sided discs that were played on a turntable revolving at 78 revolutions per minute (rpm). The discs themselves were large, breakable, easily scratched and needed to be stored carefully to survive. Yet, it was only possible to record 3 minutes of music on each side of a disc; a factor that limited the length of most popular songs.

Innovations by Columbia Records and RCA Victor meant that by the mid-1950s shellac records were gradually being replaced by 12 inch Long Play (LP) discs played at 33 rpm that held at least 25 minutes of music on each side, and 7 inch discs played at 45 rpm with 3 minutes of single play or 8 minutes of extended play (EP) on each side; all made from virtually unbreakable Vinyl, which was less prone to being scratched, and their smaller size made them far easier to store safely. Additionally, the development of small affordable portable record players, especially the Dansette Junior, de Lux and Major models, enabled teenagers to listen to records of their choosing in their bedrooms away from their parents and to play music for dancing at parties. Before then, most electric powered record players were big, bulky and far too expensive for most people to own. In 1958, an old-style Ferguson radiogram (a combination of a radio and a record player) from Fieldings Electric on Prince of Wales Road was priced at 50gns (£52.50) and an HMV radiogram at 57gns (£59.85); much more than a month's wages for an average worker. By comparison, the newly introduced Dansette Junior range was priced at only 13.5gns (£14.18) from the same retailer, a Philips Disc-Jockey Junior at 15gns (£15.75) and a Westminster Record Player at a mere 7.5gns (£7.88). The popularity of Dansette record players can be judged from the fact that, in July 1958, a Dansette Junior was awarded as the first prize in a Grand Talent Contest held at the Gala Ballroom on St Stephens Road. For those who could not afford a new record player, an active second-hand market existed

Such developments inevitably gave rise to a boom in record sales, especially the sales of popular music, and for young people this meant rock 'n' roll, skiffle or jazz rather than the sedate music enjoyed by their parents. Music that was exciting and not only provided the rhythmic beat for jive dancing but also frequently addressed issues that teenagers found relevant in the lyrics of its songs: lyrics about being in love for the first time, about jealousy and rejection, personal relationships, sex and death. Elvis sang about being in love with his best friend's girl, the Everly Brothers lamented Suzie's lost reputation and the Teenagers asked *Why do Fools Fall in Love?* Even *Heartbreak Hotel* was about a rejected lovelorn male contemplating suicide. Sex was often dealt with via double entendres or coded wording, especially in songs adapted from African-American rhythm and blues originals, which were often more sexually explicit in their lyrics. The phrase 'rock and roll' itself was a euphemism for the sex act in rhythm and blues vocabulary, a fact that did not go unnoticed by many teenagers. The Bulletin of the Songwriters Guild of Great Britain was quoted as saying:

By the shameless plugging of American records, the BBC has unnecessarily created a big public for American-idiom songs, and at present they are advertising in their programmes a great deal of unwholesome often erotically angled American rubbish.[1]

Information about the latest record releases was not easy to obtain in East Anglia during the mid-1950s. With Tacolneston now up and running, Norfolk's new television owners benefitted from programmes like the *Six-Five Special*, but for those yet to become viewers the radio was the prime source of information. Teenagers listened intently to music programmes on the BBC's Home and Light services in the hope of hearing at least one rock 'n' roll number among the plethora of musical styles on offer, especially request shows such as *Two-way Family Favourites* and even *Housewives Choice*. But for most of Norwich's young people, Radio Luxembourg continued to be the main source of information. Almost every major record company sponsored a show featuring their latest releases, including Phillips' *Record Rendezvous*, *The Capitol Show* introduced by Mal Thompson, Don Mason publicising the latest recordings from HMV and MGM in *A Date with Don*, and Benny Lee's *Record Hop* playing releases from Columbia and Parlophone. Programmes introduced by the growing number of celebrity DJs who effectively controlled popular taste in a highly competitive market by promoting certain records and selecting for their programmes only those that they personally considered likely to become best sellers.

The two most popular of all Radio Luxembourg's weekly programmes for the followers of rock 'n' roll and pop music in general were the Saturday night's edition of *Jamboree* and the Sunday night British *Top Twenty*. In May 1956 *Jamboree* replaced *Saturday Merry-Go-Round* to occupy the prime position on a Saturday evening from 8.00pm until 10.00pm. Billed as 'the most exciting show of them all', *Jamboree* was a non-stop two-hour music programme aimed at a younger audience. Most weeks the programme featured a teenage jury making predictions about the potential popularity of a selection of the latest record releases (an early template for the BBC's *Juke Box Jury*) together with a 30-minute feature in which American DJ Alan Freed introduced the latest rock 'n' roll releases from America.

From as early as 1948, Luxembourg's *Top Twenty* listing of the week's twenty most popular songs was broadcast every Sunday evening from 11.00pm until midnight, an inaccurate but highly influential listing that, until December 1959, was compiled by the Music Publishers' Association and based on data obtained from the week's sheet music sales in twenty or more selected urban music retail outlets. After 1959, it was based on the list of the top twenty best-selling records as compiled by the music magazine, *New Musical Express*. Introduced initially by Teddy Johnson and subsequently by David Gell and Keith Fordyce, by 1958 the role of resident DJ for the *Top Twenty* had passed to the influential Barry Alldis. For many teenagers, Sunday evenings were spent in their bedrooms listening to radios with their ears pressed hard against the speaker, the volume turned down low, trying to catch the latest pop music news without disturbing their sleeping parents in their bedrooms nearby. The fact that the top selling title was always played first was an incentive to stay awake until, at least, the start of the show.

Publicity relating to the latest developments in teenage culture was also disseminated through a growing number of music and other magazines aimed specifically at young people. Radio Luxembourg produced its own monthly magazine, *208*, containing articles relating to popular music, photographs of British and American singers and details of Radio Luxembourg's English language programmes for that month. The *Melody Maker* was established in 1926 to promote big band dance music and by the mid-1950s had become the voice-piece for jazz while, from 1952, the *New Musical Express (NME)* and, from 1954, the *Record Mirror* focussed on all forms of popular music including rock 'n' roll. Each eventually followed the example of the American *Billboard* magazine and began to publish their own popularity charts detailing the current most popular songs based on the weekly sales of records; the NME in 1952, the *Record Mirror* in 1955 and eventually the *Melody Maker* in 1956. Initially, the information for all three charts was obtained from a small number of retail outlets, mainly in London. Consequently, the early charts essentially reflected the preferences of London's trend-setting youth and defined what the rest of the country's teenagers should buy rather than what they had already bought.

Newspapers on the other hand, and especially local newspapers, maintained a strong resistance to the perceived Americanisation of Britain's youth culture. The record reviewers in the *Eastern Daily Press* and the *Eastern Evening News* rarely mentioned the latest rock 'n' roll releases, limiting their comments to recordings of classical music and jazz. In the rare occasions when they did mention rock 'n' roll, it was to herald its demise or to denigrate its performers. In 1956, the *Eastern Evening News'* record reviewer, John Mitchell, commented that:

> Sometimes the month's pops can make depressing listening. ... There is a nauseating version of 'Ain't Misbehavin' from Johnnie Ray. I have a great affection for this old number and just hate it to sound like the beast from fifty thousand fathoms locked in an echo chamber. ... Then there is dear little Ruby Murray in 'Please Hold Me Tightly.' I try to keep an open mind while listening to this girl. But it is no good, she gets me down. For the life of me I cannot see how she has made her reputation.[2]

In his column for the *Eastern Evening News*, Ronald Grant hopefully added that:

> Robert Earl currently has a record in the hit parade. This is quite something, for a number of reasons. First, this remarkably fine tenor has not had a big-selling record for a very long time—despite the fact that musically he is considered far ahead of the other pop stars. Secondly it shows once again the trend away from rock 'n' roll in pop music. Skiffle is virtually dead; rock 'n' roll is fading fast. Everybody in Tin Pan Alley, the headquarters of the pop

music industry feel more certain of the future of the publishing business for while rock 'n' roll had sway, nobody bought sheet music. After all, what was the point of buying sheet music when almost every song sounded like all the others?[3]

Notes

1. *Eastern Evening News*, Thursday 9 October 1958.
2. *Eastern Evening News*, Wednesday 16 May 1956.
3. *Eastern Evening News*, Friday, 6 June 1958. Robert Earl was the stage name adopted by Monty Leigh, who was born on 17 November 1926; a ballad singer with an operatic style like that of the better-known Edmund Hockridge. Earl had three minor chart hits in the late 1950s.

The Golden Age of the Disc

By the late-1950s, teenagers with spare money in their pockets were increasingly able to afford the 6/8 (33p) needed to buy a top selling 45 rpm single, the 10/- (50p) for the increasingly popular EP and, occasionally, £2 for an LP from their favourite performer. A 1959 survey concluded that 25% of all record sales in the UK were to teenagers. As early as in 1955, the *Great Yarmouth Mercury* reported that:

> Yarmouth, in common with the rest of the country is experiencing a great boom in the sales of gramophone records. Dealers in the town report that their sales are almost double those of twelve months ago. At a leading department store where the sale of records was introduced only a year ago, the popularity of records has increased considerably. Hundreds of copies of such discs as Eddie Calvert playing "Cherry Pink Mambo" and Slim Whitman's modern version of "Rose Marie" have been sold. "Indeed, so fast has Frankie Laine's "Cool Water" been selling that we cannot keep up with the demand," commented one salesgirl. She added that nearly all the records sold were of popular tunes. "We sell very little classical music," she said. Most shops find their best customers are teenagers and it is through them that the high sales of popular records are gained.[1]

John Mitchell christened the late-1950s as the 'Golden Age of the Disc':

> As fast as the turntables spin, millions of new gramophone records are churning out in an effort to satisfy the ever-increasing appetite of music-hungry teenagers. It's a fabulous new industry in the entertainment world. Norwich, as elsewhere, has been caught up in the boom in which hot numbers sell like hot cakes.[2]

In his personal review of 1958, Mitchell reported that the boom in record sales showed no let up with the year's sales totalling over one hundred million. Yet he still refused to recognise the contribution of rock 'n' roll. His own choice of the year's best twelve LPs consisted of eight jazz and four classical music collections. No rock 'n' roll or skiffle albums featured in his selection, deliberately ignoring the successful *Golden Records* and *King Creole* from Elvis Presley, *One Dozen Berries* from Chuck Berry and the best-selling debut LPs of Jerry Lee Lewis, Buddy Holly, Rick Nelson, Little Richard and the Everly Brothers. It was his opinion that:

131

Listening booths were a feature of shops selling records.

The classical and jazz issues have been more exciting, the pops rather less so. But rock 'n' roll has at last begun to tail off—not a bad thing at all.[3]

Inevitably the increasing demand for recorded music gave rise to a surge in the number of outlets selling records to the public. Most of Norwich's larger stores introduced a record department, including Jarrold's and Woolworths, often selling a cheaper record label promoting cover versions of popular songs by lesser-known singers; Gala at Jarrold's and Embassy at Woolworths. Woods Music Shop on Dove Street was a popular destination for record buying teenagers. Most shops selling musical instruments or electrical appliances added records to the products that they offered for sale. Willmotts on Prince of Wales Road, an electrical store selling radios and TVs, added a record department that was advertised by the store as containing the largest stock of records in East Anglia. As an innovation for Christmas 1958, Willmotts were among the first retailers to issue record tokens to be spent by their customers in their store. Tumilty Electric added a 'pop' record department at their shops on Wensum Street and St Giles. Charles Hall Ltd on Westlegate advertised that it had the largest and most modern record department in Norfolk, equipped with listening booths and private audition rooms. Stereophonic listening booths were also available at Herbert Robinson's, a newly opened music shop in premises on Red Lion Street previously occupied by the Peacock public house. Even the public library was considering introducing a record section for loan. In Great Yarmouth, the listening booths in Wolsey & Wolsey's store on King Street were a must-visit attraction for many of the town's teenagers.

It is likely that the change from the 12-inch 78 rpm shellac to the smaller 45 rpm vinyl discs together with improvements in the technical means of broadcasting their contents facilitated easier access to popular music for the public without the need for a live band. Recorded music played over new and improved public address systems at football stadiums, speedway, stock-car and other sports arenas, fairs and pleasure grounds were mostly drawn from the popular music genre of the time. At the Rollerdrome on Norwich's Plumstead Road, teenagers roller-skated to a musical background of rock 'n' roll songs. Portable record players enabled popular music to contribute to the activities on offer at youth clubs, pubs and other societies. The experience of the Wrentham Youth Club was typical:

> The club's pride and joy is a record player which was paid for from the proceeds of a fete and dance run within a few days of the club being formed. Members bring along their own records and take it in turns to act as disc jockey for the evening.[4]

At Norman's School of Dancing on All Saints Green, a record player provided the music for the newly introduced lunchtime rock and jive sessions, and for Tuesday's 'pop' nights when tuition in dancing to rock 'n' roll was given by dance teachers Peter and Nancy Norman. Pupils attending the Thursday evening's *Teenagers Only* session at Ken Hayden's New Dance Studio at 24 Exchange Street were encouraged by their tutors to bring and play their favourite records. Essentially, these were public dances to music played on records disguised as dance tuition, circumventing the musicians' union's objection to dances without dance bands.

American influence was best seen in the public houses frequented by American forces and where the American tradition of a jukebox was introduced. In Norwich, the Orford Arms was one of the first to install a jukebox in its upstairs lounge and its contents were frequently subsidised by imported records from America supplied by the visiting servicemen. In Great Yarmouth, the Queen's Hotel at the end of Regent Road possessed more than one jukebox for the entertainment of its American patrons. Others soon followed their example; the Woodcock Inn, the Great Eastern Hotel, the George and Dragon on the Haymarket, the Woolpack Inn, the Coach and Horses on Red Lion Street, the Staff of Life in St Augustine's and the Prince of Wales, as well as the American Club, the Norwich Supporters Club and the Norwich Industries Club to mention but a few. The introduction of jukeboxes was not without opposition from both the licensing authorities and the public. The fear was that a jukebox in a public house would not only encourage under-age drinking but also contribute to the erosion of the traditional Sunday observance. Cyril Bush, landlord of the Gardeners' Arms on Timberhill, was granted a license to install a jukebox on condition that he undertook to remove rock 'n' roll and skiffle records and turn the volume down on a Sunday. By 1960, attitudes had tempered. The Coach and Horses on Red Lion Street was granted a new Sunday music and singing licence enabling a jukebox to be used in the bar instead of a back room as hitherto. As in many other towns and cities, under-age drinking had become a problem in Norwich, more so with the advent of jazz and skiffle clubs based in public houses. Many feared that the further introduction of jukeboxes playing modern music would prove to be an undeniable attraction and amplify the problem. The landlord of the Lame Dog on Queens Road was heavily fined when twenty or more under-age teenagers were discovered by the police in a backroom dancing to rock 'n' roll records played on the jukebox.[5]

A more acceptable alternative to the public house for younger teenagers was the coffee bar. Coffee bars had become a new feature of urban society, especially in London, and had become intrinsically linked to the promotion of live popular music, especially skiffle, folk and rock 'n' roll. The '2is' coffee bar in London's Soho had become famous for launching the careers of numerous British singers. A reputation that was enhanced when an edition of the *Six-Five Special* was broadcast by the BBC from its premises. The commercial opportunity offered by a coffee bar did not go unnoticed, especially one equipped with a jukebox. Many of the ice cream parlours and milk bars that had been a fashion during the late 1940s and early 'fifties, quickly metamorphosed into coffee bars. New cafés and coffee bars sprang up everywhere mostly targeting a younger patron. In 1957, a café specifically for young people was opened in the village hall at Spixworth serving tea, coffee and soft drinks, and providing music from a jukebox. In an article in the *Eastern Evening News*, the café's organiser, George Lamb, explained that the aim of the café was to provide an alternative attraction for young people to the public house:

The Raven's Daughter Coffee Bar, Upper Goat Street.

We are trying to keep the young people off the streets and out of trouble, but in putting jukeboxes in pubs, the boys and girls are being lured into the wrong places.[6]

Coffee bars quickly became an established attraction throughout Norwich selling frothy espresso coffee served in shallow transparent plastic cups, with most of them providing music from a jukebox. One of the first was the Raven's Daughter Coffee Bar on Lower Goat Lane, majestically equipped with a Prima Espresso Coffee Machine. At Mr Effenberg's Top Twenty Café on Dereham Road, the jukebox played continuously from 9.30am until 10.00pm in the evening. The manager of the Popular Café on Botolph Street explained that a jukebox was an essential facility for a successful coffee bar:

"You don't get customers in if you don't have it," said a café proprietor in applying to the city transfer sessions today for permission to use a juke-box in the snack bar of his café at 56-58 Botolph Street, Norwich.[7]

His application was granted providing the café's jukebox was used only from 2.00pm until 10.00pm on weekdays and Saturdays, but not at all on a Sunday. Music from a jukebox was also available at Paul's Espresso Coffee Bar on Prince of Wales Road, Mac's in Thorpe St Andrews and the popular Janie's Coffee Bar, managed by Jane Cork, on Ber Street. Every Wednesday, Thursday, and Friday

The Jukebox became ubiquious in cafés throughout Europe. This one in Mariehamn, in Finland.

evenings at Janie's Café, from 7.00 until 10.00pm, it was *Juke Box Night* where all teenagers were welcome to gather, drink coffee and jive to the latest records.

As well as featuring live bands most evenings, the jukebox at the Samson's all-day cellar coffee and snack bar provided its young patrons with music for jiving as well as for listening. Ever open to a new opportunity, manager, Norman Guest, responded to the shortage of appropriate non-pub-based entertainments for younger teenagers by introducing the latest idea from London into Geoffrey Watling's entertainment facilities at the Samson, a discothèque. From 26 January 1959, Monday evenings from 8.00pm until 10.30pm were designated as *Off the Record* at the Samson. For a 1/- (5p) entry fee, teenagers between the ages of 14 and 20 were treated to a non-stop programme of recorded music from the latest top one hundred hit records played through what Guest claimed was 'the most expensive amplification equipment in the country'. Jiving was non-stop, the music was loud and intense, alcohol was banned and only soft drinks were served. *Off the Record* was an immediate success and was quickly extended by Watling to his other entertainment facilities; every Tuesday evening at Lowestoft's South Pier and every Saturday afternoon at the Lido. Wiffler of the *Eastern Evening News* commented that:

> When you consider the current price for setting a jukebox going is sixpence, it's not surprising that there's been a lot of support for those record sessions when for just double the jukebox tanner you get 2½ hours of non-stop tunes.[8]

He added later that the teenagers responded enthusiastically to the 2½ hour mixture of rock 'n' roll, pop and cha-cha music.

Most of them, it seemed to me, decided to jive and for long periods the floor was a writhing sea of young humanity. 'Sea' is the right word because as the arms came up in the jive movement, they looked like swimmers.[9]

In an interview for the *Eastern Evening News*, Harold Marsh, Entertainments Manager at the Samson said that the 'night out for a bob' had filled a gap in the provision of entertainment for the younger teenager.

They can hear the music they like and are free to jive as much as they like.

When asked, the teenagers themselves added that:

"We come because we want to jive" was a phrase heard many times when asking the teenagers what brought them to the record sessions. "There is never enough room at youth clubs" said two girls. "I like to keep up with the latest pop music," said a teenage boy."[10]

Appearing regularly at the Samson were DJs Don Robb and Don Neilson, formerly from ITV's pop programme *Wham*, together with an occasional celebrity Mecca contracted guest DJ, including big names such as the well-known and, at the time, famous Jimmy Saville. The evenings also served an important social function because following the sudden death of Birmingham's right-back and English international footballer, Jeff Hall, from Poliomyelitis, offering vaccinations against the disease to the teenagers during sessions at the disco, resulted in a substantial uptake.

Following the success of *On the Record* at the Samson, similar discothèques were instigated at other venues throughout the city, including Wednesdays and Fridays at the Norwich Supporters Club, and every Thursday at the Goode's Hotel in Great Yarmouth. On Friday 12 June 1959, *Record Round Up*, a Friday night disco began at the Gala, advertised as 'a pick of the pops', 8.00pm until 11.00pm, with the entrance price set at 2/6 (12.5p) or 2/- (10p) for Rhythm Club members. Norman Guest subsequently built upon his success at the Samson to manage a discothèque business organising discos throughout East Anglia under the title *Juke Box Jamborees*, including sessions at Cromer, Bury St Edmunds, Kings Lynn and the Goode's Hotel in Great Yarmouth; usually consisting of three hours of non-stop jiving to records from the Top 100, featuring David Ewing as resident DJ, and with an occasional 30-minute live performance by a local rock 'n roll band.

Notes

1. *Yarmouth Mercury*, Friday 7 October 1955.
2. *Eastern Evening News*, Thursday 23 January 1958.
3. *Eastern Evening News*, Tuesday 11 November 1958.
4. *Eastern Evening News*, Friday 6 November 1959.
5. *Eastern Evening News*, Wednesday 27 May 1959.
6. *Eastern Evening News*, Thursday 15 October 1959.
7. *Eastern Evening News*, Tuesday 15 July 1958.
8. *Eastern Evening News*, Saturday 31 January 1959.
9. *Eastern Evening News*, Tuesday 2 February 1959.
10. *Eastern Evening News*, Thursday 30 April 1959.

Live Music Everywhere

During the late 1950s, live music could be heard in Norwich most nights of the week despite the continued absence of a designated concert hall. Jazz and skiffle bands continued to dominate the pub and club circuits, while in the major ballrooms versatile orchestras provided the music for all styles of dancing. The Zodiacs continued to play rock 'n' roll for jive at the Ailwyn. Yet change was necessary. Norfolk's newly acquired television sets and cheaper record players had made quality entertainment readily available in the home and provided an attractive alternative to going out in the evening. Live groups competed for audiences against the best vocalists and bands appearing on TV. Not only did live performances suffer a drop in attendance; the once favoured mixed variety shows at the Theatre Royal and the Hippodrome were no longer able to compete with the better-quality programmes on television such as the *Perry Como Show*, *The Billy Cotton Band Show* and the regular Saturday evening comedy shows hosted by the likes of Charlie Chester, Ted Ray and Benny Hill. As television ownership increased, theatre audiences diminished, forcing the Hippodrome to close its doors for the final time on 1 June 1960. The building was subsequently demolished to make way for a multi-storey car park. Cinema audiences also suffered to such an extent that between 1958 and 1960 half of Norwich's cinemas closed, including the Electric Cinema on Prince of Wales Road, the Mayfair on Magdalen Street, the Regal on Dereham Road, the Capitol on Aylsham Road and the Theatre de Luxe on St Andrews. In the clubs, pubs and dance halls, live music competed with jukeboxes and discothèques.

Inevitably, those facilities that continued to provide live music found it necessary to introduce innovative ideas to attract what remained of a gradually diminishing audience. The Carlton Cinema hosted an occasional live variety show with big star attractions in between its regular film performances, while the Theatre Royal concentrated its efforts on alternating drama productions with touring live popular music shows and jazz band concerts. Both facilities benefited greatly from the paucity of good Norwich-based rock 'n' roll groups by hosting nationally recognised top 'pop' performers. Appearances by well-known rock 'n' roll artists were proving to be an undeniable attraction although in Norwich they were few and far between until 1960. In February 1958, Marty Wilde and his Wildcats topped the bill in a rare week-long variety show at the Carlton Cinema supported by singer Shirley Douglas with the Chas McDevitt Skiffle Band; Fred

139

Atkins, a ventriloquist, assisted by his wife Audrey; comedian Sonny Boy; Kisch & Valerie, an acrobatic act; and a troupe of exotic dancers.

> Winding up the programme in substitution for Terry Dene was Marty Wilde and his Wildcats, seeking to send away the youngsters hilariously content. That 80 per cent of the words of Wilde were lost in the forte of drums and three electric guitars — one played by 16-year-old Kenny Packwood, who was back in his hometown — did not seem to matter in the least.[1]

Despite being one of Britain's better-known rock 'n' roll singers, Marty Wilde was a last-minute replacement for the wayward Terry Dene. Dene had been forced to cancel his visit to Norwich due to a court appearance in Bristol. While he was appearing on a touring show in Gloucester, Dene's volatile marriage to singer Edna Savage had run into difficulties and, as a consequence, Dene embarked on a drinking spree in Bristol where he was arrested by the police for drunkenness.

Marty Wilde.
(CC BY-SA 4.0)

Norwich's misfortune in its dealings with rock 'n' roll stars continued as many entertainment organisations attempted to bring live popular music performers to the city. On 2 May 1958, Terry Dene was again booked to appear in Norwich at the Grosvenor Ballroom but failed to arrive when his car broke down on the way from London. On 12 June, the American singer Jerry Lee Lewis was due to star in a variety show at the Carlton Cinema, but his eagerly awaited performance was abruptly cancelled. Lewis' tour of the UK had been dramatically cut short when it was discovered by the press that his third marriage earlier in the year was to his 13-year-old cousin, Myra Gale Brown. Marty Wilde made another visit to Norwich in the following November when he appeared as the starring act in a show at the Theatre Royal which also included singer Nancy Whiskey, the John Barry Seven and the usual mixture of diverse speciality acts.

It was soon clear that traditional variety shows had had their day. The normal top-of-the-bill comedian was slowly being replaced by a popular singer often accompanied by other acts from the same genre. For the 1959 summer season at the Royal Aquarium in Great Yarmouth, Lonnie Donegan topped the bill in a show that included country singers Miki and Griff, Australian singer Lorae Desmond (who had represented the UK in the 1957 Eurovision Contest), singer-comedian

Des O'Connor and the Marion de Vere Dancers. It was a sign of things to come when on 30 August 1959 Marty Wilde returned once more to Norfolk to star in a one-off Sunday show at the Royal Aquarium in Great Yarmouth called *The Big Beat Show*, a touring popular music show sponsored by impresario Larry Parnes. Also appearing on the bill were other rock 'n' roll acts including the Viscounts, billed as Britain's newest vocal group; Miss Rock 'n' Roll, Sally Kelly; Vince Eager; Johnny Gentle; Duffy Power; and Dickie Pride, all backed by Norwich-born guitarist Tony Sheridan and his band of the day, the Big Beat Boys.

By 1960 touring shows attempting to replicate the excitement of TV's *Six-Five Special* and *Oh Boy!*, featuring a large cast of popular singing stars, were starting successfully to compete with the traditional variety show and were attracting capacity audiences all around the country. At Great Yarmouth, the management of the Britannia Pier, the Royal Aquarium, the Wellington Pier and the Windmill persisted for the 1960 summer season with a traditional mixed end-of-the-pier style variety show, hosted by comedians Jewel and Warris, Charlie Chester, Charlie Drake and Tommy Trinder, respectively. Competing with these and attracting capacity audiences from a younger element among the town's summer visitors were two popular music shows. Every weekday afternoon and on Sunday evenings it was another Larry Parnes production, *Meet the Beat*, at the Britannia Pier starring singers Billy Fury, Vince Eager, Dickie Pride and Johnny Gentle. In addition, Lonnie Donegan and his band were also starring in a show with the Dallas Boys at the Regal. In Norwich, the Theatre Royal successfully augmented its income every month by hosting numerous week-long popular music shows that were touring the country under the banner of *The Top Twenty Hit Parade*. Promoted by impresario Bunny Lewis, these highly popular shows starred at various times Craig Douglas, Adam Faith, the Mudlarks, Cliff Richard, Freddie Cannon, Gene Vincent, Jerry Keller and Georgie Fame. A series of shows that undoubtedly were partly responsible for the sudden boom in Norwich-based rock 'n' roll bands.

Despite the obvious attractions of television, dancing was still a favoured form of entertainment especially for the young, and in the larger ballrooms of Norwich the music for dancing was normally provided by live bands. The challenge from television and competition between the dance halls themselves effectively improved the quality of the music on offer. Viability was maintained through offering a different dance style on different nights of the week, often with music provided by different specialist bands, groups or orchestras. Patrons could dance modern ballroom, old time, cha-cha or jive to all-purpose dance orchestras, jazz bands, skifflers and, increasingly, rock 'n' roll groups, with the occasional discothèque for variety. As Steve James in the *Eastern Evening News* reported, dancing in Norwich was big business.

In Norwich….it seems that dancing is holding its own against the counter attraction of television. That's understandable for by the far greater numbers who go dancing are between the ages of 17 and 25.[2]

Based on a local survey, he also concluded that over a third of the 17 to 25 age group went dancing at least once a week. Not every ballroom adapted to the challenge posed by television. The Arlington on Newmarket Road closed and was demolished in 1960 to make way for a residential development.

As well as a vibrant and expanding club scene, special events were a regular feature especially in the local jazz year. Following the success of the previous year's skiffle competition at Bury St Edmunds, the Bury St Edmunds Round Table in collaboration with the International Jazz Club held a competition on Monday 28 May 1958, Whit Monday, to discover the best national jazz band. A disappointing number of bands accepted the challenge. On a wet and dismal Whit Monday, in front of a sparse audience, the competition between the entries was judged by trumpeter Owen Bryce and music critic Graham Boatfield. The winners were the Collegians from Norwich playing their instrumental versions of *Working Man's Blues* and *Buddy Habits*, and the song *Make Me a Pallet on the Floor* sung by the bands' vocalist Colin Burleigh. In an interview soon after being presented with the trophy by Owen Bryce, Burleigh declared that the Collegians were one of the first bands to include skiffle in their programmes, but they were now pleased to be one of the first to drop it. Skiffle, it seems, had had its day and was no longer in favour with jazz audiences. Yet that same evening, the Collegians proudly displayed their trophy at a dance in aid of the funds of the Dereham Memorial Hall where they appeared with the local Vampires Skiffle Band.

> A National Jazz Band Competition trophy which they won that afternoon was displayed by the Collegians Jazz Band of Norwich at Dereham Memorial Hall last night when they played for the Dereham Round Table's Whirligig dance. They had won the National Jazz Band Contest organised by the Bury St Edmunds Round Table under the auspices of the International Jazz Club.[3]

Inevitably, after the success of the first Riverboat Shuffle, a second shuffle took place on Sunday 15 June 1958, organised by Brian Green and the Bungay Jazz Club. Three hundred jazz fans boarded the ship *Resolute* at Great Yarmouth for a trip along the river into Norwich and back. Performing on the journey were Brian Green's Tailgate Band, the Collegians, the Mustard City Stompers and the Cliff Cannell Band from Chelmsford. The Downhomers provided skiffle interludes between the jazz sessions. Unfortunately, the *Resolute* had to turn back to Great Yarmouth before reaching Norwich as planned because of an over-extended and over-indulgent pub stop in Reedham.

The second River Shuffle on the Resolute, 1958.

All along the river the jazzmen made their presence felt and sent cows scampering over the marshes at their approach. At Reedham, the Lord Nelson's pet beer-drinking lamb, Whisky, took one look at the gaily-decorated band boat and ran indoors.[4]

A third shuffle took place on Sunday 17 May 1959 organised by the Great Yarmouth Jazz Club. Three hundred passengers paid £1 each for a ticket to board the *Golden Galleon* for a trip once again along the river to Norwich and back. Jazz was provided on the way by the Collegians, the Mustard City Stompers and the Tailgate Band. For the second time running the boat failed to reach Norwich.

> Because of the tidal conditions the Galleon turned back at Thorpe instead of going into Norwich. As a result, one of the musicians, Mr Dickie Grice, bass player with the Stompers, who had intended to get off in the city, had to make a spectacular departure—leaping ashore at Whittlingham in an effort to get back to his home in Taverham for his son's christening an hour later.[5]

The fourth shuffle on Sunday 29 May 1960 was just one element of a Big Jazz Weekend organised by the newly formed Federation of East Anglian Jazz Clubs. On Thursday 26 May, the Collegians and the Riverside Jazz Band provided a night of jazz in a packed Penrice Arms in Great Yarmouth. The next day, the Riverside Jazz Band again made an appearance at the United Jazz Club in Caister, while on the Saturday it was the turn of the Collegians at the Cottage in Thorpe. The weekend ended with a final Monday night session by the Riverside Jazz Band at their then home club by the river at Thorpe Gardens. Coaches were organised by every jazz club in the Federation to transport their club members to the various venues taking part in the weekend. The shuffle on Sunday 29 May saw an overly full Golden Galleon set sail once again towards Norwich to music from the Collegians, the Tailgate and the Riverside jazz bands. Rain showers were no deterrent to the enjoyment. While the bands played, dancers jived on a crowded top deck protected from the rain by a canopy.

> Bowler hats, jeans, deer-stalkers, sunglasses and bright sweaters caught the eye, there was continual waving to and from the other users of the river, and the musicians managed to keep the jazz flowing from their precarious position on empty beer crates and the few spare places to be found on deck.[6]

Like rock 'n roll, Traditional Jazz developed unique fashion styles in clothing among young people. For men, who were often seen sporting beards, it was often long baggy sweaters worn over blue jeans, the latter shrunken to fit tightly. Sometimes Corduroy jackets and trousers, combined with suede shoes or desert boots, often with an open-necked shirt and cravat. Duffle coats were a must. A CND badge often completed the ensemble. The term Beatnik began to be applied to those who followed this fashion. Many attempted to ape 1920s fashion styles in the manner of Acker Bilk by wearing bowler hats, waistcoats and 'grandad' shirts with white stiffly starched collars fitted by collar studs. Sometimes with no collar at all, and occasionally replaced by a colourful knotted neckerchief. For women the standard dress style was a blouse and flared skirt, suitable for dancing. As jazz became integrated into the Beat culture, this was gradually being replaced by turtle-necked sweaters over black pencil-slim skirts or tight-fitting slacks, in a style made popular by the film star Audrey Hepburn. On Friday 11 September, as part of Great Yarmouth's Battle of Britain celebrations, the First East Coast Jazz Festival was held at the Wellington Pier Winter Gardens.

As interest in jazz grew, especially by the young, visits to Norwich by big-named jazz bands also increased, sometimes by invitation from a local jazz club or promoter, but often as part of a national promotional tour that had been organised by a London-based management company. Performances by visiting bands normally took place in a major dance hall or theatre, sometimes to a seated audience and, at other times, providing the music for dancing. In April 1959, 500 jazz fans attended a fund-raising ball at Dereham's Memorial Hall at which Acker Bilk and his Paramount Jazz Band was the headline band. A follow-up ball, featuring the Dutch Swing College, had to be cancelled due to a dispute with the Musician's Union. Jazz concerts became a regular attraction at the Samson & Hercules sponsored by owner Geoffrey Watling. On Wednesday 2 September 1959, 1000 people paid five shillings each for a seat to see the Chris Barber Band in the main Samson ballroom.

> The programme was a well-chosen mixture of traditional tunes, jazzed-up 'pops' of the twenties, blues numbers, a gospel song and something that started life as a spiritual…. The opening number provided a good example of the Barber quality. It was that of the twenties, 'The Sheik of Araby', decked out strikingly in a way the twenties old favourite never dreamed of.[7]

Performing at the Theatre Royal on Sunday 14 February 1960 in front of a seated audience was a touring production called *The Big Jazz Show of 1960*, featuring music from the Terry Lightfoot Band, Cy Laurie and his Band and jazz pianist Dill Jones. Johnny Duncan and his Blue Grass Boys gave a much-appreciated performance of skiffle, despite the notion in many quarters that skiffle had at last had its day.

Jazz featured strongly in the weekly programme of events organised by the management at the Grosvenor Rooms on Prince of Wales Road. From early in 1960, every Saturday night was designated at the ballroom as a *Tradjazz* dance, with national and local bands contracted in the first instance by Guest Star Entertainments including Brian Green's Dixielanders, the East Anglian Jazz Band and the Norfolk Jazz Band from Swaffham. In July, promoters John Harrison and Don Read from London assumed control of the Saturday night programme, offering each week a nationally known band teamed up with the best of the local groups. Among those appearing at the Grosvenor's Saturday *Tradjazz* dance during 1960 were the Terry Lightfoot Band, (Read was Lightfoot's manager at the time), Micky Ashman and his Ragtime Band, the Sims Wheeler Vintage Jazz Band, the Clyde Valley Stompers and Kenny Ball. For most of 1960, the *Tradjazz* dance was the major Saturday night attraction for Norwich's entertainment seeking young people. Every weekend, between 750 and 1000 dancers made the trip to the Grosvenor for their Saturday night entertainment. Fleets of coaches brought dancers to the Grosvenor from Great Yarmouth and many other parts of Norfolk.

Even the Norwich Young Socialists were actively involved in the local jazz music scene. In describing an event organised by the Young Socialists in the historic location of St Andrews Hall, the *Eastern Evening News* declared that:

> While not unique, jiving around the stately pillars of St Andrews Hall is sufficiently rare to excite more than the usual interest in Norwich especially when the music is supplied by Humphrey Littleton and his Band.[8]

Notes

1. *Eastern Evening News*, Tuesday 25 February 1958.
2. *Eastern Evening News*, Thursday 9 April 1959.
3. *Eastern Evening News*, Tuesday 27 May 1958.
4. *Eastern Evening News*, Thursday 19 June 1958.
5. *Eastern Evening News*, Monday 18 May 1959.
6. *Eastern Evening News*, Tuesday 31 May 1960.
7. *Eastern Daily Press*, Thursday 3 September 1959.
8. *Eastern Evening News*, Tuesday 1 November 1960.

Competition for Customers

Changing tastes in popular music, competition from television and the changing dynamic of the dancing public stimulated many changes in the period from 1958 to 1960. As late as 1958, the weekly programme at the Grosvenor still catered for all styles of dancing. The management continued to assume that the dancing public would be drawn from every age range, although conceptions were starting to change. For a while, the Monday night evening of modern jazz from the Rex Cooper Quartet and the Freddie Marrison Band was abandoned and replaced by *La Fiesta*, a session catering for the late-1950s craze for dancing the cha-cha, with the ever-adaptable Bob Barbour leading a Latin-American style combo, Los Guitanos. Wednesday nights were devoted to Old Time dancing with Maestro and his Orchestra and, at the weekend, conventional strict-tempo partner dancing to music from the resident bands Jack Tubby Rogers and his Music with a Beat, and the Jock Brennan Orchestra. Roger Vickers and his Orchestra took over from Tubby Rogers as the resident dance band in April 1959 when Rogers accepted a further summer-season engagement in Skegness. Advertised as 'the band you have been waiting for,' the Roger Vickers Orchestra was an all-purpose dance band consisting of Roger Vickers, Bob Brundrett and Peter Voysey on saxophones, Ernie Gilmour on piano, Ray Stratton on bass and the popular Freddie Marrison[1] on drums. Band leader Roger Vickers, formerly a member of Brian Green's Dixielanders, described the band as:

> Essentially a dance band with an occasional vocal from bassist Ray Stratton, but we have a repertoire covering strict-tempo, modern jazz, Dixieland, cha-cha, old time and the rest.[2]

A similar programme was on offer at the Samson & Hercules; strict tempo dancing for couples of all ages to music from Leslie Douglas' Orchestra on Tuesdays and Eric Winstone and his Full Dance Orchestra on Thursdays and Saturdays. However, things were also about to change at the Samson. Harold Marsh, the newly appointed ballroom manager, was quoted as saying that he:

> Hopes to widen the scope and popularity of public dances at the Samson and Hercules so that they are of great interest to all ages from the young, who like the slightly unorthodox dances, through to the generations which prefers stately old-time dances.[3]

For the moment, changes were on hold because Geoffrey Watling, owner of the Samson & Hercules, was in the process of expanding his entertainment interests and negotiating a take-over of the Lido dance hall on Aylsham Road. At the Lido, the Tuesday evening Rhythm Club was still going strong attracting more than two hundred dancers every week and, on Saturdays, a packed ballroom danced to music from Ernest Cowell and his Band. In January 1958, the role of resident dance band was transferred to saxophonist Lionel Black and his Orchestra. Watling's purchase of the Lido was completed in the following November bringing the Samson and the Lido under a common management company. At the same time, the Norman Guest managed Cellar clubroom at the Samson became operational catering specifically for the younger members of Norwich society and completing Watling's ambitious expansion scheme.

Once both the Samson and the Lido were under Watling's control, innovation was possible. At the Samson, Wednesday evenings continued to be devoted to Old Time dancing with Eddie Gates and his Orchestra, in direct competition with a similar session at the Grosvenor. A new resident band was installed at the ballroom under the leadership of jazzman Brian Green to provide music for a Thursday night Tempo Club, playing up-tempo music for jiving, aping the successful Rhythm Club at the Lido. The biggest innovation was the introduction of the *Saturday-Night Special* at both the Samson and the Lido employing nationally recognised singers to provide cabaret style entertainment supported, where necessary, by the resident band. The first night on Saturday 11 October 1958 featured Lita Rosa at the Samson, backed by Brian Green and his Band, and Bruce Turner and his Jump Band at the Lido. At various times, the *Saturday-Night Special* attracted many well-known stars to the city including Ray Ellington, Don Lang, Russ Hamilton, Jimmy Young and Rosemary Squires. Often the star attraction was booked to perform at both the Samson and the Lido on the same Saturday evening. When she appeared in a November edition of the special, Marion Ryan was due on stage at 9.00pm at the Samson and 10.45pm at the Lido. So successful were the *Saturday-Night Specials* that the Grosvenor and Gala quickly followed suit. Many of the guest artists were rock 'n' roll stars.

Influenced by Eileen Page and her school of dancing, the tradition had been for conventional partner dances at the Gala. On Wednesday and Saturday evenings couples danced to music from Trevor Copeman and his Dance Orchestra, who had taken over the role of resident dance-band from the Bob Barbour Orchestra. Every year Eileen Page organised a competition for the best local ballroom dancers, open to both professional and amateur contestants of any age.

The Gala Cup Competition at the Gala ballroom in Norwich this week went off with commendable slickness. The whole thing including a demonstration

was over in 45 minutes leaving plenty of time for general dancing.[4]
In September 1958, Tony Howard and the New Gala Orchestra replaced Trevor
Copeman as the resident dance-band.

It soon became obvious to Watling that in offering the same style of dancing
every weekend, the Samson and the Lido were in competition with each other for
customers, especially from the younger teen-and-twenty age range, and that a large
section of Saturday night's dancing public were being neglected. As a result, at the
newly refurbished Lido a new entertainments policy was implemented with the
intention of complementing and not competing with that at the Samson. The main
aim of this new policy was to provide couples with the opportunity to combine a
conventional evening out dancing with a romantic candlelit supper served at table
in a setting of soft lights and gentle music; all at the affordable price of 8/6 (42.5p)
each. Lounge suits and evening dresses were compulsory. Music for dancing was
provided at the Lido by a newly appointed dance band, Bert Dailey & his Orchestra.
Mr Watling commented that:

> my idea is to cater for the courting couples and young marrieds who have
> no longer an interest in the boy-meet-girls public dance.[5]

The *Saturday Night Specials* continued to attract the younger dancer.

As the competition for customers between the three main dancehalls escalated,
the Saturday night appearances by nationally known singers and bands were often
supplemented at the dance by additional give-away prizes and competitions,
primarily as an inducement for the young. As an early gift for Christmas 1958,
every woman dancer at the Grosvenor was given a pair of nylon stockings supplied
by Sweet Jane Hosiery. Not to be outdone by its rival, every woman dancer at both
the Samson and the Lido also received a pair of nylon stockings manufactured by
Morley's of Nottingham. A free sherry and mini savouries were provided to all the
dancers at the Wednesday night Old Time Dance. During a New Year's dance at
the Gala on 20 January 1959, three free permanent wave or equivalent hairdos,
donated by the local hair salons Pierre Antoine of Timber Hill, Miss Norman
on London Street and Janette on Timber Hill, were awarded to the three young
women with the most attractive dresses. As the competition escalated, the prizes
became bigger. At the Samson's Jackpot dances, the prizes included tea services,
record players and washing machines.

Competitions, big and small, became commonplace. The showing on television
of Eric Morley's *Miss World* competition had created an interest in beauty
competitions. The Grosvenor had its own version.

> At the Grosvenor Ballroom they're busy holding heats each Saturday night
> in the 'Miss Grosvenor of 1958' beauty contest. There is another heat
> tonight and a further one next Saturday. The first prize is £20. Judging is

not on beauty alone. Charm, poise and personality, dress sense—these and other factors are taken into account by the independent panel of judges.[6]

The Grosvenor was home to numerous beauty contests including Norfolk's *Miss Dairy Queen*, *Miss Outdoor Girl* and *Miss Exquisite Form*. Heats for the *Queen of Industries* inter-city beauty competition were held at the Federation Club. Interest in such competitions was not universal.

Why do girls travel all over the country appearing virtually as professionals in bathing beauty contests? Many are interested solely in the money prizes. But others do so in the hope that they may be discovered for show business stardom. Quite a few like last year's 'Miss Great Britain,' Leila Williams, spend their winnings on drama lessons.[7]

Both the Samson and the Grosvenor paid lip-service to all the latest teenage crazes imported from America including Limbo dancing and Hula Hoop contests. At the Samson, demonstrations of Hula Hooping were given by the Norfolk Champion, Miss Pat Burden, and the Norfolk Hula Marathon winner, Maurice Gidney. Competitions were held at the Grosvenor for the most stylish and longest lasting performer with a Hula Hoop; each week there was £4 for the winner and £1 for the runner-up. In 1960, John Goodings, manager of the Samson, introduced a yo-yo competition for teenagers, held during the Monday night *Off the Record* discothèque, with four heats each week and a final on Monday 18 April 1960. He also introduced a regular miming contest during record sessions.

The most prestigious competition to be held at the Grosvenor was the East of England heat of the national *Find the Singer* contest, organised on behalf of ATV, which was held throughout the month of February 1959 at the Saturday night and Sunday Club dances. The winner of each regional heat was eligible to enter the televised grand-final in London on Friday 26 June for a prize of £1000 and a recording contract with Pye records. The instigator of the competition was the well-known band-leader Lou Preager. Famous as the presenter for many years of BBC radio's *Housewives Choice*, Preager and his Orchestra were the one-time resident band at the Hammersmith Palais in London and the Lyceum on the Strand. During the 1940s and 50s, the orchestra featured many times on radio and television including appearances on BBC TV's *Come Dancing* and ITV's *Palais Party*. *Find the Singer* was just one of many music contests organised by Preager, his most well-known being *Write that Tune for a £1000*, a post-war song writing contest for BBC radio that resulted in the composition of numerous popular songs, including *Cruising Down the River*. The winner of the heat at the Grosvenor and singing under his real name rather than as one of his many aliases, was a local teenage favourite, vocalist Clarence Pye, backed by a band drawn mostly from the extraordinarily successful Jailbirds Skiffle Group. Previously Pye was a finalist in a Hughie Green talent contest when aged sixteen, and in 1956 reached the semi-finals of Carroll Levis' Discoveries. He was also voted 'Singer of the Year 1958' in the Orford Cellar Skiffle Club's competition. He was greatly disadvantaged in the national final because the winner of *Find the Singer* was judged by a postal vote from the programme's viewers. Anglia Television was not yet up-and-running and, consequently, few viewers in Norfolk were able to see the show. Pye himself acknowledged that his chance of winning was slight:

> because there'll no doubt be a lot of local patriotism involved—and ITV viewers in Norwich are few and far between.[8]

When the result of the postal vote was declared by ITV on Monday 22 August, the winner of the televised final was singer Julian X, billed as Britain's Fabian[9]. Pye came second. Pye's appearance in the final, however, resulted in many local bookings and a regular spot in the Blue Room at the Norfolk Railway House.

With 1960 came many major changes. On 31 December 1959, Geoffrey Watling surprised many people in Norwich when he announced that he had sold his interests in both the Samson and the Lido to Mecca Ballrooms for £163,000. Mecca completed the take-over on 18 January 1960. On 18 February, Mecca also completed the purchase of the struggling Capitol Cinema adjacent to the Lido with the intention of combining both buildings to form a single entertainment facility for banqueting and dancing to be known as the Norwood Rooms. The Capitol Cinema closed for the last time on 4 April and work began on a £150,000 transformation of the Lido and Capitol into a single top-quality ballroom and entertainments centre. The newly named Norwood Rooms were opened on Tuesday 4 October 1960 by the Lord Mayor of Norwich, Mr A E Nicholson.

With Mecca in control, the competition with the Grosvenor intensified. At the new Norwood Rooms the focus during the week was on banqueting and special functions in its new 1000-seater Mayfair Suite. The policy adopted by Mecca at the Samson, complementing that at the Norwood, was to concentrate on popular dancing while at the same time increasing its appeal to the younger patron. The further intention was to offer a complementary dancing experience at both venues on a Saturday night. At the Samson, the local resident dance band was replaced by a Mecca contracted dance band, Jan Ralfini and his Orchestra. Previously the resident band at the Locarno in Liverpool, the 14-piece Ralfini Orchestra had featured many times on BBC's *Come Dancing* and had for a time been the resident pit-orchestra at the London Palladium. The leading vocalist with the band was Roy Green, who was advertised as a specialist in novelty numbers, rock 'n' roll, cha-cha and humour. Contracted to perform for four nights each week, the Ralfini Orchestra provided the music for private functions every Tuesday and Wednesdays;

ballroom dancing for the over twenty-ones on Thursdays and the Carnival Dance on a Saturday. To provide something of appeal to dancers of every age, Monday nights were allocated to *On the Record*, a discothèque for the teenage jivers; mid-week afternoon tea dances were introduced at the ballroom for older couples and Saturday afternoon junior record sessions to cater for the under-age teenager. Cyril Glover and his Orchestra assisted by the Chic Applin Trio were appointed as the resident all-purpose bands at the Norwood Rooms.

For a while Saturday night dancing at the Grosvenor was to the music of Yarmouth based Gordon Edwards and his Band with 19-year-old Linda Taylor as vocalist.[10] In an attempt to increase the venue's appeal to the teen and twenty age range and to compete against the Samson for popularity, a Wednesday night *Rock and Jive* dance was introduced with rock 'n' roll music from two local bands, the Big Beat 4 and the extremely popular Continentals. For those who preferred jiving to jazz, Saturday night was rebranded as *Tradjazz at the Grosvenor* with dancing to music from both national and local jazz bands. Even the more traditional Gala was forced to increase its appeal to the younger dancer and introduced a *Pick of the Pops* discothèque every Friday night.

Notes

1. Many musicians played in different bands on different days of the week. Marrison was not an exception.
2. *Eastern Evening News*, Tuesday 14 April 1959.
3. *Eastern Evening News*, Tuesday 7 January 1958.
4. *Eastern Evening News*, Saturday 24 May 1958.
5. *Eastern Evening News*, Thursday 4 June 1959.
6. Steve James, *Eastern Evening News*, Saturday 8 February 1958.
7. *Eastern Evening News*, Friday 18 April 1958.
8. *Eastern Evening News*, Saturday 11 April 1959.
9. Julian X, winner of the Lou Preager *Find the Singer* talent contest, was born Julian Lee from Camberley, Surrey. Following his success in the contest, he joined Larry Parnes' stable of rock 'n' roll singers but made negligible impact in the popular music charts. He changed his stage name to Julian Scott in 1962 and had a successful career as a versatile cabaret singer.
10. Linda Taylor from Great Yarmouth was at one time regarded as being among the top ten female singers of popular song in the UK. Nevertheless, her sole top twenty recording was a cover version of *Love is a Many Splendored Thing* in 1964.

Move It

By the late 1950s, both television and the cinema had a major influence on the musical choices of young people. Teenagers could identify more with their musical heroes when they could see them perform on a screen than they could by just listening to them on the radio. With the departure of Jack Good to ITV, the *Six-Five Special* lost its position as the prime music programme for young people on television to the Jack Good inspired rock 'n' roll show *Oh Boy!* After a six-week trial in the Midlands, *Oh Boy!* was broadcast nationwide on the independent commercial television network every Saturday from 6.00 until 6.30pm in direct competition with the BBC's ailing *Six-Five Special*. Advertised as the only teenage focussed all-music show, Jack Good had abandoned the magazine format adopted by the *Six-Five Special* for a fast-moving popular music programme. The first nationwide broadcast on 13 September 1958 had an immediate impact primarily because among the artists appearing on the show was a new up-and-coming young singer, Cliff Richard, with his group, the Drifters, performing their latest record release *Move it*. Due to its exposure on the show, *Move it* entered the Top 20 music charts at number 19 on 4 October 1958 and remained in the Top 20 for the next 14 weeks, rising to its highest position of number 3 on 1 November 1958. It was denied the number 1 position by Connie Francis' recording of *Stupid Cupid* and Elvis Presley's *King Creole*.[1]

Generally recognised as the first undeniably British rock 'n' roll song, *Move it* was written by Ian Samwell, a guitarist in Cliff Richard's backing group, the Drifters, allegedly on the upper deck of a number 715 bus while travelling to a band rehearsal. Previously, all successful rock 'n' roll recordings by British artists had been cover versions of American releases. Under the guidance of Norrie Paramour, *Move it*, was recorded by Richard at the Abbey Road Studios in London on 29 August 1958 and was initially intended to be the B-side to *Schoolboy Crush*, a cover version of a song previously released in America by country music singer Bobby Helms. The Drifters, consisting of Ian Samwell and Ken Payne on guitars, and Terry Smart on drums, were enhanced for the recording by the addition of session musician Eddie Shear on lead guitar, giving the group the formation that was to become a model for subsequent groups to follow. Jack Good much preferred *Move it* to *Schoolboy Crush* and insisted that Cliff Richard and the Drifters perform the former at their appearance on *Oh Boy!* Not for the first time did the B-side of a disc become the most influential and successful recording by a rock 'n' roll artist.

Following the success of *Move it*, Cliff Richard was invited to support the Kalin Twins on their autumn tour of the UK. In preparation for the tour, the original members of the Drifters were replaced by Hank Marvin, Bruce Welsh, Jet Harris and Tony Meehan, and the name of the band was changed to the Shadows to avoid confusion with an American singing group also called the Drifters.

Introduced on alternate weeks by Jimmy Henney and Tony Hall, *Oh Boy!* ran from September 1958 until 30 May 1959. As well as Cliff Richard, the programme's regular performers included Marty Wilde, 'Cuddly' Dudley Heslop, Adam Faith, Vince Eager and the Dallas Boys, backed by two resident bands, Lord Rockingham's XI and the John Barry 7. Glamour was provided by the Vernons Girls, a female dance group named in honour of the show's sponsor, Vernons Pools. The show was axed by ITV when a move from Hackney to a new location in Manchester failed due to the Manchester premises being unsuitable for the all-action fluid style of programme envisaged by Jack Good. Subsequent short-lived programmes by the BBC, *Dig This* and *Drumbeat*, and ITV, *Boy Meets Girl*, also failed to capture the same enthusiastic teenage following that had supported the *Six-Five Special* and *Oh Boy!*. Unfortunately, the impact of the latter was limited in Norfolk because it was axed five months before independent television, in the guise of Anglia TV, was established in the county.

Anglia Television was housed in a building on Prince of Wales Road, formerly the Agricultural Hall, renamed as Anglia House. A 1000ft mast at Mendlesham in Suffolk enabled Anglia's broadcasts to be received in most of Norfolk, Suffolk and Essex, and which was, at the time, the highest man-made structure in the country. The first hour-long programme was transmitted by Anglia at 4.15pm on Tuesday 27 October 1959 and covered the opening ceremony together with a preview of the main programmes available to view each week. Programmes for the family such as *Emergency Ward 10*, *77 Sunset Strip* and *Sunday Night at the London Palladium*. Popular music for the teenager featured in *Spot the Tune*, *Song Parade* and *Boy Meets Girl*, the latter starring Marty Wilde and Joe Brown. Reflector in the *Eastern Evening News* commented that;

> For my two sons the big event of last evening was the appearance of Cliff Richard with his guitarists and drummer, the Shadows, in ITVs 'Sunday Night at the London Palladium,' He did not shake, quiver or gaze smokily into the camera. He sang 'Living Doll' and another of his disc successes, 'Travelling Light', without any obvious aiming at the girl fans who had screamed with the delirium of delight that so often overcomes girl fans these days. His style was as sober as his dress, and to a square like myself, this was refreshing. I found Mr Richard a very agreeable performer.[2]

The opening of Anglia TV, October 1959.

Boy Meets Girl was itself replaced in the following April by another short-lived programme *Wham*, but this too was quickly axed by Anglia TV due to low viewing figures. Ronald Grant commented that:

> Part of this stay-away policy is directed at the American rock gentlemen who come over on the strength of one hit record and find the public prefer, at long last, the home-grown variety as purveyed by Messers Faith, Wilde and Richard. ... But there are many signs that the unadulterated big beat has had it. I can't say I am sorry. For far too long reputations have been made and bank balances built by young lads with virtually no idea of professional behaviour or performance.[3]

An innovative lunchtime magazine programme featuring reports and items from around East Anglia, called *The Midday Show*, not only contained interviews with local personalities, gardening advice and regional news items, but also included popular music from the region. Introduced by singers Roger Gaze and a young Susan Hampshire, the show featured local singers and groups, as well as nationally known artists appearing in East Anglia's theatres and seaside summer shows, often backed by the house band, Betty Bass and the Batchelors. Betty

Bass was a 16-year-old double bass player from Cambridge, and her band, the Batchelors, were a trio formed from three musicians well known in Norwich's modern jazz circles, Roy Webster on vibraphone, Bob Bissetto on guitar and Peter Fenn at the piano. Among the local singers appearing on *The Midday Show* were Linda Taylor from Great Yarmouth, and, on 19 February 1960, Earlham's well-known rock 'n' roller and Blue Room favourite, Larry (Clarence) Pye, singing *Oh boy, As I love you* and *Rawhide*. Music critic Roy Wilson commented that:

> Linda Taylor has an attractive voice, a vivacious personality and professionalism to match. Rock 'n roller Larry Pye, who works in a Norwich shoe factory, though not exactly my favourite kind of performer, had a way with a 'pop' version of an old song that should have pleased the teenagers.[4]

When Susan Hampshire left the programme to pursue a career in acting, *The Midday Show* was axed and replaced by the news programme *About Anglia* presented by Dick Joice. Local musicians, singers and bands continued to be featured in *Anglia Presents*, a 35 minute programme broadcast every Tuesday evening and the hour-long *Glen Mason Show* every Saturday night. Regular performers were Linda Taylor again and Barry MacDonald, formerly a singer with the Billy Duncan and Gordon Edwards' bands, billed as the singing fishmonger from Blofield. Handsome Barry MacDonald became so popular locally that he acquired his own fan club. At their first meeting in the Larkman public house on Dereham Road, he had to be rescued after being mobbed by an over-enthusiastic section of his fans stealing his clothes. In his column in the *Eastern Evening News*, Roy Wilson, commenting on the *Glen Mason Show*, said that:

> Director June Howson intends to provide non-stop jazz, nostalgic songs and ballads. I am especially glad to hear about the last two, for I am sure that the rock that has rocketed some recorded voices to (undeserved) success isn't this rich foundation it once was.[5]

The BBC's response to the continuing demand from young people for popular music programmes on TV was the adoption of an American idea called *Juke Box Jury*. A programme where four celebrity guests discuss the merits and sales potentials of new record releases. The first show was broadcast by the BBC on Tuesday 1 June 1959 with David Jacobs in the chair. The four guest celebrities were singers Garry Miller and Alma Cogan, DJ Pete Murray of *Six-Five Special* fame and teenager Susan Stranks. Among the records reviewed were contributions from an eclectic cross-section of singing stars that included Anthony Newley, Jo Shelton, Lloyd Price and Bing Crosby. Once reviewed the records were deemed by the panel to be either a hit or a miss. The initial programmes not only suffered from poor reviews in the local and national press but were also considered disappointing viewing by David Jacobs himself.

> It would be unfair to say much about Juke Box Jury which may have its fans among younger people who ought, at that time anyway, to be out of doors. 'Pop' records are not the writer's great love.[6]

In his column, Ronald Grant commented that:

> Unless this show is radically altered, it will top my list of the most pointless and unsatisfactory shows on British television. At present it is a shambling, stammering and hopeless contender for the title of 'entertainment'.[7]

and again grudgingly:

> This remains one of my top-grade television dislikes. I am still far from convinced that it serves a useful purpose—though I cannot deny the tremendous viewing figures it gates.[8]

Grant's comments were prophetic as by September, *Juke Box Jury* had attracted over five million viewers and was transferred by the BBC from Tuesday to a slot during Saturday night's prime viewing time. In an interview with the same Ronald Grant, David Jacobs suggested that the programme had done much to make pop music acceptable to adults as it involved adults talking about pop music in an adult way. Despite the initial fears and objections, rock 'n' roll was becoming respectable.

In the cinema, films from Britain as well as America continued to promote rock 'n' roll and its singers. Many films, like *Disc Jockey Jamboree*, publicised multiple singers, but the tendency was towards promoting the careers of just one starring performer and developing their profiles as actors as well as singers. *Disc Jockey Jamboree* appeared at the Regent in Norwich for a week in March 1958, featuring Fats Domino singing *Wait and See*, Jerry Lee Lewis with *Great Balls of Fire*, Carl Perkins singing *Glad all Over*, and contributions from other singing stars including Jodie Sands, Frankie Avalon and Connie Francis. In the same month, Elvis Presley starred in *Jailhouse Rock* at the Regent, Pat Boone sang about *April Love* at the Essoldo, and *The Tommy Steele Story* was told at the Regal. *Jailhouse Rock* was the story about a wild young tearaway learning to sing and play guitar while serving time in prison for manslaughter, and his bumpy road to stardom on his release. An acting role for Presley as well as publicity for his songs including the Leiber and Stoller compositions *I Want to Be Free*, *Treat Me Nice*, *Jailhouse Rock* and *You're So Square*. In April it was Tommy Steele again with *The Duke Wore Jeans* at the Regent.

The standout film of 1959 was without doubt *Expresso Bongo* starring Laurence Harvey and Cliff Richard. Richard's appearance in the film established him as an all-round entertainer rather than just simply a rock 'n' roll singer. The story tells about the attempted exploitation of a bongo-playing singer Bert Rudge (Cliff Richard) by an unscrupulous agent Johnny Jackson (Laurence Harvey) and his stripper girlfriend Maisie (Sylvia Syms). With his name changed to Bongo Herbert, Bert is teamed up with a fading American singer Dixie Collins (Yolande Donlan) who eventually helps Bert to disassociate himself from Jackson while achieving success as a singer at the same time. The film was an adaptation of Wolf Mankowitz's musical with the same name that had rave reviews when it was performed on stage at the Saville Theatre in London from 23 April 1958. The star of the show, James Kenney, suffered inappropriate attention from his many female fans. Ronald Grant in the *Eastern Evening News* describes his experience at the theatre when Kenney met his fans.

> Then it happened. They found gaggles of teenagers collecting in the gallery. James' appearances were greeted with screams and gurgles in the approved teenage fashion. And after the show he found himself mobbed at the stage door — and that is something that rarely happens in the West End of London.[9]

The film *Expresso Bongo* appeared at the Regent Cinema in Norwich from 8 February 1960 to coincide with a visit by Cliff Richard and the Shadows to the Theatre Royal. Film critic, Stargazer, reported that:

> To a self-confessed square like myself, an off-beat film such as Expresso Bongo provided something more than an opportunity of getting a close-up of a teenage ritual which is usually performed underground.[10]

Notes

1. Tony Jasper (1986), *The Top Twenty*.
2. *Eastern Evening News*, Monday 2 November 1959.
3. *Eastern Evening News*, Friday 10 June 1960.
4. *Eastern Evening News*, Tuesday 24 May 1960.
5. *Eastern Evening News*, Saturday 5 November 1960.
6. *Eastern Evening News*, Wednesday 2 June 1959.
7. *Eastern Evening News*, Saturday 19 July 1959
8. *Eastern Evening News*, Friday 18 September 1959.
9. *Eastern Evening News*, Monday 8 December 1958.
10. *Eastern Evening News*, Tuesday 9 February 1960.

Rocking on a Saturday Night

Before 1959, access to live rock 'n' roll was limited in Norwich and surrounding districts, despite its popularity on records, on the radio and on TV. Conventional dance orchestras still played music for modern and old-time dancing in the dance halls and social clubs of the city. Skiffle dominated in the pubs and youth clubs while jazz continued to grow in popularity, especially traditional jazz. Without the benefit of a large capacity concert hall, Norwich rarely qualified as an appropriate and profitable location for live performances from touring popular music shows. To halt declining audience figures, the Theatre Royal managed to buck the trend and add occasional one-night performances from touring rock 'n' roll shows to its programme of events. The first of these shows was on Saturday 5 March 1960 featuring singer Craig Douglas supported by the Avons and the Mudlarks. Thursday 7 April, saw a visit from Adam Faith and the John Barry Seven. Faith was promoted at the time as Britain's number one recording artist because of his recent chart successes with *Poor Me* and *What Do You Want*. But the most popular visit of all was that by Cliff Richard and the Shadows on Sunday 24 April. Tickets for the show became available at the Theatre Royal box office from 10.00am on Monday 11 April. As early as 7.00am that morning, over 250 excited fans, mainly girls, were already in the queue. When the show eventually took place, it was in front of the largest audience ever to attend a performance of any kind at the Theatre Royal. An excitable audience was greatly entertained by Cliff Richard and the Shadows, Kathy Kirby, The Jones Boys and singer-comedian Norman Vaughan. Not everyone was impressed:

> I was unfortunate enough to book a seat to see but not hear Master Cliff Richard and was amazed at the behaviour of our so-called 'teenagers' of the fair sex. They certainly were 'sent' although regretfully not far enough away from Cliff or myself. Thanks to the screaming, clapping idiots, I was not able to appreciate Cliff's rendering of pop songs.[1]

A showing of the film *Expresso Bongo* at the Norvic Cinema was conveniently scheduled by the cinema to coincide with Cliff's visit to Norwich. Not everything ran smoothly. Cliff's car had been stolen while he was performing in a show earlier in the tour, and, as a result, he was reliant on being transported to and from venues by coach with the rest of the cast. Unfortunately, after the show at the Theatre Royal, the designated coach driver became lost somewhere in Norfolk and arrived

159

three hours late to pick up and convey the show's personnel to the next location in Bradford. Consequently, the show in Bradford began two hours later than planned. On Thursday 2 June, it was the turn of Freddie Cannon, Gene Vincent and Jerry Keller to entertain at the Theatre Royal, the last show before the start of the summer season.

It seems likely that it was Cliff Richard and the Shadows, together with their successful recording of *Move it*, who were the inspiration for the sudden influx of locally based British rock 'n' roll bands, including the many amateur and semi-professional bands based in Norwich, such as the newly formed Vampires Rhythm Group based in Hellesdon.[2] To imitate American style rock 'n' roll proved not to be an easy task and required a degree of musicianship lacking in most amateur performers. Rock 'n' roll in America evolved through a long tradition of music stretching back to African-American rhythm and blues. It was a musical style that was not a major component in Britain's musical history and was performed often with instruments unfamiliar to most amateur British musicians. To replicate accurately the sounds of Bill Haley and his Comets with guitars, saxophones and double bass, or the frantic piano playing of Little Richard and Jerry Lee Lewis, or even the close harmonies of the Platters were not easy tasks. Consequently, most early British rock 'n' roll bands were made up from experienced musicians, mainly jazz musicians such as Tony Crombie, and, locally, Bob Barbour, musicians who could cope with the demands of an unfamiliar style of music. But with Cliff Richard and the Shadows there had developed a form of rock 'n' roll evolved from foundations in skiffle, essentially British and easy to copy. While initially

The Vampires Rhythm Group in rehearsal.

formed to play skiffle, many groups morphed into rock 'n' roll bands based on the model promoted by Cliff Richard and the Shadows, a band that was ideally composed of a singer backed by lead, rhythm and bass guitars, and a drummer. Following their example even more closely, many guitarists replaced their often-home-made amplification equipment with a Vox AC15 or similar. As a gift, Cliff Richard had ordered a Fender Stratocaster with a tremolo arm for Hank Marvin from America which had arrived just in time for the 1960 tour in March. This too became the desired instrument for aspiring lead guitarists. With the addition of an echo chamber like the one given to Hank Marvin by Joe Brown, the prototype of a typical five-piece rock 'n' roll band and its equipment was complete. The Shadows, without Cliff Richard, were also influential, not only for popularising synchronised dance movements by the band while playing, but also for promoting pop instrumentals. Their first instrumental, *Apache*, was composed by musician Jerry Lordan as a tribute to a 1954 western film of the same name. The piece was first recorded by guitarist Bert Weedon but failed to gain any chart success. Lordan introduced the Shadows to the composition while accompanying them on their 1960 tour, and it was eventually recorded by the band at the Abbey Road Studios in the June of that year. Released by the Shadows as a single in July 1960, *Apache* soon entered the popular music charts and reached number 1 in November. From that moment on, instrumentals became a normal part of most rock 'n roll groups' repertoires.

With the temporary closure of the rock 'n' roll club at the Ailwyn in February 1959, the Zodiacs, fronted by vocalist Terry Reed, together with the Tom Lloyd Trio, relocated to the newly rebuilt Raven public house on Gaol Hill. The Raven had been severely damaged by bombs during World War II and was completely rebuilt and modernised in the mid-1950s. To bring customers into a city centre public house, the landlord, John Armstrong, attempted to provide a different musical attraction every night of the week except for Sundays. Among the regular performers were organist Eddie Gates, singer Frank Spalding, and pianists Frank and John Lofty. Monday night was rock 'n' roll night for the younger drinker with the Zodiacs.[3] As was the case with skiffle, most local bands began their musical careers performing in the function rooms and bars of Norwich's public houses. Ricky Lee and the Heartbeats were the resident band in the back parlour of the Larkman public house on Dereham Road, colourfully called the Purple Room. Lee's first performance at the Purple Room on 23 May 1959 caused some amusement as he had been advertised as Ruby Lee and the Heartbeats. Most people were expecting a woman. The Larkman also advertised itself as being one of the first places in Norwich to serve hotdogs. Roger Moon and the Toffs, described in the press as an outstanding rhythm group, entertained the drinkers in the Horse Barracks public house. The Toffs were essentially the Footprints Skiffle Group renamed. Dave and

Monday night was rock 'n' roll night at the Raven.

the Gay Cavaliers, previously the Four Deckers Skiffle Band, performed regularly at the Spread Eagle and the Red Lion in Thorpe, as did the Vampires Rhythm Group. Ricky Rich and his Band entertained in the similarly named Red Lion in Aylsham, while Peter Wild and his Wildcats rocked in the Bakers Arms on Heigham Street. The Double E Rhythm Group, an offshoot of the 8T8 band, performed regularly in the Morning Star public house on the junction of Pottergate with St Gregory's Alley. The landlord of the Morning Star was fined £10 in 1960 for allowing underage drinking during performances of the band. As well as jukeboxes, live rock 'n' roll bands in public houses posed a growing problem for landlords with the rise of underage drinking. Another issue was the noise. Amplified rock 'n' roll bands were a different form of entertainment to the more sedate un-amplified skiffle. While rock 'n' roll bands attracted young customers, the noise deterred the older drinker. By November, Monday's rock 'n' roll sessions in the Raven had been replaced by a quieter Eddie Gates on the organ, while the drinkers in the Blue Room on Prince of Wales Road conversed to an unobtrusive background sound of piano music.

Concerns over underage drinking and the issue of large groups of teenagers roaming the centre of Norwich on a Sunday with little to do, led the management of the YMCA on St Giles Street to consider plans to establish a Sunday Rock Café to occupy those:

> Young people between the ages of 16 and 21 who do not belong or have any loyalties to any youth group, church or organisation. "Most of them have nothing to do and nowhere to go on Sundays and they spend their time on the street corners or at the cinema." Most teenagers have one great interest, rock 'n' roll.[4]

When the café opened on Sunday 15 November 1959 in the gymnasium of the YMCA, it not only provided young people with a place to go on a Sunday but also an opportunity for new up-and-coming Norwich rock 'n' roll bands to demonstrate their skills. Every Sunday, the resident band, the Thunderbirds, was supported by one or two other guest groups. The members of the Thunderbirds—Roy Bell, rhythm guitar and vocals, Alistair Thorne, lead guitar, David Cameron, bass and Terry Saye, drums—were all students from the Avenue Road Senior School in Norwich. One of Norwich's most successful bands, the Cadillacs, made its first appearance at the opening night of the YMCA Rock Café. When the Monday night rock 'n' roll sessions ceased at the Raven, the Zodiacs disbanded and two members of the group, Stewy McIntosh and Micky Woodcock, had joined forces with Derek Shepherd and the three Zagni brothers, John, Ivan and Frank, of the Jailbirds to form this new and phenomenally successful ensemble.

The Rock Café proved to be an instant success. On opening night, over 120 boys and girls between the ages of 16 and 21 paid the 1/- entrance fee to listen to the music. Unfortunately, in supporting the YMCA's application for a Sunday Music and Singing Licence, the Chief Constable said that it was a good idea to provide some kind of entertainment for young people on Sundays, but then assured the chairman of the licensing committee that rock n roll dancing would not be allowed.[5] A major disappointment for many of the teenagers at the opening night and could have been a problem had it not been for the latest craze, the hand jive—a form of dance involving a rhythmic repeated pattern of up to 24 different hand movements and body pats carried out while seated. The bands played while rows of seated youngsters sang to the music and jived with their arms in unison. For a time, the YMCA's Rock Café attracted large numbers of young people to its Sunday shows and was a favoured venue for Norwich's best rock 'n' roll bands. Mr Souter, secretary of the Norwich YMCA, said that the café had been a bold but successful social experiment and that:

> Open house has been extended to all Norwich teenagers at a 'Continental Café' where the unattached could listen to the type of music young people today appear to enjoy most. Average attendance had rarely fallen below 100-120 and it was regarded as a successful method of contact with youngsters who were neither members nor had loyalties to any church or youth organisation in the city.[6]

On 31 January 1960, one of Norwich's newest top bands, the Continentals, played for the first time at the Café. With the disbanding of the Orford Cellar's resident band, the Jack O'Diamonds, guitarists Micky Large and Barry Butcher had joined forces with David Blyth, Sid Bezant, Pat Wood and Johnny Pratt to become the first of a frequently changing line-up in this long lasting and popular city band.

In April, the facilities at the YMCA were temporarily closed for improvements that included a new gym and accommodation for a boys' club. Sunday 3 April, the last night at the Café, was advertised as a 'Big Band Jamboree with all your favourite bands', featuring the Continentals and the Kings Men. To compensate for the closure of this popular venue, Johnny Thompson and the Kings Men hired the nearby Herbert Frazer Hall and provided regular rock 'n' roll sessions until the Café eventually reopened on Sunday 2 October 1960 with a session from yet another newly formed band, the Big Beat Four. Over the next few Sundays, club members were entertained by performances from the Cadillacs, the Nomads Skiffle Band, the timeless Bob Barbour and his Bobcats, and Lester Roberts and the Jetblacks. Secretary Souter again commented that sessions were 'going with a swing' and of the teenagers:

They were very well behaved and we had no trouble. There was an average attendance at the café of more than one hundred young people aged between 16 and 21 and many of them said how much they enjoyed the Sunday sessions.[7]

No doubt influenced by the success of the rock café, other venues began to open in the city. On Monday 17 November, rock 'n' roll sessions were restarted at the Ailwyn. Monday nights were designated 'Gee Wizz' nights at the Ailwyn with live music from the Cadillacs and the Big Beat Four. The City Supporters Social Club introduced rock and jive nights with the Mellotones, an Everly Brothers tribute duo, and Bob Barbour and his Bobcats. Tragedy struck Bob Barbour when, on 30 December 1960, his unique £150 handmade electric guitar was stolen from his parked car. At the time, he reported that only six others in the country were made to the same design. Even Norwich City College had its own band. In June 1960, the college band was invited to perform in London by Betty Foster, Queen Ratling of the Grand Order of Water Rats, at her Spring Charity Ball. The band, all aged sixteen, were Tony Webster, vocals and guitar; Lloyd Baker, piano; Mac McIntyre, guitar; John Cole, bass; and Peter Jay, drums. Peter Jay eventually achieved nationwide success with his Yarmouth based band, Peter Jay and the Jaywalkers. In the countryside too opportunities were opening. On Thursday 30 June 1960, a weekly rock 'n' roll dance began in the Hemsby Village Institute. Holidaymakers and villagers alike were invited to rock in the Institute to music from the Cadillacs and Roger Moon and the Toffs.

The major dance halls were also forced to respond and add live rock 'n' roll sessions as one of their weekly offerings. With live rock 'n' roll, discos and jazz, jiving became the main dance choice of the week. At the Grosvenor, Friday night was advertised as *Hooray Friday* with rock and jive to the Continentals and the Big Beat Four. The Big Beat Four was a combination of Rodney Kidd and Pat Barriskill from Blue Star with the remnants of the Neptunes Skiffle Band.[8] On Sunday, dancers jived to the Off Beats at the Grosvenor's Sunday Club. At the Samson & Hercules, Monday nights were advertised as *Dig the Rock* with jiving to the Jetblacks, another rock 'n' roll band formed by an amalgamation of musicians from the Nomads, Toff and the Tigers, and the Downhomers skiffle bands.

Notes

1. Letters to the editor, *Eastern Evening News*, Tuesday 3 May 1960.
2. The personnel of the Vampires Rhythm Group, not to be confused with the Dereham Vampires Skiffle Band, were Clive Dyball (vocals), Johnny Crossfield (lead guitar), Eric Nichol (rhythm guitar), Bob Sutton (bass) and Tony Napper (drums).
3. The Raven was renamed as Freshers in 1985 and eventually ceased trading in 2009. Currently, the building is the location for Paolo's Italian Restaurant and the St Giles Tattoo

Parlour.
4. *Eastern Evening News*, Thursday 1 October 1959.
5. *Eastern Evening News*, Tuesday 17 November 1959.
6. *Eastern Evening News*, Saturday 9 April 1960.
7. *Eastern Evening News*, Thursday 24 November 1960.
8. The Big Beat Four featured Pat Read as Ricky Southern (vocals), Rodney Kidd (guitar), Mike Lorenz (guitar), Pat Barriskill (bass) and Denny Royal (drums).

Into the Swinging Sixties

This story ends in 1960 not because teenage culture and its music ceased to evolve but simply because my life as a university student meant that I spent more time in Leicester and less in Norfolk, especially when I met and eventually married my Leicester girlfriend. From that point onwards, the university's Students' Union together with the Mecca Dance hall and various music clubs in the Leicester city centre provided most of my musical entertainment. My attachment to Norfolk and Norwich waned, albeit temporarily. Nevertheless, teenage culture continued to develop both in Norwich and throughout the whole of Great Britain, even more rapidly than before, eventually flowering into that era known now as the swinging sixties. Yet this may not have happened had it not been for the changes that occurred in the late 1950s. Royston Ellis in his book *The Big Beat Scene* suggests that it was the American influence on the culture and music of young people together with the ending of National Service for eighteen year olds in 1960 that ultimately resulted in the cultural liberation of Britain's youth in the 1960s. Billy Bragg in his book *Roots, Radicals and Rockers* also identifies the period from 1955 until 1960 as being a defining influence on the culture of the young. The period when American jazz, blues and rock 'n' roll became anglicised under the motive force that was skiffle.

> British pop music, for so long a jazz-based confection aimed at an adult market, was transformed (by skiffle) into the guitar-led music for teens that would go on to conquer the world in the 1960s.[1]

A less romantic view suggests that changes to the culture of young people were manufactured by business and commercial interests intent on relieving teenagers of that surplus of money appearing in their pockets for the first time since World War II. That it was the manufacturers and producers rather than the consumers that determined the fashions and trends in youth culture.

For me, my love for popular music saw no bounds. By 1960, the separate and initially independent strands of popular music—jazz, skiffle and rock 'n' roll—had coalesced to create a British beat music scene unified by a dance, the jive. Skiffle might be dying but it was skiffle that bridged the gap between jazz and rock 'n' roll. It was skiffle that also popularised the guitar as the main instrument of popular music, created a general interest in folk music and laid the foundation for the popular music strands defined by the Beatles and the Rolling Stones that erupted in 1963. At university, my musical interests were diverse. I was an active member of the university folk club, occasionally played banjo in a student jazz band and, following the success of *Crumbeat* in the 1960 Rag Revue, was a founder member of Leicester university's first rock 'n' roll band, Aztec and the Incas. Together with a partner band, the Farinas, formed by students at the Leicester College of Art and Technology, we provided a rock 'n' roll contribution to the popular music scene of Leicester's student population. For a time, I also played bass guitar in a city band called Johnny Angel and the Mystics.

In many ways, these three bands accurately reflected the prevailing trends in British popular music at that time. Aztec and the Incas were formed by five competent musicians from various parts of the country and from different musical backgrounds; Rod, Trev, Russ, Eric and me. Rod was primarily a folk singer while Trev had previously played guitar in a skiffle band, Russ and Eric were jazz musicians and I preferred rock 'n' roll. Not only did we play our versions of current popular songs, but we also played rocked-up jazz standards and penned songs of our own. In 1961 we wrote and performed on stage at the university a rock musical, *A Million Miles to the Moon*, which gained some positive reviews in the Leicester press. The Farinas was formed by a group of Leicester born students who were studying at the Art college. They too had their own style, composed songs of their own and had the advantage that they stayed together in Leicester after completing their studies. Johnny Angel and the Mystics was a rock 'n' roll band formed by four young Leicester office workers, which enjoyed a brief period of success in the early 1960s while appearing in various dance halls and nightclubs throughout the East Midlands. They were essentially an imitation band, copying as accurately as possible the music of established pop stars, particularly Cliff Richard and the Shadows. The most successful of the three was the Farinas who, by 1965 had teamed up with singer Roger Chapman to form the band, Family.[2] For Aztec and the Incas, a career in music had failed to materialise before graduation happened and the members dispersed onto various career paths in different parts of the country. Like many bands who simply copied other artists' performances, Johnny Angel and the Mystics were eventually replaced by a disco.

By 1960, Norwich supported a vibrant local beat music scene. Nationally recognised jazz and rock 'n' roll bands visited the city on a weekly basis, usually performing in front of a dancing rather than seated audience. Most were supported by local singers and bands. On 17 May 1963, the Norwich-based band, Ricky Lee and the Hucklebucks, supported the Beatles when they appeared at the Grosvenor. Yet despite a corpus of competent bands—the Stompers and Collegians playing jazz; the Cadillacs, Continentals and the Big Beat Four rock 'n' roll; and Albert Cooper rhythm and blues—few from Norwich made an impact nationally. Gifted musicians, the likes of Beryl Bryden, Tony Sheridan and Kenny Packwood, needed the opportunities that London provided for their talents to be properly appreciated. Maybe the lack of suitable premises where music in all its forms could be heard, played and appreciated was a contributing factor, including the absence of a major concert hall with good acoustics. Theatres, cinemas and dance hall ballrooms were not always ideal as a venue for promoting any musical style. Even in its heyday during the late 1960s, when it featured the likes of Jimi Hendrix and David Bowie, the Orford Cellar had poor acoustics and an audience capacity of just over three hundred. Another disadvantage suffered by Norwich, especially in the period 1955 to 1960, was the lack of either a university or a major higher education establishment. The UEA was not established until 1963. Not only would such an institution have provided an opportunity for talented young musicians in their late teenage years to meet and play, share ideas and form bands, but also a regular venue where their music could be performed. One band from Norfolk did make the national stage by the early 1960s. Great Yarmouth's Peter Jay, formerly a student at the Norwich City College, and his band, the Jaywalkers, was the first nationally known rock band to headline a Saturday dance at the Students' Union in Leicester University. Small world.

Notes

1. Billy Bragg (2017), *Roots, Radicals and Rockers* pxv.
2. Family, described as a progressive rock band, was officially formed in 1966. Best remembered for its first two long play discs, *Music in a Doll's House* and *Family Entertainment*, both of which had some success in the LP music charts.

Appendix I
Popular Music in Norwich: A Timeline of Key Events

1952	25 Nov:	The East Coast Jazz Club opens at the Cat & Fiddle—the first trad-jazz club to be established in Norwich.
1953	n/k	A jazz club was established at the Gibraltar Gardens on Heigham Street.
	16 Feb:	Norwich's First Jazz Band Ball was organised by the East Coast Jazz Club at the Chantry Hall.
1954	n/k	The refurbished Samson & Hercules and the Gala Ballrooms open for dancing.
	3 May:	The first Jazz Band Ball to be held at the Samson & Hercules featured Ken Colyer and his Band.
	5 May:	The Norwich Jazz Club was established in the Orford Arms cellar on Red Lion Street.
	20 Dec:	The Norwich Industries Club opens.
	n/k	The Norwich Jazz Club relocates to the RAFA Club Headquarters in Spencer House on Lobster Lane.
1955	22 Jan:	*Shake, Rattle & Roll* by Bill Haley and his Comets reaches its highest position of number 4 in the UK Top Ten Singles Charts.
	1 Feb:	A temporary transmitter at Tacolneston becomes operational—BBC TV available in Norwich.
	11 Mar:	The Norwich Jazz Club moves to the St Giles Parish Hall on Cow Hill.
	14 May:	Alex Welsh and his Dixielanders perform at the Samson & Hercules.
	16 May:	Cy Laurie becomes the first London based jazz band to appear at the Norwich Jazz Club.
	11 Jul:	Norwich Jazz Club's first Jazz Jamboree.
	5 Sep:	Norwich Jazz Club organises a Jazz Cavalcade at the St Giles Hall.
	20 Oct:	The Chris Barber Jazz Band plays live at the Lads' Club.
	7 Nov:	*Blackboard Jungle* at the Regent cinema.
	7 Nov:	The Norwich Jazz Club moves to Boulton & Paul Sports Club at Rosary Corner.
	12 Nov:	Bill Haley's recording of *Rock around the Clock* reaches number 1 in UK record charts.
1956	5 Jan:	Ken Colyer's Jazz Band plays in concert at the Lads' Club.
	7 Jan:	Lonnie Donegan's recording of *The Rock Island Line* enters UK record charts.

15 Mar: Stan Kenton's Big Band appears at St Andrews Hall.

19 Mar: The American Club opens on Lobster Lane.

16 Apr: The 59 Jazz Club opens in the Herbert Fraser Hall on Bethel Street.

19 Apr: Elvis Presley enters the UK record charts with *Heartbreak Hotel*.

30 Apr: *Davy Crocket* at the Gaumont cinema.

19 May: Mick Mulligan and his Band perform at the Lads' Club.

29 June: The Chris Barber Jazz Band appear in concert at the Samson & Hercules.

9 July: Cy Laurie and his Band play live at the Gala.

20 Aug: *Rock around the Clock* at the Gaumont cinema, its first showing in Norwich.

3 Sep: Sydney Bechet and the Reoweliotty Jazz Band play live in the St Andrews Hall.

10 Sep: *Jazz in the Air* festival organised by the Norwich Jazz Club.

9 Oct: A 2nd Tacolneston Transmitter becomes operational. BBC TV now available over most of Norfolk.

18 Oct: *Rock around the Clock* returns to the Regal.

29 Oct: First rock 'n' roll dance in Norwich was held at the Ailwyn Hall, jiving was to records.

30 Oct: Lionel Hampton's Big Band performs at St Andrews Hall.

1 Nov: Bob Barbour and the Rockets play rock 'n' roll music for the first time at the Industries Club.

11 Dec: Gt Yarmouth's first rock 'n roll dance was held at the Queens Hotel: jiving was to records.

20 Dec: Opening night of the Grosvenor Rooms Dance Hall on Prince of Wales Road.

1957   4 Jan: Seven hundred people dance to the Chris Barber Jazz Band at the Samson & Hercules.

10 Jan: The first rock 'n' roll evening at the Grosvenor.

4 Feb: Art Baxter and his Sinners appear at the Hippodrome.

16 Feb: The first edition of *The Six-Five Special* on BBC TV.

17 Feb: The Speedway Jazz Club opens at the Firs Stadium.

17 Feb: The 59 Jazz Club relocates to the Grosvenor.

18 Feb: Lonnie Donegan appears at the Theatre Royal.

6 Mar: Bill Haley and his Comets perform at the Carlton Cinema in Norwich.

21 Mar: Bob Barbour and the Rockets replace Les Hague as resident band at the Gala.

14 April: The Chris Barber Jazz Band appear in concert at the Carlton Cinema.

1 Jun: The first edition of the *Saturday Skiffle Club* on BBC radio.

9 Jun: The first *Riverboat Shuffle*, organised by the Bungay Jazz Club.

10 Jun: The *Bury St Edmunds Skiffle Competition*.

12 Jun: A Skiffle Competition was held at the Industries Club and was won by the Saints Skiffle Band from Thorpe.

15 Jul: George Melly sings at a meeting of the Norwich Jazz Club in the Boulton & Paul Social Club.

27 Jul: An English Folk Dance and Song Society weekend was held at Wymondham College.

2 Sep: The Federation Club replaces the Norwich Industries Club at Oak Street.

28 Oct: Count Basie's Orchestra appears at the Samson & Hercules.

? Nov: The *Downhomers Skiffle Club* opens in the Herbert Frazer Hall on Bethel Street.

1958   20 Jan: The *Norwich Jazz Club* moves to the Bedford Arms PH.

18 Feb: Norman Guest opens a jazz and skiffle club in the Orford Arms Cellar.

14 Mar: The Neptunes win the Norwich heat of the *Daily Sketch National Skiffle Competition*.

27 Mar: The last performance of the BBC's radio programme *Off the Record*.

11 Apr: The Jailbirds win the Norwich heat of the Rank Organisation's *Teenage Entertainer of 1958* competition.

18 Apr: The Sinners Rhythm Club opens at the Sportsman PH, Barrack Street.

3 May: A *Festival of Folk Song and Dance* was held at the Lads' Club.

28 May: A *National Jazz Band Contest* at Bury St Edmunds was won by the Collegians.

11 Jun: A *Festival of Skiffle* at the Dereham Memorial Hall.

15 Jun: The Second Riverboat Shuffle.

30 Jun: The *East Anglia's Skiffle Group of the Year* competition held in the Orford Cellar was won by the Sidewinders from Coltishall.

14 Aug: Ronnie Hanton, drummer with the Jack O'Diamonds Skiffle Group, dies from an asthma attack.

8 Sept: Norman Guest's Jazz Club moves from the Orford Arms to the new cellar club at the Samson & Hercules.

11 Oct: Geoffrey Watling, owner of the Samson takes over the management of the Lido.

15 Oct: Jazz and skiffle clubs re-open under new management in the Orford Cellar.

4 Nov: *Move It* by Cliff Richard & the Shadows enters the UK Top 20 charts.

	26 Nov:	The Norwich City Supporters Club opens at Rosary Corner.
	1 Dec:	Opening night of Ailwyn Hall's 8T8 Rhythm Club, featuring rock 'n' roll from the Zodiacs.
1959	20 Jan:	The Gt Yarmouth Jazz Club opens at the Penrice Arms PH on King Street.
	26 Jan:	The first *Off the Record* disco was held at the Samson & Hercules.
	17 May:	The Third Riverboat Shuffle.
	12 Jun:	The first *Record Round-up* disco was held at the Gala.
	2 Sep:	The Chris Barber Jazz Band performs at the Samson & Hercules.
	27 Oct:	Anglia TV broadcasts for the first time from Norwich.
	15 Nov:	The Sunday Rock Café opens at the YMCA on St Giles Street.
	31 Dec:	Geoffrey Watling sells the Samson & Hercules and the Lido dancehalls to Mecca Ballrooms.
1960	4 Jan:	The Riverside Jazz Club opens at the Rushcutters PH in Thorpe.
	18 Jan:	Mecca Ballrooms buy the Capitol Cinema.
	3 Apr:	The YMCA Rock Café closes.
	24 Apr:	Cliff Richard and the Shadows perform at the Theatre Royal.
	26-30 May:	A *Big Jazz Weekend* was organised by the Federation of Norfolk Jazz Clubs.
	28 May:	The Fourth Riverboat Shuffle.
	1 June:	The Hippodrome Theatre on St Giles Street closes.
	18 June:	The Riverside Jazz Club moves to Studio 4 at the Cock Tavern PH.
	30 June:	A Rock 'n' roll club was established in Hemsby's Village Institute.
	1 July:	The Orford Cellar Jazz Club moves to the Lamb Inn and renamed as the Green Turtle Jazz Club.
	20 Aug:	The Shadows recording of *Apache* reaches number 1 in the UK Top Singles Charts.
	2 Oct:	The YMCA Rock Café reopens.
	4 Oct:	The Norwood Rooms open on the site of the Lido and Capitol Cinema.
	3 Nov:	A Jazz Club opens at the Garibaldi in Great Yarmouth.
	17 Nov:	Monday night's rock 'n' roll dance restarts at the Ailwyn.
	22 Nov:	Johnny Byles opens a modern jazz club in the cellar at the Orford Arms.

Appendix II
Norfolk based singers and bands with a mention in the text

8T8 Band, The
Allez Katz, The
Applin, Chic   *The Chic Applin Trio.*
Ayres, John
Barbour, Bob   *Bob Barber and the Rockets, Bob Barber's Modern Seven, The Bob Barbour Orchestra, Bob Barbour and Los Guitanos, Bob Barbour and the Bobcats.*

Barker, Len
Bass, Betty   *Betty Bass and the Batchelors.*
Bates, Colin   *Colin 'Barney' Bates, Colin Bates and his Jazzmen.*
Bates, Eddie
Baxter, Ben
Bear, Brenda   *Brenda Bear with the Billy Roy Band, Brenda Bear and the Mustard City Stompers.*

Beech, George
Big Beat Four, The
Bishop, Neville   *Neville Bishop and his Band.*
Black, Lionel   *Lionel Black and his Orchestra.*
Blue Stars, The
Bosomworth, Charles   *Charles Bosomworth and his Oceanaires.*
Brennan, Jock   *The Jock Brennan Orchestra.*
Bryden, Beryl
Bullen, Jock   *The Jock Bullen Skiffle Group.*
Burleigh, Colin   *The Collegians with singer Colin Burleigh.*
Cadillacs, The
Capocci, Mike   *Mike Capocci and the Ray Stratton Quintet.*
Caryl, Ronnie   *Ronnie Caryl and his Orchestra.*
Cobras, The
Collegians, The   *The Collegians with singer Colin Burleigh.*
Collins, Al   *The Al Collins Dance Band.*
Continentals, The
Cooper, Albert   *Albert Cooper and the Jolly Butchers Skiffle Band, The Albert Cooper Blues and Boogie Band.*
Cooper, Rex   *The Rex Cooper Quartet, Rex Cooper and the Neuwe Quintet, The Rex Cooper Combo.*
Copeman, Trevor   *Trevor Copeman and his Dance Orchestra.*
Cowell, Ernest   *The Ernest Cowell Dance Band.*
Cox, Harry
Cygnets, The
Dave and the Gay Cavaliers
Dices Skiffle Group, The
Dixielanders, The   *Brian Green and his Dixielanders.*
Double E Rhythm Group, The

Douglas Leslie	*The Leslie Douglas Orchestra.*
Downhomers, The	
Dugdale, Bernard	
Duncan, Billy	*Billy Duncan and his Dance Orchestra.*
Dury, Brenda	*Brenda Dury and the Tailgate Jazz Band.*
East Anglian Jazz Band, The	
East Landers, The	
Edwards, Gordon	*The Gordon Edwards Band.*
Fenn, Peter	*The Peter Fenn Quartet.*
Five Sided Squares, The	*The Thetford Sideliners.*
Footprints Skiffle Band, The	
Freeman, Brian	*Brian Freeman and the Bob Barbour Orchestra.*
Galey, Bert	*Bert Galey's Dance Band.*
Gates Eddie	*The Eddie Gates Orchestra.*
Gaye, Barbara	*The Barbara Gaye Band.*
Gibraltar Jazz Band, The	
Glover, Cyril	*Cyril Glover and his Orchestra.*
Gray, Mireille	
Green, Brian	*Brian Green and his Dixielanders, Brian Green's Oom-cha Jazz Band.*
Hague, Les	*The Les Hague Orchestra.*
Hannant, Anna	*aka Black Anna.*
Hanton, Ronnie	*The Ronnie Hanton Skiffle Band.*
Hewitt, Dick	
J T Skiffle Quartet, The	
Jack O'Diamonds	
Jailbirds, The	
Jay, Peter	*Peter Jay and the Jaywalkers.*
Jetblacks, The	
Jolly Butchers Skiffle Band, The	
Jones, Trevor and Copeman, Colin	*The Trevor Copeman Band.*
Jordan Larry	*aka Clarence Pye, Larry Jordan and the Jailbirds.*
Kestrels, The	
Kingfishers Skiffle Band, The	
Kings Men Rhythm Band, The	
Larner, Sam	
Lee, Ricky	*Ricky Lee and the Heartbeats.*
Locke, George	
Lofty, John	
MacDonald, Barry	
Maestro	*Maestro's Old Tyme Dance Band, Maestro and his Orchestra.*
Marrison, Freddie	*The Freddie Marrison Four.*
Marshlanders Skiffle Group, The	
McGinnity, Tony	*aka Tony Sheridan, Tony McGinnity and the Saints Skiffle Band.*
Moon, Roger	*Roger Moon and the Toffs.*
Mustard City Stompers, The	
Neptunes Skiffle Band, The	
Neuwe Quintet, The	
Norfolk Jazz Band, The	

Norwich Modernists, The
Off Beats, The
Oom-cha Jazz Band, The
Packwood, Kenny
Pye, Clarence   *aka Larry Pye, Larry Jordan, Larry Jordan and the Jailbirds.*
Ramblers Skiffle Group, The
Randall, Chic
Rebels, The
Red Cap Skiffle Band, The
Reptiles, The
Riverside Jazz Band, The
Rockets, The   *Bob Barbour and The Rockets.*
Rodents, The
Rogers, Jack/John   *Jack 'Tubby' Rogers and his Orchestra.*
Roy, Billy   *The Billy Roy Band.*
Saints Skiffle Band, The   *Tony McGinnity and the Saints Skiffle Band.*
Sheridan, Tony   *formerly Tony McGinnity.*
Sidewinders Skiffle Band, The
Sinners Skiffle Group, The
Spalding, Frank
Stebbings, Sylvia
Stratton, Ray   *The Ray Stratton Quintet.*
Tailgate Jazz Band, The
Taylor, Linda   *Linda Taylor and the Gordon Edwards Band.*
Thetford Sideliners, The
Thunderbirds Rock Band, The
Thunderbolts, The
Toffs, The   *Toff and the Tigers, Roger Moon and the Toffs.*
Tom Lloyd   *The Tom Lloyd Trio.*
Tooes, Ivan   *The Ivan Tooes Quartet.*
Vampires, The (Dereham)
Vampires Rhythm Group, The
Vickers, Roger   *Roger Vickers and his Orchestra.*
Warne, Derek   *The Derek Warne Skiffle Men.*
Wild Four Skiffle Band, The
Wild, Peter   *Peter Wild and his Wildcats.*
Winstone, Eric   *Eric Winstone and his Full Dance Orchestra.*
Woodchoppers, The
Yare Valley Skiffle Group, The
Zagni Brothers
Zodiacs, The

Appendix III

UK Top Twenty Singles Charts.
The Number One Record, 1955–60

1955

Mambo Italiano	Rosemary Clooney	Jan 22–Feb 5
Naughty Lady of Shady Lane	Dean Martin	Feb 12
Give Me Your Word	Tennessee Ernie Ford	Feb 19–Mar 5
Softly, Softly	Ruby Murray	Mar 12
Give Me Your Word	Tennessee Ernie Ford	Mar 19–Apr 30
Stranger in Paradise	Tony Bennett	May 7–June 4
Unchained Melody	Al Hibbler	June 11–July 2
Dreamboat	Alma Cogan	July 9–16
Rose Marie	Slim Whitman	July 23–Sept 24
Cool Water	Frankie Laine	Oct 1
The Man from Laramie	Jimmy Young	Oct 8–Nov 5
Rock Around the Clock	Bill Haley and his Comets	Nov 11–

1956

Rock Around the Clock	Bill Haley and his Comets	–Jan 7
Sixteen TonsTennessee	Ernie Ford	Jan 14–Feb 11
Zambesi	Lou Bush	Feb 18–25
Memories are Made of This	Dean Martin	Mar 3–10
It's Almost Tomorrow	The Dream Weavers	Mar 17–31
Poor People of Paris	Winifred Atwell	Apr 7–May 5
No Other Love	Ronnie Hilton	May 12–June 2
I'll be Home	Pat Boone	June 9–July 14
Blue Suede Shoes	Elvis Presley	July 21–28
Why Do Fools Fall in Love	Frankie Lymon and the Teenagers	Aug 4
Whatever Will Be	Doris Day	Aug 11–Sept 15
Saints Rock 'n' roll	Bill Haley and his Comets	Sept 22–29
Lay Down Your Arms	Ann Shelton	Oct 6–13
Woman in Love	Frankie Laine	Oct 20–Nov 3
Just Walking in the Rain	Johnny Ray	Nov 10–Dec 22

1957

Singing the Blues	Guy Mitchell	Jan 5-12
Singing the Blues	Tommy Steele	Jan 19
Singing the Blues	Guy Mitchell	Jan 26
Garden of Eden	Frankie Vaughan	Feb 2—16
Young Love	Tab Hunter	Feb 23—Apr 6
Cumberland Gap	Lonnie Donegan	Apr 13—May 4
Butterfly	Andy Williams	May 11 -June 1
Yes Tonight Josephine	Johnny Ray	June 8—29
Gambling Man	Lonnie Donegan	July 6
All Shook Up	Elvis Presley	July 13 - Aug 24
Diana	Paul Anka	Aug 31—Oct 19
That'll be the Day	The Crickets	Oct 26—Nov 16
Mary's Boy Child	Harry Belafonte	Nov 23—Dec 21

1958

Ma He's Making Eyes at Me	Johnny Otis Show	Jan 4—11
Great Balls of Fire	Jerry Lee Lewis	Jan 18
Jailhouse Rock	Elvis Presley	Jan 25—Feb 8
The Story of My Life	Michael Holliday	Feb 15—22
Magic Moments	Perry Como	Mar 1—Apr 12
Whole Lotta Woman	Marvin Rainwater	Apr 19—May 10
Who's Sorry Now	Connie Francis	May 17—June 21 i
All I Have To Do Is Dream	The Everly Brothers	June 28—Aug 23
When	The Kalin Twins	Aug 30—Sept 27
Stupid Cupid	Connie Francis	Oct 4—Nov 1
Bird Dog	The Everly Brothers	Nov 8—22
Hoots Mon	Lord Rockingham's XI	Nov 29—Dec 19
It's Only Make Believe	Conway Twitty	Dec 26—

1959

It's Only Make Believe	Conway Twitty	- Jan 17
I Got Stung/One Night	Elvis Presley	Jan 24—Feb 21
Smoke Gets in Your Eyes	The Platters	Feb 28—Mar 28
Side Saddle	Russ Conway	Apr 4—11in'
It Doesn't Matter Any More	Buddy Holly	Apr 18—25
A Fool Such As I	Elvis Presley	May 2—June 13
Roulette	Russ Conway	June 20
Livin' Doll	Cliff Richard	Aug 8—22

Only Sixteen	Craig Douglas	Aug 29–Oct 10
Travellin' Light	Cliff Richard	Oct 17–Nov 28
What Do You Want	Adam Faith	Dec 5–

1960

What Do You Want	Adam Faith	- Jan 16
Why	Anthony Newley	Jan 23–Feb 27
Poor Me	Adam Faith	Mar 5
Running Bear	Johnny Preston	Mar 12–19
My Old Man's a Dustman	Lonnie Donegan	Mar 26–Apr 23
Cathy's Clown	The Everly Brothers	Apr 30–June 25
Good Timin'	Jimmy Jones	July 2–23
Please Don't Tease	Cliff Richard	July 30–Aug 13
Apache	The Shadows	Aug 20–Sept 24
Tell Laura I Love Her	Ricky Valence	Oct 1–8
Only the Lonely	Roy Orbison	Oct 15–29
It's Now Or Never	Elvis Presley	Nov 5–Dec 31

Information from

Tony Jasper (1986) *The Top Twenty, The Official British Record Charts 1955–85*, Javelin.

Bibliography and Source Material

Primary sources

Newspapers & Magazines

Eastern Daily Press (Archant Newspapers) 1955-60.

Eastern Evening News (Archant Newspapers) 1955-60.

Yarmouth Mercury (Archant Newspapers) 1955-60.

Directories

Kelly's Directory of the City of Norwich, 1956.

Bibliography (local history)

Cossey, P. (2015)   *Continuous Performances; Memories of Norwich Cinemas 1946-1961* The Norwich Movie Shop.

Fakes, A.(ed) (2011)   *The Story of Hemsby on Sea; Based on the Writings of the late George William Beech 1901-1979 Davies* Great Yarmouth.

Harris, K.(2003)   *Albert Cooper; A Chronicle of Norwich's King of the Blues* HannaH Publications.

Holmes, F. & Holmes, M. (2015) *Norwich Pubs and Breweries Past and Present* Norwich Heritage Projects.

Holmes, F. & Holmes, M. (2017) *Norwich 1945 to 1960: a Journey from Austerity to Prosperity* Norwich Heritage Projects.

Lindsay, B. (2020)   *Two Bold Singermen and the English Folk Revival* Equinox Publishing Ltd.

Mann, A. (2013)   *The Teacher: The Tony Sheridan Story* AMPS.

Miller, C. (2005)   *Country Boy: Growing up in Norfolk 1940-60* Sutton Publishing.

Miller, C. (2008)   *The Fifties Replayed: A Norfolk Youth at Leisure* Sutton Publishing.

Miller, C. (2012)   *A Degree of Swing* Derby Books Publishing.

Bibliography (general background)

Bell, R. (2013)   *The History of British Rock 'n Roll: The Forgotten Years 1956-1962* Robin Bell Books.

Betts, G. (2005)   *Complete UK Hit Singles 1952-2005* Collins.

Bradley, D. (1992)   *Understanding Rock 'n' Roll: Popular Music in Britain 1955-1964* OUP.

Bragg, B. (2017)   *Roots, Radicals and Rockers: How Skiffle Changed the World* Faber & Faber.

Booker, C. (1969)   *The Neophiliacs* Fontana.

Chilton, J. (1997)   *Who's Who of British Jazz* Cassell.

Dawson, J. (2005)   *Rock Around the Clock: the Record that Started a Revolution* Backbeat Books.

Dewe, M. (1998)   *The Skiffle Craze* Planet.

Doggett, P. (2015)   *Electric Shock; From the Gramophone to the iphone—125 Years of Pop Music* Bodley Head.

Ellis, R. (1961/2010)   *The Big Beat Scene* Music Mentor Books.

Evans, J. (2016)   *Rock & Pop on British TV* Omnibus Press.

Flattery, P. (1975)   *The Illustrated History of British Pop* Drake Publishing.

Foster, M. (1997)   *Play it Like Elvis* Sanctuary Publishing.

Frame, P. (2007)   *The Restless Generation: How Rock Music Changed the Face of 1950s Britain.* Rogan House.

Frame, P. (1980)   *Rock Family Trees* Omnibus Press.

Frith, S., Brennan, M. Cloonan M. & Webster E. (2013)
    The History of Live Music in Britain: Vol 1: 1950-1967 Ashgate.

Gammond, P. & Clayton P. (1960)
    A Guide to Popular Music. Phoenix House.

Gelly, D. (2014)   *An Unholy Row: Jazz in Britain and its audience 1945-60* Equinox.

Gillett, C. (1970)   *The Sound of the City* Souvenir Press

Green, J. (1998)   *All Dressed Up: The Sixties and the Counterculture* Jonathon Cape.

Greil, M. (2015)   *Mystery Train; Images of America in Rock 'n' Roll* Faber & Faber.

Hennessy, P. (2006)   *Having it so Good: Britain in the Fifties* Allen Lane.

Horn, A, (2009)   *Juke Box Britain: Americanization and Youth Culture 1945-60.* Manchester University Press.

Humphries, (2012)   *Lonnie Donegan: the Birth of British Rock & Roll* Robson Press.

Jasper, T, (1986)   *The Top Twenty: The Official British Record Charts 1955-1985* Blanford Press.

Kynaston, D, (2009)   *Family Britain 1951-57* Bloomsbury.

Larkin, C. (ed.) (1993)   *The Guinness Who's Who of Fifties Music* Guinness Publishing Ltd.

Lindsay, B. (2020)   *Shellac and Swing: A Social History of the Gramophone in Britain* Fonthill Media Ltd.

McDevitt, C. (1997)   *Skiffle: the definitive story* Robson Books.

Miller, J. (1999)   *Flowers in the Dustbin: the Rise of Rock 'n Roll 1947-1977* Fireside Books.

Napier-Bell, S. (2015)   *Ta-ra-ra Boom De-ay: The Business of Popular Music* Unbound.

Nichols, R. (1983)   *Radio Luxembourg: the Station of the Stars* Comet.

Sandbrook, D. (2005)   *Never Had it so Good: From Suez to the Beatles* Little, Brown.

Strong, M. (2006)   *The Essential Rock Discography* Cannongate.

Turner, A. (2008)   *Halfway to Paradise: The Birth of British Rock* V&A Publishing.

Websites

geoffreywatling.or.uk/history   (for information about Geoffrey Watling)

musicfromtheeastzone.co.uk   (interesting information about singers and bands in the eastern region, collected with the aim of producing an encyclopedia of popular music from East Anglia. Some of the information is based on personal recollections which would need substantiating, but a good starting point for any research.)

definitions.net/definitions/popular+music

Index